$\frac{1}{24}$

PREFABULOUS
+ ALMOST OFF THE GRID

PREFABULOUS

+ ALMOST OFF THE GRID

YOUR PATH TO BUILDING AN ENERGY-INDEPENDENT HOME

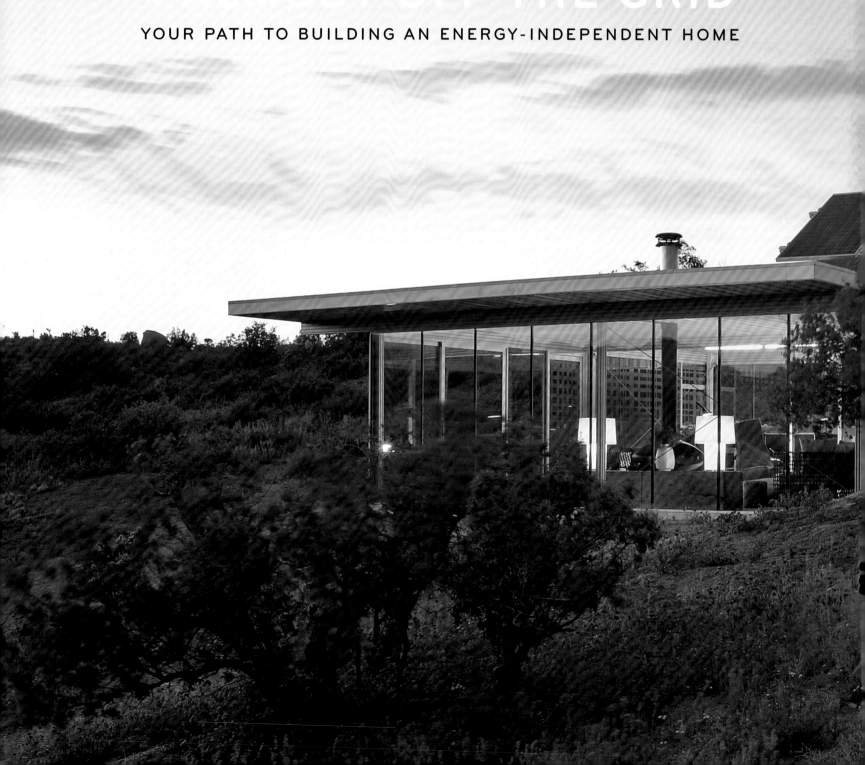

SHERI KOONES   FOREWORD BY ROBERT REDFORD

ABRAMS, NEW YORK

For Alex and Jesse,

with the hope they will live in an environmentally healthy world

ACKNOWLEDGMENTS

I am indebted to all of the homeowners, architects, builders, manufacturers, organizations, and suppliers who graciously shared their knowledge and experience with me. Each time I write a book, these people become new friends, and this is one of the joys of writing books.

I'm always amazed at the creativity and beauty of the houses I review—and the ones I found for this book were no different. The houses included here are among the most terrific I have ever come across. The methods and materials are new, creative, remarkably energy efficient, healthy, and environmentally friendly. I learned so much while writing this book and was so inspired by the creativity exhibited.

Thank you to Joyce Deep for your kindness—you are a joy to work with. A special thank-you to Robert Redford, my environmental hero, screen idol, and just a wonderful human being. I appreciate your encouragement and participation in this project—it means a great deal to me to have the support of such an important environmentalist who not only talks the talk, but walks the walk.

Rob, Alex, and Jesse are always a great source of inspiration and encouragement as I muddle through these projects. A special thank-you to my dear son Jesse, who, while preparing to begin college, helped me with some of the research for this book.

Thank you to all of the photographers who graciously contributed their fine work.

My thanks to the National Association of Real Estate Editors, a wonderful organization that has been so supportive of my work, with two Gold Robert Bruss Book awards and numerous wonderful friendships. My gratitude to my friends, who always help me more than I can say—Lucy Hedrick, Denise Marcil, Dave Wrocklage, and John Connell. Thank you to my brother and friend, Mark Warman, who is a continuous source of great support.

Abrams has been a joy to work with. Thanks to Eric Himmel for your continued support, Laura Dozier for your fine editing skill, and Darilyn Carnes for the excellent design.

The world needs to conserve energy, water, and resources—I hope these houses will help to inspire future homeowners as much as they've inspired me.

OPPOSITE The Snowhorn House in Austin, Texas, earned LEED Platinum certification. (Photo courtesy of Casey Dunn)

CONTENTS

Acknowledgments	5
Foreword by Robert Redford	9
Introduction	11
New World Hudson Home	22
New England Farmhouse	28
The Sea Breeze Cottage	36
Lakeside Green Cottage	42
Green Retreat	48
Superb-A House	54
Stillwater Dwelling	62
Newport Beach House	68
Modern Cottage	74
Riley's Rosemary Beach Retreat	80
C3 Prefab	88
New World Whitman-Annis Home	94
The Evolution	100
PLACE House	106
Greenfab House	112
Sheth House	118
Snowhorn House	124
Hilltop Craftsman	132
G•O Logic Home	138
Zero Energy Idea House	144
Lancaster Project	152
Unity House	158
High Desert itHouse	164
Rock Reach House	172
ART House	178
Passive Craftsman	184
4D Home	192
Kenmore Road House	198
Sungazing House	204
Schaller Eco-Home	210
SmartHome Cleveland	218
Taliesin Mod.Fab	224
Index of Important Terms	231
Resources	232

When I was a teenager working summers as a roustabout in what is now the Chevron Oil fields south of Los Angeles, I got firsthand knowledge of the consequences of offshore drilling. Over the years I've watched the dire consequences it has had on people, wildlife, local fisherman, and other industries. In some cases residents along waterways have relocated because of the oil spills. Imported oil has created other problems, putting our country in a precarious political position.

The recent Chilean mine accident and the nuclear meltdown in Japan have proven that seeking fuel the way we have been can have dangerous and unhealthy consequences. Even "clean-burning" natural gas, the bridge fuel between fossil and sustainable, is highly toxic and polluting in the hydraulic fracturing process necessary to access it.

A perfect solution to this energy challenge is to reduce our dependence on fossil fuel. Over the years clean energy options have become more available, more technologically sophisticated, and more financially feasible. There is new technology available in solar, geothermal, and wind power, and beyond.

In 1975 when I built my own passive solar home in Utah, it was incredibly difficult to find materials and systems to achieve the efficiency and energy independence I sought. Today, these technologies have evolved and there are many options available for the construction of energy-independent homes and other buildings. The variety of systems and the prices for these systems have been reduced over the years. In addition, there are government, state, and local subsidies and tax breaks to encourage their use. Nobody's asking for perfection but even walking down this road partway will go a long way toward a better future.

Since homes use approximately 38 percent of the energy in this country, constructing more energy-efficient homes is an excellent way to reduce consumption. *Prefabulous + Almost Off the Grid: Your Path to Building an Energy-Independent Home* demonstrates many examples of houses that require minimal energy; some of which even give back as much energy as they use. The methods and materials used in the construction of houses in this book demonstrate how houses can be built to reduce energy and water consumption, while also being healthy and sustainable. The houses are beautiful, comfortable, and vastly reduce their footprint on the earth.

With the heavy cost we pay for energy—environmentally, politically, and financially—the hope is to embrace the new and reduced cost of natural energy. The houses in this book set an excellent example of the types of houses that should be built today—with reduced energy use, healthy products, and more sustainable materials.

We need to learn from our past mistakes regarding energy consumption and embrace new ways to reduce our needs. It's time for everyone to consider more clean energy options in our lives. *Prefabulous + Almost Off the Grid: Your Path to Building an Energy-Independent Home* will inspire and help you do that.

—Robert Redford
Environmentalist, Actor, Director

PAGES 2-3 AND 6-7 The High Desert itHouse in Pioneertown, California, is totally off the grid, generating its own energy with solar photovoltaic and solar hot water panels. (Photo courtesy of Art Gray Photography)

OPPOSITE At the Frank Lloyd Wright School of Architecture in Arizona, the breezeway in the Taliesin Mod.Fab, separating the bedroom from the main living area, provides an opportunity to experience nature—a concept often used by Frank Lloyd Wright in his structures. (Photo courtesy of Bill Timmerman)

BELOW Modular manufacturer Royal Homes in Canada built this cottage on Starr Island in just seven months. Limiting the impact on the environment, energy and heated water are created from the adjoining lake through a filtration system, using solar energy. (Photo courtesy of Riverstore Photography)

OPPOSITE The modules and materials were brought over to Starr Island on a barge from Honey Harbour, Ontario. (Photo courtesy of Royal Homes)

continue to be amazed at the number of houses built, even today, with neither energy-efficient design nor factory-manufactured quality. The first saves money from the initial day of occupancy while the second ensures the long-term value of the investment. Simply put, prefabrication addresses these two critical issues, offering the least complicated and most reliably scheduled path to the green home of your dreams.

The downturn in the building industry has forced everyone to revisit fundamental home-building assumptions. Whereas houses were getting bigger and bigger in the boom years of the 1970s and '80s, today's homeowners are shopping for smaller, better-designed houses that utilize space more purposefully and reduce waste of energy, water, and other resources.

When the cost of energy was lower, the political world situation less turbulent, oil spills more contained, and nuclear energy seemingly fairly safe, energy efficiency was not a major issue. Today we pay a high price for the energy we use.

As more homeowners, architects, and builders begin to understand these consequences, they are looking for more efficient and cost-effective methods of building. They are looking for ways to build houses that use much less energy, with more efficient building "envelopes," and in some cases, generate some or all of the energy they require with solar, wind, and geothermal means. Houses are being built that are off the grid and almost off the grid—both of which require dramatically less energy than has been needed in the past. Some of these houses are even returning excess energy to the grid.

Although there are various degrees of energy independence presented here, being almost off the grid is optimal, since it indicates a minimal need for energy use from the utility company, while also presenting the possibility of returning energy back to the grid. However, this book celebrates the efforts by builders and homeowners throughout the United States who have achieved varying levels of energy independence, to preserve our natural resources for future generations. A variety of strategies are presented to achieve that independence.

GREEN VALUE

As home buyers become more educated, they are realizing that there are *two* price tags to consider when pricing a new home. What the house will cost to operate and maintain has become almost more important than what the house will cost initially to build. The small added cost of installing energy-saving systems is quickly recouped in the first few years of operating the house.[*] After that, it's like getting a dividend check every month! Moreover, when homeowners eventually decide to sell their energy-efficient home, the low utility records will allow them to put a higher price on it, thus profiting further.

Sadly, if informed homeowners want to live in an energy-efficient home today, they will probably have to build one. In spite of current media coverage of all things green, relatively few energy-efficient houses have been built in recent years. This is shortsighted since this type of construction will not only pay for itself in a short time but also makes a home more salable in the future, when building codes become much more stringent. This is already starting to happen as the new energy codes are embraced across

---

[*] ROI (return on investment) for green upgrades is commonly between eight and twelve years.

the country. In the not too distant future, energy-hog homes will become obsolete and will sell more slowly. We're finally entering a time when bragging rights are about energy efficiency rather than granite countertops.

A recent study by Earth Advantage Institute, a nonprofit in Oregon, found that new homes that were certified green sold for 8 percent more than noncertified ones. Additionally, the organization's year-to-year sales reports indicate that this figure can be as high as 30 percent for many homes, even during an economic downturn.[*] This suggests that homeowners value all the benefits of a green home—comfort, quality, healthy environment, and energy efficiency—and are looking for the assurance a green label provides. They are clearly willing to pay a premium for a greener home. Reports also indicate that green houses sell in less time and closer to the asking price.

Until this recent national trend becomes the standard way of building, homeowners will continue to pay more for the relatively rare homes designed with efficiency in mind. At the same time, according to a recent study by the National Association of Home Builders (NAHB), called "The New Home in 2015," homes will get smaller and have more green features. The typical house in 2015 is expected to average 2,152 square feet, which is 10 percent smaller than those started in the first three quarters of 2010, attributable to the consumer focus on lowering heating and cooling costs. NAHB concludes that consumers will purchase homes "based on need more than want."

It goes far beyond just the HVAC system (heating, ventilation, and air-conditioning). Almost 68 percent of the surveyed builders expect houses in 2015 to feature a whole constellation of green technologies, including water-saving toilets, low-flow faucets and showerheads, energy-efficient windows, better-insulated wall assemblies, and at minimum an

ENERGY STAR rating for the entire house. Energy monitoring and smart house optimization (using digital systems to tune performance) will also be very common.

ENERGY INCENTIVES

Today many homeowners are willing to pay a premium for green features so they can save on energy costs and live in a more comfortable house. Federal, state, and local tax incentives are widely available to offset the cost of this investment. To check incentives anywhere in the United States, visit www.dsireusa.org, the Database of State Incentives for Renewables & Efficiency. This website serves as a comprehensive source of information about incentives, as well as policies that promote renewable energy and energy efficiency.

Homeowners may also qualify for the Federal Residential Renewable Energy Tax Credit, which allows tax credits of up to 30 percent of what they spend on solar energy systems, geothermal heat pumps, fuel cells, and wind energy systems through 2016. Homeowners can claim the value of their credit against their tax liability. For further information on this tax credit, check out the website www.energysavers.gov.

GUIDELINES FOR BUILDING GREEN

In the last fifteen years several national and innumerable regional programs have been developed to guide the construction of more efficient homes.

In 1998 the U.S. Green Building Council (USGBC) established the Leadership in Energy and Environmental Design (LEED) program to provide a framework for green construction. At this writing, there are 8,662 LEED-certified homes and 31,075 registered homes under construction.

In 2005 the National Association of Home Builders published "The Model Green Homebuilding Guidelines," and in 2008 the NAHB Research Center launched the National Green Building Certification Program. This program's goal is not only to certify green homes but also to educate the building community and the general public about green

---

[*] These reports are based on countywide averages from the Portland Regional Multiple Listing Service for the period 2007–11.

This Savannah modular i-house was built at Green Bridge Farms in Savannah, Georgia, crafted by Clayton Homes, a division of Berkshire Hathaway. The house has several renewable energy sources including a geothermal heat pump, solar hot water, and photovoltaic panels. A very tight envelope greatly reduces the need for energy for heating and cooling. Charles Davis, the owner of Earth Comfort Company, built the house as a model for future developments. The house is net-zero, producing as much energy as it uses; Davis purchases energy at off-peak, reduced rates, from Georgia Power at night to charge his electric car and sells back energy during the day at increased rates. Davis says his largest energy bill to date has been $35. An energy monitor shows the wattage used by each appliance in the house, the power produced by the solar panels, and the number of watts sold back to Georgia Power. The house was awarded Mainstream Green Home of the Year in 2011 by GreenBuilder magazine. (Photo courtesy of Shawn Heifert)

building. There are currently 3,061 certified houses in this program.

These are the two largest national programs, and both use a point system and third-party verification to establish that certified homes are green and sustainable. Although there are slight variations in emphasis, these programs certify structures that are healthy, maximize energy and water efficiency, reduce carbon dioxide emissions, minimize embodied energy (the energy used to make and transport the building materials), and curtail adverse impacts on building sites and their surrounding neighborhoods. Many regions around the country have established local versions of these programs to encourage the construction of greener homes.

Before any of this, in 1990 Dr. Wolfgang Feist quietly founded the Passivhaus Institut (PHI) in Germany. He sought the principles for creating very low-energy structures at an affordable price. Toward this end, Feist developed software—the Passive House Planning Package (PHPP)—to model homes as well as commercial structures. He explored thoughtful designs and a thermal shell that could reduce the need for heating, cooling, and ventilating systems to almost nothing. Homes designed using this software can reduce energy for heating and cooling by 90 percent and overall energy consumption by 60 to 70 percent!

More than twenty thousand structures are already certified by Passivhaus in Europe, achieving this standard through the use of "superinsulation,"* high-performance windows and doors, heat recovery ventilators, passive solar design, and sophisticated energy modeling. This movement has come to the United States as the Passive House Institute US, a nonprofit program established to further research and consult with homeowners and builders. It is a growing trend—creating houses that are energy neutral or even energy producing. In 2008 there were three completed Passive Houses (PHs) in the United States and twenty certified PH consultants. By 2010 there were sixteen completed homes and 160 certified Passive House consultants, plus fifteen more houses under construction and forty going through certification review. PHs tend to cost an additional 7 to 10 percent up front but yield long-term savings of 60 to 70 percent in energy efficiency. Many are built without using expensive "active" technologies such as photovoltaic or solar thermal hot water systems. The focus for Passive House is almost entirely on energy conservation, which differentiates it from programs such as LEED and NAHBGreen with their broader considerations.

In 2002 the first Solar Decathlon event took place on the Mall in Washington, DC. This international competition was established by the US Department of Energy to demonstrate the potential of houses designed to both collect and convert sunlight into usable energy. It was held again in 2005 and then every two years thereafter. In 2010 the first Solar Decathlon Europe took place in Madrid, and

* This term was originally coined in 1976 by Wayne Schick of the University of Illinois at Urbana-Champaign while designing his famous "Lo-Cal House." Superinsulation is typically in the range of R-40 to R-60 and works in large part by eliminating all thermal bridging through advanced framing.

future events are planned again in Madrid in 2012 and China in 2013, as well as in the United States. For each Solar Decathlon, universities around the world submit plans, and twenty are selected to be built. The students travel to the events to demonstrate their houses, sharing ideas and increasing awareness of new technologies in energy efficiency (for more information on the Solar Decathlon, see page 196). One of the excellent houses presented at the 2011 event, the 4D Home, is included here (see page 192).

All of these programs attest to the great interest developing in this country and worldwide for energy-efficient buildings—both residential and commercial. In the United States, energy used to heat and cool homes has typically accounted for 40 percent or more of our total energy consumption. But recently people have begun to discover how easy and cost-effective it is to build homes that are dramatically more energy efficient. Many beautiful and comfortable houses have been built to high energy and environmental standards. Yet the question remains why more homeowners don't insist on this option. In the 1960s and '70s there were still some challenges to building an energy-efficient, healthy, sustainable home. Today there are really none!

WHY BUILD GREEN?

As codes become more stringent and the cost of energy continues to rise, energy-efficient homes will become the norm. Wouldn't it be better to build such a house now rather than building one that will be passé in ten years? According to a 2008 study conducted by McGraw-Hill Construction and the U.S. Green Building Council, green homes will account for 12 to 20 percent of the housing market by 2013, up from 2 percent in 2005. It's predicted that green homes will be on the market for less time and bring a higher resale value than comparable but less-efficient homes.

It used to be said that the energy-saving products available in the United States—windows and doors are good examples—lagged behind the technologies available in Germany, Canada, and other countries. But each year, when I attend the NAHB

International Builders' Show (the most comprehensive product display and demonstration of building products in the world), I see more and more green products brought to the American market. This is great for US homeowners as well as the economy. According to the USGBC, the green building market will support 7.9 million US jobs and pump $554 million into the economy over the 2009–13 period.

On October 5, 2009, President Obama signed Executive Order 13514, setting sustainability goals for federal agencies. Leading by example, this legislation requires all agencies to set 2020 greenhouse gas (GHG) emission reduction targets, increase energy efficiency, conserve water, reduce waste, decrease use of energy for fueling vehicles, and use their purchasing power to promote sustainable products. It is only a matter of time before higher goals will be set for residential structures. The bar is moving up!

A wonderful aspect of energy-efficient construction, beyond the long-term financial savings, is the comfort created by these homes. When properly designed and engineered (two practices that are increasingly becoming one), they are toasty warm in winter and refreshingly cool in summer. Some designs use almost no motors or pumps, producing a rare and calming quiet throughout the house.

SAVING WATER

Although a large portion of the world is covered with water, about 97 percent is salt water and only about 3 percent is potable. Depletion of reservoirs and groundwater can put humans at risk, raise concentrations of pollutants in the water supply, reduce the supply available for industrial and agricultural purposes, and put a strain on aquatic ecosystems and their dependent species. Water efficiency in new homes can easily reduce water usage by 30 percent or more. Outdoor uses, primarily landscaping, account for 30 percent of the 26 billion gallons consumed daily in the United States (according to the EPA). Because they are so easy to implement, water-saving techniques are found in most of the houses profiled in this book. They range from simple

BELOW The challenge for this home, called Residence for a Briard, was to build the greenest possible modern house on a very tight budget. Architect Whitney Sander and Icaza Construction were able to meet the challenge for this house in Culver City, California, using a prefabricated recycled structural steel frame and panels with recycled denim insulation. The house is three thousand square feet, has twenty-eight-foot ceilings, and cost $160 a square foot to build. The house has radiant heat, a gray water system, tankless water heaters, passive heating and cooling, four-layer acrylic windows with twice the insulating value of one-inch insulated glass, little construction waste due to the prefab shell, low-flush toilets, low-VOC paints, soy-based stain for the concrete floor slab, bamboo flooring, a superinsulated envelope (nine-inch-thick walls and roof), and SCIP (structural concrete insulated panel) walls at the front. (Photo courtesy of Sharon Risedorph)

OPPOSITE ABOVE This 1,600-square-foot modular house on Orcas Island in Washington was built by Method Homes, a manufacturer of modern prefab houses. It has an energy monitoring system (TED, the Energy Detective) so the homeowners can keep track of how much energy they are using. (Photo courtesy of Lannie Boesiger)

OPPOSITE BELOW The beautiful timber frame, built by Hugh Lofting Timber Framing, provides the skeleton for the Murus structural insulated panels, which create a seamless insulation shell for this off-the-grid residence named Solitude Farm, located just south of Annapolis, Maryland. Storm water is managed through rain gardens and bioswales (drainage courses designed to remove silt and pollution from surface runoff). This residence utilizes solar thermal energy for the domestic hot water system and has in-floor radiant heat. A geothermal heat pump provides backup heat during cloudy weather, as well as air-conditioning with in-floor radiant cooling during the hot and humid summer months. Passive solar orientation with seasonal shading was maximized through the high-efficiency windows and the high-reflectivity roofing system, which reduces heat gain in summer. The concrete floors and chimney mass placed for maximum heat absorption allow passive heating. The house was built using all natural, local, and recycled materials, with minimal construction disturbance or waste. (Photo courtesy of Brian Spirt)

The different labels for energy-efficient houses can be confusing. To help clarify, here is a small glossary for some of the terms used in this book:

• **Zero-energy (or net-zero) house:** A house that produces as much energy as it uses within a typical year.

• **Off the grid:** This refers to any house considered energy independent and not connected to a local grid-based power company. Today it is sometimes broadened to mean the house must produce enough energy for heating, cooling, and to power all its lighting and appliances.

• **Almost off the grid:** Many of the houses profiled in this book, although not off the grid, are almost off the grid, requiring minimal energy from the utility company. This is accomplished by building a very efficient "envelope" and with some houses creating energy using renewable means. Some of the houses included here have net metering, which means that at times they can produce extra energy that can be fed back into the grid.

• **Passive solar:** Much of the thermal energy needed for space heating or hot water is collected merely by configuring the geometry of the house to collect solar heat. Passive solar usually accomplishes this without any moving parts, equipment, or additional systems. In contrast, "active" systems include solar collectors, wind generators, hydrogenerators, pumps, fans, and so on.

• **Passive House:** A stringent US building standard related to efficiency requirements developed by Germany's Passivhaus Institut.

• **Carbon-neutral home:** A house that produces zero carbon emissions.

strategies—such as low-flow faucets and shower-heads and dual-flush toilets—to more elaborate gray water systems and water storage tanks. In some climates, xeriscaping (landscaping requiring mini-mal water use) is the easiest, most effective way to reduce the water use around the exterior of a home (see Sungazing House, page 207).

WHY BUILD HOUSES PREFAB?

I'm still surprised when I run into someone who clings to the disproven stereotype that prefabricated houses are all double-wides and ugly little boxes. Having written three books and presented at count-less conferences on the subject, I'm saddened that this ill-founded bias persists. Unfortunately many people still have no idea what prefab construction is and are ill-informed of the many options that now exist in this industry. People who still think prefab is synonymous with little ticky-tacky boxes should take a look at all of the beautiful prefab houses that have been built in the last ten years. They easily rival the beauty of any site-built home.

There are many ways to prefabricate a house; the most popular methods include using modu-lar components, structural insulated panels (SIPs), panelization, prefabricated concrete walls, timber frames, and steel frames. These techniques are show-cased in the pages that follow. Moreover, several new and innovative approaches are included in this book, such as the Open-Built system used for the Unity House (see page 158) and the patented panel sys-tem in the Rock Reach House (see page 172), usually used for commercial applications.

The benefits of prefabrication are as numerous as the ways to achieve them. One of the most obvious advantages prefab has over site-built construction is the minimization of waste. On-site construction cre-ates lots of wasted materials that end up in Dump-sters and ultimately in landfills. The homeowner pays for all of this material, the cost of hauling it away, plus the tipping charge at the dump when it arrives there. In contrast, factories have the opportunity to recycle materials and thus keep waste to an absolute minimum. Wood is used on other projects, and many

materials, such as drywall and metal, can be returned to the manufacturer.

As a modern society, we expect things to happen quickly. When a website doesn't open right away, we become frustrated. When we order something online, we want to receive it the next day. We are an immediate gratification society. We should not have to wait two years to move into a new and well-built house. Prefabrication meets our need for faster, high-quality construction. Unlike on-site construction, which typically requires sequential construction starting with the footing and founda-tion, all of the elements can be fabricated at the same time, reducing overall construction time. One exam-ple is the Rock Reach House (see page 172) with a panelized wall system that was factory fabricated in one day, while the steel frame was fabricated in four days. These elements could be fabricated while the footings were being installed. The house itself was then "dried in" (the frame, floor, roof, walls, and win-dows were installed) in just five days.

Factory construction drastically reduces con-struction time for larger components as well. The New World Hudson Home, a modular house, was fabricated in the factory in five days and completed in a little over a week at the exhibit in New York (see page 22), and the Greenfab House (see page 121) was built in a modular factory in two weeks, set in six hours, and completed in forty-five days.

Several of the houses in the book are built with structural insulated panels, and a study has found that this method of construction is dramatically faster than typical methods: "Field erection of struc-tural insulated panels is faster than for conventional framing. A conventionally framed and insulated house of similar size and design would take approxi-mately 122 percent longer to erect. Wall erection was the most efficient task, taking about a third of the time that it would take to build and insulate a con-ventionally framed wall."[*]

Frank Baker, founder of Insulspan and River-bend Timber Framing and owner of the Lakeside Green Cottage (see page 42), one of the SIP houses in the book, says the production time for both the

SIPs and the timber frame was about three or four days, which occurred simultaneously. Assembly of the house took about a week. All of these examples attest to the time saved by building houses using prefabricated components.

Moreover, just as we wouldn't consider having our car assembled in our driveway, we shouldn't consider building our houses on-site. Homeowners should expect the expertise and experience in the construction of their home that comes with controlled factory conditions, experienced professionals, and close supervision of each part of the house.

Many of today's factories employ computer-controlled machinery to produce higher-quality work at lower cost. These machines are faster and more accurate than site-based workers using conventional hammers and saws. Such technologies can be deployed only in a factory setting. In every area of the digital age, we expect faster, more exacting, less costly answers to our needs. Should we not require the same for the most expensive, important projects we undertake—namely, building our homes?

Another key advantage of prefab modular construction is the inherent resilience of the structure. After the Federal Emergency Management Agency (FEMA) surveyed the damage left by Hurricane Andrew (Category 4), it determined that modular housing "provided an inherently rigid system that performed much better than conventional residential framing."[†] Almost by definition, modular construction must be stronger and more durable. After all, it experiences a 65-mph ride for several hours on the highway between the factory and the site and is lifted with a crane by two cables and set on the foundation. No site-built house could withstand that type of stress! It excels at one of the most important aspects of green construction—durability. Homes that last longer produce less waste and fill fewer landfills over the years.

---

[*] RSMeans Business Solutions by Reed Construction Data, November 2006.

[†] "Building Performance: Hurricane Andrew in Florida," FEMA, December 1992.

The Hawkins residence in Gilmer County, Georgia, is not connected to the grid and depends entirely on photovoltaic panels on the roof of the shed (which houses the battery backup system, stores wood, and contains a wood shop), a masonry heater, a geothermal heat pump, and a backup generator. Water is heated by an on-demand water heater powered by the photovoltaic panels. It was constructed using ICFs for the walls and SIPs for the roof of the house. The house was built using optimal solar orientation, high-efficiency windows, and other green features. The house was designed by Bob Bourguignon and built by Rick Wood Construction. (Photo courtesy of Ken Hawkins)

In addition to the many commonly quoted reasons for building prefab, such as saving time and money, protecting our natural environment, and conserving materials, there are also some less advertised facts that are equally compelling. According to Fred Humphreys, president and CEO of NAHB's Home Builders Institute, there is a shrinking interest in construction work among young people. Forty percent of the current construction workers are baby boomers and getting ready to retire. At the same time, high schools are shutting down many of the vocational programs that could teach construction skills to a new generation. Moreover, there is an increasing lack of interest in construction work in general. It is perceived, correctly, as dangerous and offering less than ideal working and weather conditions.

Many of these labor problems are eliminated with prefab construction, where the work is done in comfortable surroundings, in less dangerous conditions, with safety regulations and regular oversight. Factory work is steady, without the interruptions caused by poor weather conditions. The prefabricated industry attracts serious, disciplined workers who receive paid benefits, vacations, and necessary training. This labor is also highly supervised in the factory setting, which means a very carefully built house.

EDUCATING CONSUMERS

One of the biggest reasons more people don't build energy-efficient prefab homes is because they are simply not aware of the options. Building homes has become more of a science than ever before, and even many professionals are hard-pressed to stay current with the latest developing knowledge in construction.

Computer simulations and "energy modeling" allow architects and engineers to experiment with various configurations until they find the very best results. But they need to understand the principles and learn the software. Similarly, there are many new materials and methods for integrating unprecedented efficiencies into a new house—but only if people are aware of them. The technologies are developing quickly, and homeowners are challenged to educate themselves about the latest methods. At the very least, they must become informed enough to choose an architect, manufacturers, and a builder that understand these concepts.

Building a home is one of the largest projects most people will ever undertake. It is important to consider all of the options and do the research before proceeding. *Prefabulous + Almost Off the Grid: Your Path to Building an Energy-Independent Home* will provide homeowners with information about some of the wonderful options available to them. Containing profiles of thirty-two homes, this book explains many of the materials, systems, and techniques available to create a more energy-efficient, comfortable, and healthy home.

In these difficult economic times, efficiency should be at the top of every homeowner's priority list. But I also show that aesthetics don't have to be compromised for efficiency and affordability. The houses profiled in this book are proof that one can have both.

In addition, the homes in *Prefabulous + Almost Off the Grid* are at various degrees of energy independence. There are houses that are completely independent of the grid, requiring no outside energy sources, as well as those that call for only minimal outside energy.

The book features strategies for building an energy-efficient home that focus on conservation, including ways to superinsulate the walls, roof, and floors. It explores optimal orientation, high-performance windows and doors, and deep overhangs. The latest methods for heating and cooling your house with renewable energy are also reviewed—including solar collectors, photovoltaic panels, geothermal heat pumps, and wind turbines. Additionally, I've outlined methods for cutting down energy use with high-performance appliances, efficient lighting fixtures, and energy-reporting systems. Finally, all of the houses include healthy and sustainable aspects, explained in sidebars and in the text.

A variety of methods have been used to attain these efficiencies, with the houses varying in size, style, and location. The amount of energy they require, as well as the energy they can produce, depends on climate and the design of the house. The houses in the book appear in order of increasing efficiency, although this is a very casual arrangement, since all of the houses are efficient in different ways.

One of the important messages of this book is that homeowners should not be deterred from building an efficient home because they are concerned about the cost. In some cases, green houses do cost more than less efficient houses, but in most of these homes, the energy savings will equalize the additional cost within a few years. In some cases energy-efficient houses have been built at no additional cost of construction. There are many ways to achieve efficiency, and I hope you will be inspired by some of the methods used in this book.

In the end, the most important aspect of home construction today is how a house performs. All of the new technology that is available and incorporated into the home is inconsequential if the house doesn't function in a healthy and energy- and water-efficient manner. When available, statistics are included that verify the efficiency of the houses that are featured in this book with HERS ratings (Home Energy Rating System), blower door test results, and other certifications. The houses are varied in style, location, type of construction, and materials, but all will encourage you to build a healthier, more efficient home that is kinder to the environment.

The best solution to our energy problems is to conserve energy and take advantage of renewable energy when required. I hope this book will inspire you to do both.

New World Hudson Home

Modular

PHOTOGRAPHER:
Courtesy of New World Home (unless
  otherwise noted)

ARCHITECT:
New World Architecture

MANUFACTURER:
Haven Custom Homes

BUILDER:
New World Home

LOCATION:
New York, New York, and Hardyston,
  New Jersey

SIZE:
1,607 square feet

HERS RATING: 48

BLOWER DOOR TEST: 1.59 ACH @ 50
  Pascals (see page 27)

CERTIFICATION:
LEED-H—Platinum
National Green Building
  Certification Program—Emerald
ENERGY STAR
Indoor airPLUS Program

GREEN ASPECTS:
Small footprint
Fiber cement siding
Thermally modified yellow pine decking
Recycled-content carpet
Dual-flush toilets—WaterSense labeled
Low-flow water fixtures—WaterSense
  labeled
No-VOC paint
Engineered quartz countertop
Permeable pavers
Rainwater collection
Reclaimed engineered flooring
Manifold plumbing system (see page 27)
Formaldehyde-free fiberglass insulation
FSC-certified wood
Foot pedal (kitchen sink)

ENERGY ASPECTS:
ENERGY STAR–rated windows and doors
ENERGY STAR–rated appliances
ENERGY STAR–rated metal roofing
High-efficiency HVAC system
Programmable thermostat with moisture control
Energy monitoring system
Insulated joists and sill plates
Precast insulated concrete form (ICF) foundation
Tankless water heater
Spray foam insulation—open cell
LED and CFL lighting
Motion-detector lighting controls
Lighting timer controls
Advanced framing to minimize thermal bridging
Heat recovery ventilator (HRV)

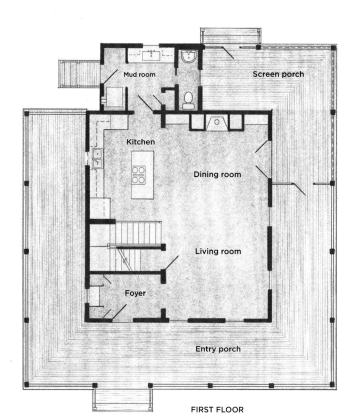

FIRST FLOOR

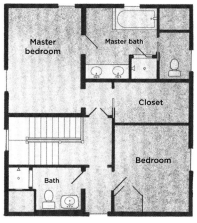

SECOND FLOOR

From June 4 to June 17, 2010, over ten thousand people toured the New World Hudson Home on display in lower Manhattan at the World Financial Center on a beautiful site overlooking the Hudson River. The house was designed in cooperation with *Country Living* magazine. It took just one day to set the house and make it "dried in," or weatherproof. The finishing touches took five days, and the house was then open to the public for almost two weeks.

The reaction of the crowds ranged from surprise that the house was modular to delight at hearing that this very traditional-looking house was so technologically modern. Visitors were delighted to hear about the wide array of green attributes and features that were incorporated into the house. Tyler Schmetterer, founder of New World Home, says, "There is still a very steep learning curve taking place throughout the country about modular, and visitors were surprised that a modular can include state-of-the-art green features, capable of achieving the highest certification levels in the industry."

Inspiration for the design of this house is rooted in the heritage of the Hudson River Valley architecture, including its cottage style, wraparound porch, thoughtful details, and functional use of space. New World Home considered this design to be particularly appropriate for the New York City exhibition at the World Financial Center, where the home was perched above the North Cove Marina, overlooking the Hudson River.

NEW TECHNOLOGY, OLD-WORLD CHARM

The concept behind New World Home is to evoke the spirit of the past while integrating modern conveniences and amenities. This house has traditional clapboard siding, but here it is fiber cement, which is more durable and requires less maintenance than wood. Whereas more traditional old houses had small, drafty windows, New World Home uses larger, ENERGY STAR–rated, highly efficient windows to provide a good source of light and natural ventilation. Like more traditional old houses, New World uses shutters to protect windows from inclement weather and cool the house from intense sunlight, while giving the house old-world charm. These shutters are made of composite wood and fiberglass, which is more durable and longer lasting and requires less maintenance than traditional shutters.

CONSERVING ENERGY AND WATER

The house was built with a variety of energy-saving methods, which began in the factory with the open-cell spray foam insulation and advanced framing to minimize thermal bridging (see Unity House, page 162). New World provides a long list of requirements to the modular manufacturer to meet its standards. Tyler says, "Our green standards typically exceed anything a plant has attempted in the past, and as such, requires exacting specifications and methodologies that are third-party inspected for undergoing certification (e.g., USGBC)." As is the case with all modular houses, this house also has the advantage of producing minimal waste and being built in a protected environment where there is less chance of damage from moist weather conditions.

By closely monitoring the house with a whole-house monitoring system, New World has been able to evaluate and control the efficient use of energy.

In addition to using LED (light-emitting diode) and CFL (compact fluorescent) bulbs to reduce energy, a motion detector is used to activate the

BELOW The dishwasher and refrigerator are ENERGY STAR certified. A foot pedal at the sink limits water waste by controlling flow. Recycled barn siding is used on the kitchen island.

BOTTOM The flooring in the living and dining rooms, as well as throughout the house, is made from elm engineered wood rescued from abandoned buildings. Even the furnishings in the house are sustainable—the chairs are upholstered with recycled-fiber fabric, and the dining table is made from salvaged antique elm doors.

lights, and a lighting timer control is used to shut them off.

Water savings are accomplished with a rainwater catchment system and low-flow fixtures in the kitchen and bathrooms. A foot pedal (see New World Whitman-Annis home, page 99) gives a more controlled flow in the kitchen sink, cutting down on wastewater. The manifold plumbing system (see sidebar page 27) is also designed to conserve water.

CONSERVING NATURAL RESOURCES

Attempts have been made throughout the house to use as few resources as necessary. The elm flooring on the lower floors and carpet on the upper floors are from recycled materials. The dining table is made from rescued elm doors. The engineered wood flooring (a sandwich of finished wood on top and plywood underneath) consists of reclaimed elm, which has more strength than solid wood, and the wood used is harvested from small-diameter, fast-growing trees. Even the decorations are mostly green and include recycled, reclaimed, or organic content.

A PERMANENT LOCATION

After the demonstration was over, the house was dismantled in a single day and transported to a permanent location in Hardyston, New Jersey. It was quickly reset on a precast insulated concrete foundation, which was prepared in advance. Although several visitors wanted to purchase the display house, the company opted to retain it as an interactive design/education center and a major sales hub.

BELOW LEFT <u>Horizontal wainscoting</u> helps make this narrow room appear wider. The four-poster bed is made from sustainably grown mindi wood (which has a natural resistance to decay and fungus), and the mattress is 100 percent organic cotton and hemp.

BELOW RIGHT The hallway is decorated with recycled prints from an old copy of *Art Forms in Nature*. The window is situated to flood the area with light.

BOTTOM LEFT Making practical use of all available space, this alcove on the second floor is used as a small work area with an antique desk.

BOTTOM RIGHT The vintage-looking tub and wainscoting add to the hominess of this bathroom. Bathtub and sink faucets are all water saving.

Blower Door Test

The blower door test is a diagnostic tool used to measure the airtightness of a structure. A powerful fan is mounted in the frame of an exterior door. The fan pulls air out of the house, lowering the interior pressure and pulling air in from the outside through unsealed cracks and openings. A pressure gauge measures the amount of air the fan pulls out of the house, revealing any leaks in the air sealing, which can then be amended. Adequately sealing a house can increase comfort, reduce energy costs, and improve air quality. This test is required for some certifications, including the ENERGY STAR Program. The result of the blower door test for the New World Hudson Home was 1.59 ACH @ 50 Pascals. This means there are 1.59 air changes in the house per hour at a standardized 50 Pascals of pressure (a measure of force per unit area).

Manifold Plumbing Systems

A manifold plumbing system (or simply "manifold system") is a circulatory system for the home. Each flexible pipe, hot or cold, goes directly from the manifold to the individual fixture or appliance—rather than through a series of branches off two larger ¾-inch pipes—so any given line can be disconnected from the water supply if it is not functioning and requires maintenance. The water lines are typically made of ½-inch PEX (cross-linked polyethylene), which won't rust and endures freezing much better than metal. These lines supply water (hot/cold) directly to the fixture along the most efficient path. The shorter distances between supply and fixtures and the narrower pipes achieve greater water conservation.

New England Farmhouse

Panelized

PHOTOGRAPHER:

Eric Roth

PROJECT ARCHITECT:

Stephen Haskell, Connor Homes

GREEN ARCHITECT:

Stephanie Horowitz

ZeroEnergy Design

BUILDER:

Aedi Construction

INTERIOR DESIGNER:

Lisa Kauffman Tharp

LOCATION:

Concord, Massachusetts

SIZE:

2,700 square feet

HERS RATING: 50

CERTIFICATION:

ENERGY STAR

GREEN ASPECTS:

Low-flow faucets

Dual-flush toilets

Metal roof

Modest footprint

Flexible space

Reclaimed wood flooring

Recycled brick patio

Salvaged kitchen cabinetry

FSC-certified wood

Allergy-free native plantings

No-VOC paints and finishes

HEPA whole-house filtration system

Fiber cement siding

ENERGY ASPECTS:

Spray foam insulation—open cell

Passive solar orientation

Stone flooring (thermal mass)

Interior windows

Daylighting (skylights and clerestory windows)

Ceiling fans

Cooling chimney

Radiant heating and cooling

High-performance windows

Exterior rigid insulation

ENERGY STAR–rated appliances

ENERGY STAR–rated lighting

Wired for future photovoltaic and solar thermal panels

Heat recovery ventilator (HRV)

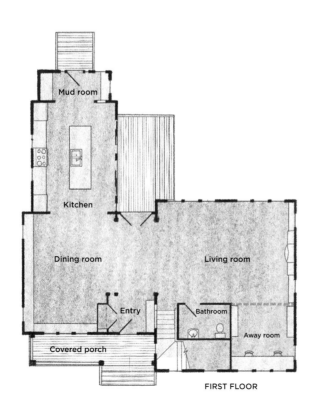

FIRST FLOOR

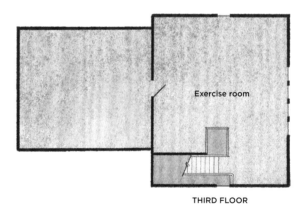

THIRD FLOOR

SECOND FLOOR

This house, built with cutting-edge green technology, fits in perfectly with the historical neighborhood.

isa Kauffman Tharp says it has been her mission to exemplify healthier building techniques in her own home and to help others learn about the many healthy options open to them in home construction.

Lisa took time off from her busy interior design practice to build her own house, which became a full-time job. She did a lot of research and made *A Pattern Language* by Christopher Alexander her architectural bible. Published in 1977, this has been an important guide for those interested in building a healthy home. Being chemically sensitive herself, Lisa wanted to be sure that she created a very healthy environment in her own home.

PUTTING TOGETHER A TEAM

She started out by putting together a team of architects who would combine the newest modern techniques of healthy green design and panelization construction with the traditional farmhouse design that would fit into this historical district.

Stephanie Horowitz of ZeroEnergy Design (ZED) worked to combine the green aspects of the house with cutting-edge healthy techniques. Stephanie says, "One of the challenges was to develop a design that captures both the park view at the front of the house and the direct sunlight at the back for passive solar heating and daylighting. The tight, L-shaped lot turned out to be ideal for maximizing the south-facing glazing in the first-floor living spaces."

Jordan Goldman, the mechanical designer at ZED, also worked on this project. Jordan says, "Two of our biggest design criteria were great energy efficiency and excellent indoor air quality. To reduce the energy demands, we designed an extremely energy-efficient building envelope that is well insulated and airtight. Along with the efficient envelope, we included high-efficiency mechanical equipment to meet the reduced demands in a highly efficient manner. Furthermore, the building envelope is designed to properly manage moisture flow, which eliminates the risk of condensation in the walls, which in turn can cause mildew, mold, and rot. Eliminating mildew and mold is incredibly important for excellent indoor air quality."

At Connor Homes, designer Steve Haskell was asked to transform the ZeroEnergy concept into a historically credible architectural design. His task was all the more challenging because Connor Homes manufactures its houses as precut panel assemblies.

Building the house with panelized construction appealed to Lisa because it is a method of closing a house up quickly and minimizing the intrusion of moisture and mold that can develop when a house is exposed to the elements. Lisa says there was a lot of back-and-forth communication among this team of professionals, but in the end they were the perfect combination of "yin and yang."

FINDING THE PERFECT LOCATION

The L-shaped lot on which the house was built was carefully selected. After looking at lots for nearly a year, Lisa and her husband, Sam, found the perfect site in historic Concord, Massachusetts, which offered them the lifestyle they sought. The location allowed them to walk to town and spend time in the adjacent park, rather than having to drive everywhere. Their child was also delighted to achieve a new sense of independence as friends, stores, and public transportation are within walking distance.

BELOW The local bluestone in the entranceway matches the exterior front walkway, thereby connecting indoors to out, while providing thermal mass.

BOTTOM There is more glazing on the rear of the house for passive solar gain and excellent daylighting.

Why Panelization?

The exterior and interior walls of a house, as well as the roof and floor components, are produced in a factory and then shipped to the site to be assembled together like a jigsaw puzzle. Panels can include windows and doors, but very often are shipped without those items already in place. Because they're built in a controlled environment, these component panels are not exposed to the elements and have less chance of later developing mold. Sophisticated machinery is often used in factories, including Connor Homes', which allows for more precise panels. The New England Farmhouse was erected in seven days, which is much faster than a house can be built on-site.

Indoor Air Pollution: Keeping the Air Clean

Spending time in the home should be a healthy experience—not one that can make you sick. Reports indicate that since people spend approximately 90 percent of their time indoors, they are exposed to two to five times and occasionally up to one hundred times more pollutants than they would be from outside air alone. Indoor air quality has had an adverse effect on many people in their own homes, some suffering from sick building syndrome (SBS), causing acute health problems and discomfort. Those with asthma and chemical sensitivities may be particularly affected by the chemicals and toxins used in building components, paints, finishes, adhesives, upholstery materials, and even the fire retardants and protective coatings used on various items, including mattresses. With

houses being built tightly sealed for energy efficiency, these toxic materials are trapped in the home environment. Forced hot air systems can disperse particles around the house and air-conditioning can trap moisture, which may cause mold. More and more houses are being built today with careful consideration of all items used to build, furnish, and clean the house. HVAC systems are being designed to keep indoor pollution to a minimum and maintain a well-ventilated house.

Nontoxic Mattresses

People might be surprised to find out what chemicals have been used in their mattresses. The Consumer Product Safety Commission requires all mattresses in the United States to contain some sort of flame retardant, which can potentially be toxic. Materials often include boric acid, formaldehyde, and other chemicals that can be toxic to adults and even more so to babies. With most people spending approximately eight hours in their beds each day, exposure to these toxins can have serious health effects. Some people believe that the dangerous effects from the toxic chemicals may outweigh the risk of the mattress catching fire. A doctor's note is required for consumers trying to purchase a chemical-free mattress. One manufacturer offers a removable flame-retardant layer that can be zipped off. White Lotus Home at www.whitelotus.net has an array of choices. For further information about mattress safety, check the website of the Consumer Product Safety Commission and www.peopleforcleanbeds.org.

BELOW The space-saving bed alcove provides a cozy sleeping nook, while leaving most of the square footage in the room available for full use during the day.

OPPOSITE All appliances in the kitchen are ENERGY STAR–rated in order to limit energy use. Larger windows on this southern side of the house flood the interior with sun. Skylights were added for additional daylighting.

BUILDING "CLEAN"

A great deal of time was spent on research and design before construction began. Lisa scrutinized every item that went into the building and interior design of the house for its health and efficiency.

The building shell contains increased insulation to reduce energy consumption and to maintain a comfortable year-round environment in the home. Building the house airtight limits air and moisture infiltration, avoiding the possible growth of mold and fungus.

Instead of using engineered beams in the floor and roof, which might include toxic finishes and glues, plain lumber was selected. This could have limited the expanse of open areas in the house, but with the combined efforts of the architects, the floor plan was executed to avoid that problem.

Lisa did not want a forced hot air and air-conditioning system, which would keep allergens and other contaminants airborne. Instead she and ZED chose a hot water radiant and radiator system, which would provide quiet, healthy heat.

No-VOC (volatile organic compound) paints and finishes were selected throughout to prevent toxic materials entering the interior air. Lisa says, "Every piece of material that came into the building envelope was evaluated for its toxicity before it entered—from the insulation to the grout to the floor finish to the sofa."

Mattresses (see page 31), which in the United States are required by the Consumer Product Safety Commission to contain flame retardants, can be toxic and even carcinogenic. Lisa obtained a doctor's note to purchase flame-retardant-free mattresses, which is the only way they can be obtained in this country. (Canada does not have this requirement.)

All fabrics used in the house are 100 percent cotton or linen, which have not been treated by stain guards, Teflon coatings, or antimicrobial finishes. Lisa says everyone's immune system is affected by some of these chemicals but that those with heightened sensitivities may respond to them faster.

NATURAL VENTILATION

It was very important to Lisa to "work with nature, reducing reliance on mechanical systems." Every floor plan decision was made around the sun, wind, and shade. This excellent team of architects designed the house so that room and window placement would ensure cross-ventilation and natural sunlight.

An advantage of this lot is the beautiful tall maple trees on the south side of it, which help block out some of the sun in the hot summer. The layout was designed with the kitchen and other family rooms in the rear of the house, where they could take advantage of the solar gain in the winter. The breezes from the open park across the street help to cool the house in the summer.

ZED designed a continuously operating ventilation and filtration system that's composed of a whole-house HEPA filter and an energy recovery ventilator (ERV). The HEPA filter constantly circulates and filters the air while the ERV exhausts stale air from the house and brings fresh air in. The ERV recovers heat and humidity from the exhaust airstream so that the incoming air is preheated and humidified. This can keep energy loss 90 percent lower than that caused by some ventilation systems.

Steve Haskell at Connor Homes says that in order to take advantage of the solar gain and "daylighting" of the southern exposure, larger windows were used on the rear of the house where the kitchen and family rooms are located. Smaller, more historically correct windows are on the north-facing front. This is the side that is seen from the street.

ACCESSIBLE AND UNIVERSAL

Lisa's major priorities in building her house were to make it comfortable and healthy, but she also wanted the house to be practical for her family's current situation and the future.

The downstairs has a "wet room" bathroom, which is wheelchair accessible, instead of a powder room. On the wall is a showerhead but no enclosure, with the floor pitched to the floor drain. This can be used by someone who is not able to get upstairs to the more conventional showers or it is a good place to wash a dog or clean muddy boots. This bathroom and the study next door could someday be turned into a master suite, so the couple can age in place in the house they have worked so hard to create.

FUTURE ENERGY MEASURES

ZED provided the infrastructure for future photovoltaic panels and a solar hot water system. These renewable energy systems will allow the house to offset some of its energy consumption. Lisa and Sam may decide to add these systems after they see what their future energy requirements will be.

BLOGGING AS AN AID TO OTHERS

Lisa started a blog (www.concordgreen.blogspot .com) so she could share all that she learned through her research and construction. "This house has become more than just my own health challenge, which I've made huge strides in," says Lisa. "I wanted to learn and then spread the word to help other people so they could be aware of how simple choices that we make when building or redecorating our home can dramatically impact our health."

The New England Farmhouse is not only healthy but also beautiful and efficient. It is no wonder that Lisa is inspiring others by her construction decisions; through her blog she is also bringing together an entire community of people who are dealing with chemical sensitivity issues similar to her own.

The Sea Breeze Cottage

Modular

PHOTOGRAPHER:

David Brown

Brown Photography (unless otherwise noted)

DESIGNER:

Don Aheron

Nationwide Homes

MANUFACTURER/BUILDER:

Nationwide Homes

INTERIOR DESIGNER:

Margie Wright

Nationwide Homes

LOCATION:

Orlando, Florida FARM

SIZE:

2,679 square feet

CERTIFICATION:

National Green Building Certification Program—Silver

ENERGY STAR

GREEN ASPECTS:

No-VOC paints and sealants

Dual-flush toilets

Low-flow showerheads and faucets

Metal siding

Materials with recycled content

Engineered wood

Covered entryways

ENERGY ASPECTS:

Solar shingles (see page 39)

Spray foam insulation—closed cell

ENERGY STAR–rated appliances

ENERGY STAR–rated lighting

ENERGY STAR–rated windows and doors

CFL lighting

Backup generator

High-efficiency heat pump (see page 39)

Tankless water heater

Efficient HVAC ductwork (to ensure no leakage)

No plumbing in exterior walls

Advanced framing techniques (insulated headers, single top plates at interior walls, engineered headers)

Direct-vent fireplaces (see page 40)

Ventilation fans

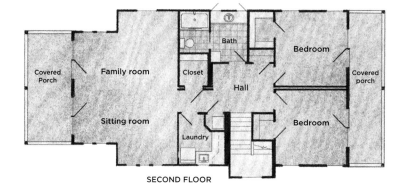

SECOND FLOOR

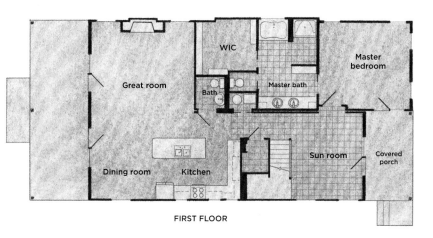

FIRST FLOOR

ABOVE The house was constructed at the Nationwide Homes factory in Martinsville, Virginia. (Photo courtesy of Nationwide)

OPPOSITE The house was set on a back lot at the International Builders' Show in Orlando in January 2011.

n just fifteen days the Sea Breeze Cottage was built in the Nationwide Homes factory in Martinsville, Virginia; in two days it was delivered to Orlando; and in seven days, twelve people erected it on-site at the International Builders' Show in 2011. Over 4,700 people visited the show, with an overwhelmingly positive response. (I was fortunate to be one of them, having attended that conference.) A general reaction to the modular aspect of the construction was surprise. Although a great deal of information is available about modular construction, people still seem to be amazed at how attractive modular houses can be.

The house was designed as a modern beachfront cottage, and it can be situated on a narrow lot, the house measuring just thirty feet in width. The design combines modern technology with traditional styling, with plenty of indoor conveniences and an abundance of outdoor living space.

BUILDING IN EFFICIENCY

Among the highlights of the house are the innovative integrated solar shingles (see opposite), first seen at this show. Closed-cell foam insulation was installed in the factory and advanced framing techniques (insulated headers, single top plates at interior walls, engineered headers) were used to ensure a well-insulated, tight envelope.

An energy-efficient 15 SEER heat pump (see opposite) was specifically designed for the Florida climate. The air ducts were sized exactly as needed and sealed to eliminate air leakage. Plumbing was protected from the effects of heat by locating the pipes in more protected areas of the house and away from exterior walls.

The Sea Breeze Cottage was designed to be very energy efficient and to meet the National Green Building Standard. The house was certified to the second highest level, Silver.

During the show, the house produced energy, with the electric meter running backward, and the excess energy was sold back to the local utility company.

LIMITING ENERGY USE

To limit the energy used in this house, all appliances, lighting, windows, and doors are ENERGY STAR rated. The two innovative direct-vent gas fireplaces (see page 40) use a minimum of energy. The ceiling fans installed in several rooms help to move air around, making the house feel cooler and reducing the need for air-conditioning.

After the show, the house was sold to a customer and moved just north of Tampa to a lakefront property.

BELOW   A special item in the master bathroom is this glossy red soaking tub, which adds a punch of brightness to the room.

BOTTOM   The upstairs family room has reclaimed stained maple hardwood flooring.

Solar Shingles

The Dow Powerhouse Solar Shingle is a groundbreaking photovoltaic; it is a solar roofing shingle that is integrated into residential rooftops along with standard asphalt shingle materials. It reduces installation time and complexity by using a proprietary interconnect system design that eliminates on-roof wiring, it minimizes through-roof penetrations, and it can be installed in the same manner as a standard roofing shingle. These shingles are revolutionary because they incorporate photovoltaic (PV) cells into standard roofing shingles, protecting the home while converting the sun's energy into electricity. They are an aesthetic improvement over traditional, bulky PV panels because they are installed flush to the roof and blend seamlessly to create an attractive, integrated appearance. A Dow-certified roofing contractor installs the shingles, and an electrician connects the array to an inverter, which converts the direct current (DC) to the alternating current (AC) that powers the home. There is no wiring on the roof thanks to Dow's unique connector system, and the Powerhouse Solar Shingles are the first residential solar roofing shingle with an integrated connection system to receive Underwriters Laboratories (UL) safety certification—as both a roofing and a solar product. Typical residential solar arrays offset approximately 40 to 80 percent of a home's electricity, but that is dependent on many factors including the home's orientation and homeowner goals. For additional information about Dow's Powerhouse Solar Shingle system, check out the website www.dowsolar.com.

Heat Pumps

In more temperate climates, heat pumps offer an alternative to furnaces and air conditioners. Using a small amount of energy, they can pull heat out of the air or ground (geothermal) to heat a house. The process can be reversed to cool a structure. They are more efficient than other types of HVAC systems because they transfer air instead of burning fuel. Heat pumps can vastly reduce utility bills but will not function well in very cold climates. ENERGY STAR–qualified heat pumps have a higher seasonal energy efficiency ratio (SEER), a higher energy efficiency ratio (EER), and a higher heating seasonal performance factor (HSPF) than standard models. Since December 2009, homeowners with ENERGY STAR–qualified air-source heat pumps have been eligible for a 30 percent federal tax credit. For more information about heat pumps, check the website www.energystar.gov, and also see www.rheem.com, which sells the product used in the Sea Breeze Cottage.

BELOW The direct-vent gas fireplace uses a minimum of energy. The ENERGY STAR–rated fan reduces the need for air-conditioning. The sliding doors expand the house to include a generous outdoor living space.

BOTTOM This open kitchen includes all ENERGY STAR–rated appliances and solid-surface countertops, which include recycled content.

Direct-Vent and Vent-Free Fireplaces

Direct-vent (DV) fireplaces do not require a masonry chimney and can be vented directly through a wall, or through the roof using a chimney as a traditional fireplace does. It is one of the most efficient types of fireplaces because it draws its combustion air from outside and does not consume warm house air, as most traditional fireplaces with chimneys do. Exhaust air is expelled through concentric pipes or through separate intake and exhaust vents. This type of fireplace eliminates drafts and heat loss, does not interfere with indoor air quality, and is easier to install in a remodeled house. It can burn natural gas or propane. One limitation, however, is that the fireplace must be close to an outside wall, or if in the center of house, it needs to vent vertically. There are two types of DV fireplaces, some that are principally decorative and some that are heaters. All eliminate drafts, unlike traditional wood-burning fireplaces, but decorative gas units are just decorative, while heater units can warm up a major portion of the house.

There are also vent-free fireplaces available today that do not require any venting and can be installed almost anyplace in the home. Because there are no vents, all the heat remains in the house. A by-product of combustion is water, and that remains in the room if there isn't a vent for the moisture to escape. This can be a plus in houses that are very dry in the winter, but may create condensation on cold windows in houses that are already moist. Vent-free fireplaces can burn ethanol or gas. For further information, check the websites www.hpba.org and www.ventfree.org.

This circular fireplace gives the appearance of infinity with LED lights and mirrors, although it has a shallow depth.

Lakeside Green Cottage

Structural Insulated Panels/Timber Frame

PHOTOGRAPHER:

Peter Baker (unless otherwise noted)

DESIGNER:

Dennis L. Feltner

FRAME AND SIP DESIGNER:

Brian Faulkner

CONTRACTOR:

Tom Dearth

MANUFACTURER:

Insulspan

Riverbend Timber Framing

SIZE:

1,652 square feet

LOCATION:

Lakeside, Ohio

BLOWER DOOR TEST:

0.27 ACH @ 50 Pascals

CERTIFICATION:

National Green Building Certification
Program—Gold

GREEN ASPECTS:

Small footprint

Salvaged stove

Low-flow showerhead and faucets

Metal roof (with recycled content)

Salvaged wood for trim, flooring, and
timber frame (see page 46)

Salvaged doors and hardware

Salvaged claw-foot tub, sink, and low-
flow toilet

Permeable pavers (see page 46)

FSC-certified wood

Engineered wood

No-VOC paint

Rain barrel capture for irrigation

Locally grown white cedar siding

ENERGY ASPECTS:

SIPs

Passive solar orientation

Tankless water heater

LED and fluorescent lighting (see page 46)

Roof overhangs

Insulated concrete form (ICF) foundation

Spray foam sealant (joints, windows, doors)

High-efficiency windows

ENERGY STAR–rated appliances

ENERGY STAR–rated flat-screen television

ENERGY STAR–rated ceiling fans

Expanded polystyrene (EPS) insulation in basement
and crawl space

Wired for future photovoltaic and solar thermal panels

Heat recovery ventilator (HRV)

SECOND FLOOR

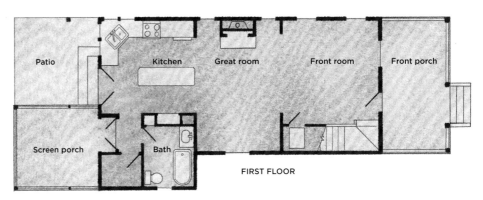

FIRST FLOOR

ABOVE A fallen tree damaged the original house beyond
repair. Many parts were salvaged for the new structure.

OPPOSITE The home was rebuilt in the style of the hundred-
year-old house that was previously on that property.

When a storm dropped a large tree on Brenda and Frank Baker's vacation cottage, their first impulse was to save the original structure. But after a thorough inspection, it was determined that the house was too compromised to be reused. So the Bakers decided to rebuild the house from the ground up, with the same character as its hundred-year-old predecessor, but as a model of energy efficiency and sustainable construction.

THE RIGHT PEOPLE FOR THE JOB

As industry icons, the Bakers probably know more about sustainable construction than most. Founders of Insulspan, maker of structural insulated panels (SIPs), and Riverbend Timber Framing, they have worked in the industry for over thirty years. During the developing stages of structural insulated panels, they were able to make their own SIP product more efficiently and economically, with increased quality. With the use of CNC (computer numerical control) machines, using CAD and CAM programs, in the early 1990s, SIPs became an even more practical building material because these technologies reduced the cost of labor and allowed panels to be cut more precisely, producing a higher-quality product. So when it was time to rebuild the cottage, SIPs and timber framing were natural choices.

The Bakers enlisted designer Dennis Feltner to re-create the cottage to fit the narrow thirty-three-foot-wide site and to accommodate the Bakers and their two grown sons. Having worked for the Lakeside Historic Preservation and Design Review Board, Feltner is familiar with the community's building requirements and architectural styles, and he is also an advocate for eco-friendly design.

A GREEN MODEL

The Bakers use the cottage not only as their vacation retreat but also as a model project to help educate the public on sustainable construction. "We want to show people that eco-friendly building technology and historic character can go hand in hand," says Frank. They give lectures at their community, one of the largest historical communities in the country, and invite people to visit their cottage.

BUILDING A TIGHT ENCLOSURE

The house incorporates several effective insulating products. The foundation is concrete poured into an arrangement of insulated concrete forms (ICFs), which are interlocking blocks of expanded polystyrene (EPS) insulation. The blocks stay in place and function as an efficient barrier against air infiltration. The SIPs form an excellent insulating envelope, as infill with the timber frame and high-efficiency windows.

COST EFFICIENCY

Frank emphasizes the cost of ownership rather than the cost of the house structure. Comparing a SIPs-built house to a "code-minimum" house, he says the cost of ownership of the former will stay flat over time while the cost of ownership of the latter will continually increase, because of the dramatic rise in the cost of energy.

ADVOCATE FOR NET ZERO

Frank says the pitch of the roof is perfect for photovoltaic panels and solar hot water panels, which he plans to install in the future to make the house a zero-energy home. Frank was one of the founding members of the Structural Insulated Panel Association and is on the board of directors of the Net-Zero

BELOW   The metal roof is durable and environmentally friendly, made from recycled content.

RIGHT TOP   The timber-frame is being erected. The Bakers' name and the year it was built can be seen on the beam.

RIGHT BOTTOM   A blower door test was conducted to show where there was air leakage, so this could be corrected. (Photo courtesy of Marty Birkenkamp)

Energy Home Coalition, a not-for-profit organization working to encourage net-zero-ready construction. The organization is promoting structures to be designed as net zero or net zero ready so that renewable systems can be easily attached, allowing the structures to become net-zero-energy homes later on. This permits homeowners to add renewable systems, such as solar panels, at a later date, after the construction of their house, when they can better afford them or the systems become more economically feasible. This vision of zero-energy performance by all residential structures is shared by the California Energy Commission and was proposed in a bill in the United States Senate.

BELOW A salvaged bureau holds a vessel sink in the guest bathroom upstairs.

BOTTOM The beautiful timber frame can be seen in the second-floor hallway.

LED Lighting

Until recently LED (light-emitting diode) lights were not a reasonable option for residential applications because of the cost and limitations in design. This technology is rapidly expanding and becoming a viable option for new home construction as well as remodels. LED lights use at least 75 percent less energy than incandescent lighting; last a minimum of 25,000 hours, or twenty-two years based on average household use (for comparison, an incandescent light lasts about 1,000 hours, and fluorescent lights last between 10,000 and 20,000 hours); do not contain mercury (as fluorescents do); come with a three-year warranty; are now available with Edison (screw-in type) bases; and can be used with some dimming systems and motion sensors. LEDs also perform well even with frequent on-off cycling. They are less fragile than incandescent and CFL bulbs and produce very little heat. LEDs are available for indoor and outdoor use. They are still more expensive than other bulbs and not as readily available, but that should change in the near future. When purchasing LED lights, check for the ENERGY STAR qualification and the warranty on the bulbs.

Salvaged Materials— What's Old Is New Again

In the Lakeside Green Cottage, many materials, including the doors, trim, and hardware, were salvaged from the original house on the property, which was destroyed by a fallen tree during a storm. Several advantages to incorporating recovered materials into new construction include: less debris in landfills, conservation of resources, saving money, and owning unique objects that may no longer be readily available. There are some disadvantages: Some restoration work may be required, no warranties or assembly instructions come with these treasures, and you may have to transport them. But many people enjoy discovering some wonderful reclaimed items and connecting in a small way with the past. Today there are many places to find salvaged materials for the home. For information about finding salvaged materials (or donating your own), the following are two websites that may be helpful: www.ecobusinesslinks.com /recycled-building-materials.htm and www .builder2builder.com.

Permeable Paving

Permeable paving allows water to drain into the ground and filter out some of the pollutants and contaminants, preventing pooling of rainwater and reducing the amount of pollutants entering natural waterways in runoff. The initial cost for permeable pavers may be higher than for more traditional paving materials such as asphalt; however, they will probably reduce the cost of other drainage and storm water management systems on the property and can add to curb appeal. There are several different types of systems. Some are as simple as mulches, which include pebbles, gravel, and sod. More sophisticated systems can include pavers made of concrete, cut stone, or plastic with voids, where grass can grow or where water can simply drain through. Using permeable paving in cold climate areas holds some challenges: sand used in plowing may clog the porous areas, road salt containing chlorides can filter down into the water system, and plowing may destroy the integrity of the pavers. For further information about permeable pavers, check the website www.paversearch.com.

BELOW LEFT The posts and beams provide definition for the large open space—with the dining area in the front of the house, the living room in the middle, and the kitchen in the rear.

BOTTOM LEFT Ceiling fans in several of the rooms help keep the family and guests cool in the hot summer. The beautiful timber frame trusses add a warm look to the rooms.

BELOW RIGHT All appliances in the house are ENERGY STAR rated. The island countertop is made from a slab of mahogany bought at auction, and the other countertops are made from pieces of oak that had been stored in the barn on the property for almost fifty years.

Green Retreat

Post and Beam

PHOTOGRAPHER:

Patrick Barta Photography (unless
  otherwise noted)

DESIGNER:

Tom Schuch

Lindal Cedar Homes

CONTRACTOR:

MC Construction

BUILDING PACKAGE:

Lindal Cedar Homes

LOCATION:

Seattle, Washington

SIZE:

2,400 square feet

CERTIFICATION:

ENERGY STAR

Built Green—4 Star (see page 53)

National Green Building Certification
  Program—Bronze

GREEN ASPECTS:

Recycled materials

Metal roof from recycled content

Locally sourced materials

Insulation made from postconsumer
  recycled bottle glass

Dual-flush toilets

Bamboo and cork flooring

No-VOC paint

Recycled decking

Recycled glass/concrete countertops
  (C2C certified)

Native plants

Rain garden

Separate garage

ENERGY ASPECTS:

Passive solar orientation

Energy-efficient windows

Radiant heat

ENERGY STAR–rated appliances

ENERGY STAR–rated lighting

Wired for future solar hot water and
  photovoltaic panels

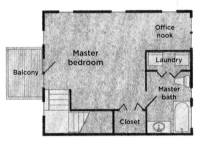

SECOND FLOOR

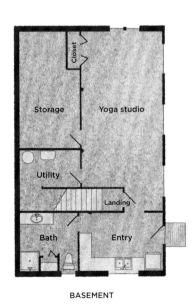

BASEMENT

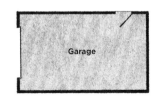

Garage

FIRST FLOOR

Red was used for the doors and trim to add a hint of color to an otherwise unpainted wood exterior. The standing seam metal roof is also red, coordinating well with the red cedar wood.

Wendy decided her six-hundred-square-foot cottage was too small for her family and yoga studio, but she still adored her beautiful wooded lot where the house was situated. With no foundation, the cottage was not expandable, so the only alternative was to start building a new house from scratch at her current location. Wendy wanted to replace her old cottage with a house that had more space, was very green, and could be built within the constraints of her tight budget.

She was also aware of the health hazards related to toxic products used in construction and the energy wasted in many homes. After doing much research on green building, Wendy became committed to making hers a healthy, energy-efficient, environmentally friendly home.

She chose the Lindal building system because the company was able to meet her priorities, which included high ceilings, an open floor plan, and lots of windows so the house would be filled with light. Lindal project consultant Tom Schuch walked her through the construction and green certification process. Wendy says she never could have done this on her own.

DECONSTRUCTING THE OLD HOUSE

In keeping with her objective to build the house environmentally friendly, she opted to have the old house deconstructed—a greener alternative than simply demolishing it. Olympia Deconstruction Company was hired to take apart the old house and salvage as many materials as possible. Wendy says, "I loved the idea of not contributing to a landfill unnecessarily, and figured that if I was investing in a green home, I should do the green version of demolition." It took

a little over a month to demolish, much longer than if she had quickly torn down the house and put the materials in Dumpsters. But with the deconstruction process, most of the material was salvaged, and Wendy received a small tax credit.

The only parts of the old house that were used for Wendy's new house were cement blocks and rocks used for "hardscaping" the garden; the remaining materials, such as wood, cabinetry, and sinks, were sold in a salvage store owned by the people who did the deconstruction.

BUILDING GREEN

The house was positioned to take the best possible advantage of passive solar energy and to bathe the interior in natural light. Wendy anticipates adding solar hot water and photovoltaic panels in the near future. Currently she has radiant floors, which are quiet and keep the house warm even on the coldest days.

Tom recommended several green builders in the area. Wendy chose MC Construction, a company with strong credentials in constructing environmentally friendly homes. She stayed involved in the process from beginning to end, selecting materials and systems. Pam Worner of Green Dog Enterprises guided Wendy as a third-party verifier for the green certification process.

All of the materials were consolidated in Lindal's plant in Burlington, Washington, and shipped in containers to the site. Lindal precut the posts and beams and the wall parts, prehung the doors, and even made the windows in the plant. The posts and beams were erected in much the same way many old barns used to be raised (see page 53). Unlike two-by-four-type

LEFT The owner has a yoga studio on the lower level of the house. The large picture window adds serenity to the space.

BELOW A workshop was set up in the old carport to remove nails from the wood in the deconstructed house, which was donated for other purposes. (Photo courtesy of the owner)

BOTTOM The post and beam construction is conducive to building a house with an open floor plan and limited interior walls.

framed houses, most walls in the house do not support the roof—the posts and beams do.

The Green Retreat is the first house in Washington State to be certified under the National Green Building Certification Program developed in part by the National Association of Home Builders.

The standing seam metal roof is made from recycled metal and adds an attractive design feature as well as being very durable. The roof also has a lifetime guarantee. The house is wired for photovoltaic panels and has plumbing for solar hot water panels, which will be installed on the roof in the future.

BELOW The flooring in the kitchen is cork, which Wendy says is the "softest material to stand on." The countertops are polished concrete and the cabinets were built locally using alder wood that is free of formaldehyde and other toxic substances.

BOTTOM The bathroom countertops are made from 100 percent recycled glass and concrete surfacing that has received Cradle to Cradle certification (see sidebar).

Built Green

Built Green is a nonprofit residential building program of the Master Builders Association of King and Snohomish Counties in Washington. It provides consumers and builders with a rating system to quantify environmentally friendly building practices for remodeling and new home construction, both single and multifamily units. They provide standards for energy efficiency, indoor air quality, conservation of natural resources, and water quality. The Built Green website offers a list of builders in the area who are able to build to its standards, which exceed local building codes. The owner of the Green Retreat used the checklist on this website as a guide for her construction. For additional information about the Built Green program, check the website www.builtgreen.net.

Post and Beam/Timber Frame Construction

Post and beam and timber frame construction are similar; both are methods of building that create a frame that is self-sustaining and that carries the weight of the house. Timber frames are always made with solid wood with mortise-and-tenon connections, and secured with wood pegs. Post and beam construction can be constructed using engineered wood such as glulams and can have metal connectors. Because the frame carries the weight of the house with both methods, interior load-bearing walls aren't necessary, allowing for large open interior spaces and high ceilings. Often the frame is left exposed, adding a natural beauty to the look of the house; in some cases the frame is hidden behind walls. Most post and beam/timber frames are preconstructed in a protected environment, then are labeled and trucked to a site where they are quickly erected. Often the wood used for these frames is recycled wood or standing dead timber. If the house is later deconstructed, these timbers can then be used for future structures. For additional information about timber frame construction, check out the website of the Timber Framers Guild: www.tfguild.org.

Cradle to Cradle (or C2C)

Cradle to Cradle (C2C) is a design concept based on natural principles—everything is a resource for something else; use renewable energy; and celebrate diversity. Cradle to Cradle certification is a program designed to support manufacturers in a process of continuous improvement. Such companies create materials and products that cycle continuously in one of two nutrient systems: biological (things that can safely return to the soil) or technical (things that can be upcycled in perpetuity). In their 2002 book, *Cradle to Cradle: Remaking the Way We Make Things*, American designer William McDonough, in partnership with German chemist Michael Braungart, developed this concept and popularized its importance. Their program identifies products and materials that are safe for humans and the environment. The program presently has four levels of certification—basic, silver, gold, and platinum—which are based on five categories, including material health, material reutilization, renewable energy use, water stewardship, and social responsibility. For further information about the Cradle to Cradle Certified program, check the website www.mbdc.com.

Superb-A House

Panelized

PHOTOGRAPHER:

Art Gray Photography

ARCHITECT:

Minarc

MANUFACTURER:

mnm.MOD

BUILDER:

Core Construction

LOCATION:

Venice, California

SIZE:

2,400 square feet

GREEN ASPECTS:

No paint, no tiles, no carpet

Separate carport

Cooling pond with accent of recycled glass

RUBBiSH (recycled rubber sinks; see page 60)

Eco-smart fire

Native vegetation garden (no water consumption)

Recycled rubber finish on kitchen cabinets and
   Hide-n-Sit disappearing island chairs

Dual-flush toilets

Materials used in their organic form whenever
   possible

ENERGY ASPECTS:

LED lights

Natural ventilation (no air-conditioning),
   including cross-ventilation

Radiant floor heating

Passive solar orientation

Solar thermal panels

Thermally broken panel system

Thermally broken windows and doors

Energy-efficient appliances

ABOVE The fencing is tilted at an angle so the owners can
see out but passersby can't see in, allowing for privacy.

OPPOSITE The exterior siding is made of concrete panels
and certified cedar.

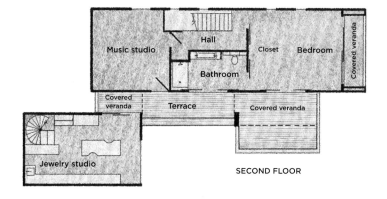

SECOND FLOOR

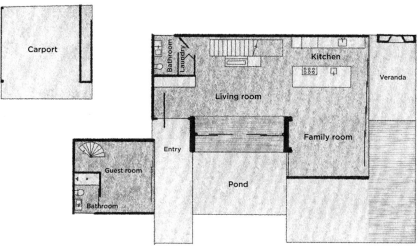

FIRST FLOOR

L   ess is more" is the general philosophy of architectural and marriage partners Erla Dogg Ingjaldsdottir and Tryggvi Thorsteinsson. What are the chances that two students from Iceland would meet at an architectural college in California? But these two did, and for ten years, they have been designing houses that reflect their vision of the natural aesthetic of Iceland. Since it is an island where everything needs to be imported, natives are more likely to recycle materials and use ones that will last longer.

Erla and Tryggvi believe that materials are beautiful in their natural state, so they avoid layering them unnecessarily. They also believe homes should be built requiring minimal energy, with very energy-efficient envelopes. Erla and Tryggvi say people work too hard to make things beautiful, when they are already beautiful. Instead of adding paint to a skim-coated wall, it is left in its natural state, without any other embellishment, which they say looks good and conserves materials, energy, and waste.

When asked to design a modern, very energy-efficient house for clients in Venice, California, it was an opportunity for Erla and Tryggvi to employ many of the techniques they'd developed over the years. By limiting the use of materials and conserving energy, they say they are able to design a beautiful house that will cost less than a typical house and will be less costly to maintain.

WHAT THE HOUSE DOESN'T HAVE

Erla and Tryggvi say, "It is not what the building has, it is what the building does not need." The Superb-A House was built using no paint, no tile, no carpet, and no traditional HVAC system. They avoided layering materials; so instead of using tile in the bathrooms

over concrete, and then grout, they used concrete on the walls without embellishment. Whenever possible, materials were left in their natural state. All lighting is LED to minimize energy use and to adhere to their quest to use materials that will last as long as possible.

NATURAL HEATING AND COOLING

Erla and Tryggvi say their designs are "not about creating energy but saving energy." No air-conditioning system was installed in the house. Cooling is achieved through the passive orientation of the house, lots of windows for natural cross-ventilation, and a cooling pond, which serves to cool the air before it enters the house. "Night flush cooling" is one of the energy-saving features. This takes advantage of the temperature swings that occur over a twenty-four-hour period in California. Window openings placed close to the floor draw cool night air into the house, and exhaust openings near the ceiling draw warmer air out into the night.

Radiant floor heating is used on cool days, and the water for the system is heated by solar hot water panels on the roof. Lots of mass in the floors and walls create thermal mass, which aids in the heating and cooling of the structure.

PREFAB CONSTRUCTION

All of the parts of the house were built in a factory, with walls precut, predrilled, and numbered for easy assembly on-site. Erla and Tryggvi developed and patented a panelized system with metal structural members and insulation calculated to meet the energy requirements at the various exposures of the house. The walls are designed with thermal breaks so there is minimal air infiltration. Patented expanded

The landscaping of the house includes only local plantings. Herbs are located close to the barbecue area so that they can be used while cooking outdoors.

BELOW In the evening, air blows over the pond, where it is cooled, and then comes into the house through the windows, which are close to the ground. The lift-and-slide wall of glass opens almost fully to encourage indoor/outdoor living.

BOTTOM The upstairs bathroom opens to a deck, allowing natural ventilation and bathing in the fresh air.

All decking is ipe (see Snowhorn House, page 131), a highly sustainable, very durable wood.

polystyrene (EPS) insulation, a Cradle to Cradle Certified product (see Green Retreat, page 53), is used in the wall, ceiling, and roof structure. Erla and Tryggvi did extensive research and energy modeling before any construction was to begin. They say they are now able to achieve R-6 per inch with their panel design; this achieves R-30 for a five-inch wall.

The design methods were also intended to streamline the manufacturing process, with less handling, less processing, less cutting, and less waste. Wherever possible the house was built using standardized, off-the-shelf products to save time and money. Erla and Tryggvi say the entire house can be taken apart and restructured on another site.

Because the method for this prototype was so different from anything the building department in Los Angeles had ever seen, it took over a year for inspectors to issue a building permit. Now that the methods and materials have been approved, Erla and Tryggvi say it will take far less time to replicate the next house using the same method; the house could be completed in four or five months.

For this project mnm.MOD, the design arm of their company, received a Sustainable Quality Award for Excellence in Stewardship of the Environment from the California State Assembly and an Award for Economic Development from the Senate of the State of California.

Tryggvi says, "If a building's orientation, massing, window area/shading, insulation arrangement, and air tightness are not properly optimized, no amount of latest mechanical systems and or sustainable materials can make the building a true low-energy building."

The kitchen cabinetry and kitchen chairs are made from material that was manufactured from recycled tires.

Recycled Rubber

According to U.S. Rubber, a flooring manufacturer, more than 40.2 million reusable and waste tires are generated each year in California alone. It is estimated that 1.5 million waste tires are illegally dumped or stockpiled. Some companies have decided that since there is so much rubber already in existence they could use it to produce useful and attractive items for the home. Minarc produces rubber bathroom sinks, which are lightweight and very durable. Its disappearing chairs fit neatly under the counter, and when not in use, they disappear from sight and create less clutter in the room. Both of these items are made from recycled tires. For more information about these products, check the website www.minarc.com. For more information about rubber, check the website www.usrubber.com.

A very open floor plan allows air to circulate throughout the house.
The wall of glass, when open, extends the living space.

Stillwater Dwelling

Modular

ARCHITECT/BUILDER:

Matthew Stannard

Stillwater Dwellings

MANUFACTURER:

Guerdon Enterprises

LOCATION:

Sauvie Island, Oregon

SIZE:

2,300 square feet

HERS RATING: 87

CERTIFICATIONS:

LEED-H—Gold (targeted)

GREEN ASPECTS:

Reclaimed teak flooring

Low-VOC paint

Dual-flush toilets

Low-flow faucets

Fireplace with renewable energy
   source—denatured ethanol

Standing seam recycled metal roof

ENERGY ASPECTS:

Passive solar orientation

Energy monitoring system

ENERGY STAR–rated appliances

Photovoltaic panels (to be installed)

Formaldehyde-free batt insulation

Electric hybrid heat pump

Extended roof overhangs

Cool roof metal coating

Increased thermal mass in basement walls and floors

Clerestory awning windows and operable skylights
   (for stack-effect cooling)

High-efficiency glass

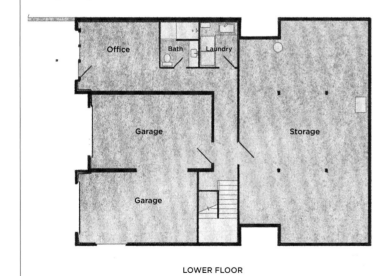

LOWER FLOOR

UPPER FLOOR

The high butterfly roof is a signature feature of the Stillwater Dwelling. The extended ceiling height was made possible by hinging the living room roof at the low end and lifting it up higher on-site. The factory put hinges on one end, and the windows and walls above the door header were installed on-site.

The owners of the Stillwater Dwelling went through the design process with several architects and contractors, only to find out that their site-built dream house would be priced at double their plan. Frustrated by the over-budget cost, the owners turned to the Internet and found Stillwater Dwellings.

BUILDING MODULAR

"We were immediately struck by the Stillwater Dwellings designs, but it was the upfront pricing that made it real for us. Once we visited one of their client's homes in Bend, Oregon, we were sold . . . we had to have one!" noted homeowner Todd. "Savings on the cost of the home were $880,000, or over 50 percent, based on what we paid Stillwater Dwellings and the estimates we received from site-built contractors for a home of the same size and quality."

Stillwater generally offers a package with interiors complete, as well as exteriors. However, homeowners John and Todd had already amassed a significant amount of interior fixtures for their initially intended on-site-built design: wood flooring, porcelain tiles, light fixtures, and artwork including many Balinese pieces from their travels to Southeast Asia. Stillwater Dwellings therefore worked with them to supply a fully completed exterior but only a partially completed interior, including all of the mechanical systems, drywall, and millwork; the owners focused their attention on customizing the interior finishes.

TILT-UP ROOF

The owners John and Todd wanted the house to have high ceilings. Stillwater was able to accommodate them with a tilt-up roof section. The entire roof over the great room was transported flat, on top of the home module, from the Stillwater factory to the homesite. Once the module was installed on the foundation, the crane tilted the entire roof section up and the additional wall panels were inserted to create an interior ceiling space twelve and a half feet high, complete with two-and-a-half-foot-high operable clerestory windows above the already nine-foot-high wall of glass.

LIVING IN A GLASS HOUSE

Although there's a preponderance of glass in this house, it was designed to be highly energy efficient. The windows have high-performance glass that blocks ultraviolet (UV) rays and, according to the glass manufacturer (Cardinal), performs 96 percent better at winter nighttime insulation (measured by its R-value—see page 67) than other forms of glass. A heat pump supplies both air-conditioning and heat when needed. The house is wired for photovoltaic panels, which will be added in the near future.

PRESERVATION OF THE EXISTING LANDSCAPE

The home was assembled on a ten-acre site with a 360-degree view capturing its island and river surroundings as well as Mount St. Helens, Mount Hood, and Mount Rainier. The original homesite featured an incredible collection of rare trees, exotic rhododendrons, and a mature garden landscape, which John and Todd wanted to leave entirely untouched. Modular off-site construction turned out to be the perfect solution. Needing minimal staging and work areas, the modules were picked up from the driveway and lifted over the trees and bushes, and then placed carefully down onto the foundation, with minimal impact on the site.

The kitchen features all ENERGY STAR–rated appliances. Many of the interior components were purchased from the owners' travels in Southeast Asia.

BELOW The house was situated on the property for optimum
solar advantage.

BOTTOM LEFT Large sliding glass doors open to a small patio,
expanding the space of the house and aiding in natural ventilation.

BOTTOM RIGHT On the rear deck, the owners can have breakfast
watching the sun rise over Mount St. Helens! The oversize doors and
multiple windows allow for natural lighting and ventilation.

Smart Home Systems

Systems are available today that can monitor the energy produced by or coming into the house from outside sources. They can keep track of the energy and water being used; regulate the thermostat; and turn on and off appliances, security systems, lights, and music. All of this can be controlled by keypads in the house, computers, and even iPads and cell phones from remote locations. Residents can communicate with these and additional items through home automation. These systems provide comfort and security by doing things for you (such as turning on the coffeemaker in the morning, turning up the heat so the house is warm when you return home, monitoring fire and security systems, reminding the elderly to take meds, or shutting off the water before a tub overflows). They can also save energy. When people know how much energy they are using, they tend to reduce their usage. Some systems can put devices at a reduced level of functionality and turn off lights when people aren't in the room. For more information about smart home systems, a good website to check is http://home.howstuffworks.com/smart-home.htm. For information about the energy monitoring system in the Stillwater Dwelling, check the website www.control4.com.

R-value

R-value is the measure of thermal resistance to heat flow through a given insulating material. The higher the R-value of a material, the greater the insulating effectiveness. The R-value of a material depends on the type of material, its thickness, its density, and how it is installed. If thermal bridging (see Unity House, page 162) is created around the insulation through studs and joists, for example, the R-value of a material can be compromised. Proper installation is required to achieve the maximum insulation of a structure. The amount of insulation required depends on the climate and the exposure of the particular wall. For more information, check the website www.energysavers.gov or www.ornl.gov/sci/roofs+walls/insulation/ins_01.html.

Clerestory Windows

Clerestory windows are located in the upper part of a wall, allowing light to shine down into the center of the room. They can increase daylighting, passive solar energy, and aid in cross-ventilation. Hot air, which rises, can also be expelled through them in summer, reducing air-conditioning requirements. In cold climates they can add to heat gain when located on the south side of the house; awnings and overhangs can minimize heat gain in the warmer months (when the sun is at a higher angle in the sky). Clerestory windows bring light into a room without compromising privacy and in small rooms add to the usable wall space.

Newport Beach House

Modular/Steel Frame

PHOTOGRAPHER:

Scott Mayoral

Mayoral Photography (unless otherwise
   noted)

ARCHITECT:

KieranTimberlake

DEVELOPER/BUILDER:

LivingHomes

MANUFACTURER:

Profile Structures

INTERIOR DESIGNER:

Kristin Kilmer Design

LOCATION:

Newport Beach, California

SIZE:

2,200 square feet

CERTIFICATION:

LEED-H—Platinum

GREEN ASPECTS:

No-VOC paints

Low-VOC stains

Small footprint

Automatic ventilation

Dual-flush toilets

Low-flow faucets and showerheads

Gray water ready

Recycled composite decks and fence

Biocomposite wood siding

Recycled glass tiles

Recycled steel

Engineered wood

Wheat-core doors

Bathroom vents on timers

GREENGUARD Indoor Air Quality
   Certified Quartz countertops

ENERGY ASPECTS:

Photovoltaic panels

High-performance windows

Transom windows

Recycled-content blown-in insulation

Tankless water heater

ENERGY STAR–rated appliances

ENERGY STAR–rated lighting

Mini-duct air distribution (see page 72)

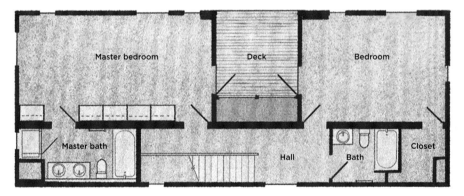

SECOND FLOOR

ABOVE The modules are lifted and set into this tight space. (Photo courtesy of LivingHomes)

OPPOSITE The exterior cladding is composed of eco-friendly, UV-protected panels made of a 50/50 blend of 100 percent postconsumer recycled paper and rapidly renewable bamboo fiber, which is an FSC-certified fiber.

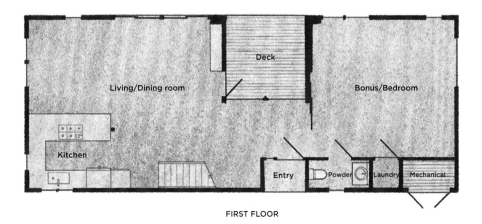

FIRST FLOOR

To the amazement of local residents, a 250-ton crane lifted four preconstructed modules and set them on a small lot, where they were assembled in about five hours. Originally built in a factory and installed as a model home at the 2009 International Builders' Show in Las Vegas, Nevada, this home was later displayed at the 2009 TED Conference in Long Beach, California. Soon after that, it was sold to a private owner and installed about twenty miles down the coast, in Newport Beach. Once installed at its permanent site, the house received a LEED Platinum rating from the U.S. Green Building Council's LEED for Homes program. An earlier home built by LivingHomes was the first in the country to receive this designation.

HOUSE COMPOSITION

The 2,200-square-foot house comprises four simple, modern, stacked modules that have open and flexible interiors promoting passive solar and daylighting. The two lower modules contain an open kitchen, dining area, and living room arrangement and a spacious multipurpose room, while the two upper modules contain a master suite, an additional bedroom, and a bathroom. All of the home's mechanical, plumbing, and electrical systems are located in two "smart" modules aligned in a stacked configuration, resulting in labor and materials savings compared to conventional building methods.

Because the modules arrived 95 percent complete, with finishes preinstalled, on-site installation time was minimal. The entire process from start of construction to finish took less than four months.

CONSERVING ENERGY AND WATER

The house was designed to reduce energy demand with such features as daylighting, high-efficiency insulation, an efficient HVAC system, low-energy lights, a tankless water heater, and ENERGY STAR–rated appliances. Electrical energy is generated for the house with photovoltaic panels on the roof, which offset grid-supplied energy.

Water is conserved with the use of low-flow faucets and dual-flush toilets. The house was built gray water ready, which means a dual pipe system was installed that can carry wastewater from the shower, sinks, dishwasher, and washing machine to be used for toilets and watering the landscape.

An automatic ventilation system, central vacuum system, and mini-duct air distribution (see page 72) help improve indoor air quality.

CREATING A LIGHT FOOTPRINT

By constructing the house in a factory setting, Living-Homes claims a reduction in waste to about 2 to 10 percent of materials used. Most of the materials used to construct the house—for instance, the glass tiles and composite wood for decking—are recycled. Even the window frames are constructed of recycled content. The steel that makes up the frame of the house is also composed of recycled content, and the lumber is engineered, meaning it is composed of scrap wood.

Most of the furnishings in the house are made from salvaged, recycled, or rapidly renewable content; fabrics are organic, and paints and finishes are all low VOC.

BELOW The floor plan is open, with sliding doors extending the space to an open porch. All kitchen appliances are ENERGY STAR rated. Countertops are solid surfacing made from recycled content.

BOTTOM Most rooms in the house, including the master suite, have direct access to the outdoors, extending the living space and promoting natural ventilation.

EDUCATION OF THE HOMEOWNERS

An important aspect of building an environmentally healthy home is educating the homeowners in the use and maintenance of the house. LivingHomes provides training and information so residents will make lifestyle choices that reduce waste of resources and energy.

In addition, a resource monitoring system displays water, energy, and gas usage in real time. When homeowners know exactly how much energy and water they are using, they often monitor themselves and reduce usage.

LUXURY WITH GREAT QUALITY

The cost of this house was $275 a square foot, but its luxury price comes with a design from the award-winning architectural firm KieranTimberlake, exceptional structural stability, a steel frame, factory precision, and a low environmental impact. Also, the house has a coveted location; it is a block from the beautiful Newport Beach.

Large windows and sliding glass doors promote natural daylighting and cross-ventilation. Flooring throughout the house is engineered from rapidly renewable eucalyptus trees.

Mini-duct Air Distribution

Mini-duct air distribution systems force air through flexible, insulated feeder ducts that are only 2 or 2¾ inches in diameter. These ducts can be threaded through cavities in walls, floors, and ceilings, requiring less space than traditional ducts. Because they are highly pressurized, they can be turned and T-jointed, forming arrangements that can create problems in traditional systems. Air moves through this tubing at about 2,000 feet per minute (fpm) (whereas standard duct systems move air at 500 to 600 fpm); this pressure eliminates the buildup of dust in the ductwork, which in turn improves indoor air quality. Air goes through a filter to remove airborne dust and allergens and is expelled through round outlets, set in walls, floors, and ceilings, that can blend in with their surroundings. These systems are often used in remodels where there is no room for more standard-size ductwork, but in many cases they are also used in new construction such as the Newport Beach House. The systems are quieter to operate and can improve dehumidification by about 30 percent (according to manufacturers), which encourages the homeowner to raise the temperature and use less air-conditioning. For more information about the system used in the Newport Beach House, check the website of Hi-Velocity Systems at www.hi-velocity.com.

BELOW Transom windows add to the natural daylighting in this open living room, dining room, and kitchen area. No space is wasted in this house. The rooms are designed for flexibility and multiuse.

BOTTOM The countertops are GREENGUARD-certified quartz and contain 25 percent postconsumer recycled content. The tiles are produced with 10 percent postconsumer recycled glass content. The toilet is dual flush and low flow.

Modern Cottage

Modular/Structural Insulated Panels/Site Built

PHOTOGRAPHER:

Philip Jensen-Carter (unless otherwise noted)

ARCHITECT:

Joel Turkel, Turkel Design

MANUFACTURER:

Epoch Homes

BUILDER:

Modern Cottage LLC

LOCATION:

Ancram, New York

SIZE:

2,734 square feet

HERS RATING: 65

BLOWER DOOR TEST:

1.97 ACH @ 50 Pascals

CERTIFICATION:

National Green Building Certification
program—Emerald
ENERGY STAR

GREEN ASPECTS:

Low-flow faucets and showerheads

Bamboo flooring

Cement flooring

Native planting

FSC-certified wood

ENERGY ASPECTS:

Geothermal system

Insulated engineered wood (see page 78)

Passive solar orientation

Spray foam insulation

Advanced framing

SIP roof

Radiant heat (see page 78)

Induction stove (see page 77)

ENERGY STAR–rated appliances

CFL lighting

Triple-glazed windows

Energy recovery ventilator (ERV)

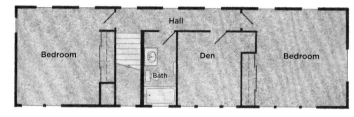

SECOND FLOOR

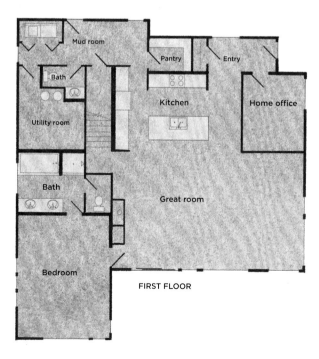

FIRST FLOOR

TOP LEFT The framing of the house was constructed at the Epoch factory with the EnviroWall system. (Photo courtesy of Dave Wrocklage)

BOTTOM LEFT The second module is lifted in the air and placed perpendicular to the first module, which is set on the prepared foundation. (Photo courtesy of Modern Cottage)

OPPOSITE The exterior of the house is western red cedar, and the windows are fiberglass clad, both of which are low maintenance. Overhangs help to deflect summer heat gain.

Brenden Maloof had always been interested in alternative energy. As a teenager, he searched for dams to create hydroelectric power under the Public Utility Regulatory Policies Act (1978) and he interned for a windmill company while still in law school. After graduating, Brenden worked as an attorney in Japan and says he got an excellent education on how energy and space can be conserved.

Back in the United States, Brenden began building and remodeling houses, always with the goal of finding more affordable, energy-efficient methods of construction. He became interested in prefabricated modern design and teamed up with Scot Cohen, an upstate New York builder and real estate broker. Scot shares an interest in modern pre-fab green construction and was happy to collaborate with Brenden on this new project.

DEVELOPING A DESIGN

Brenden had worked with Joel Turkel in the past and thought he was the perfect architect to design the Modern Cottage because of his specialty in modern, flat-roof design.

Brenden and Scot came up with the idea of building the house using two modular boxes stacked perpendicularly. The modules are coupled with a site-built wall of windows in the great room and a site-built back wall supporting the upper modular box. The resulting configuration was placed on a concrete slab that is totally insulated to avoid any thermal bridges. Unlike most modules, these were shipped with a temporary floor that was removed, so that the house could be set on the thick concrete slab, which serves as thermal mass and contains the embedded radiant heating system. This concept of completing the rectangular shape with a site-built portion was done to create a wide-open first-floor space. The site-built portion allowed Modern Cottage the flexibility to exceed some of the dimensions that could be produced by modular construction for this house.

BUILDING GOALS

Three methods of construction were used to build the Modern Cottage. There were two modulars built in a factory; prefabricated SIPs were installed for the roof; and the great room was site-built. The goal was to utilize the advantages of modular factory production—for cost savings, efficiency, quality control, and time savings—along with the ability to add particular design features with a small amount of on-site building. Brenden says, "The idea of 'less is more' was a guiding force to the project. Therefore, good modern design, livable layout, significant energy efficiency, lower cost to build, and reduced time to market were the driving objectives of the project."

BUILDING A TIGHT SHELL

Brenden and Scot chose Epoch to build the two modules because of the company's expertise in custom modular construction. The frame uses insulated engineered wood (see page 78) and includes open-cell foam insulation between the studs. Windows are triple pane and highly efficient with an R-9 rating (see Stillwater Dwelling, page 67). Foam was placed between the concrete foundation and the ground for energy efficiency. Care was taken throughout the construction of the shell to eliminate thermal bridging (see Unity House, page 162) anywhere there could be potential heat loss or gain from the outside. This allowed them to minimize the size of the HVAC system while still allowing for a large amount

BELOW The floors on the first floor are poured concrete that has been sanded and stained, giving them a beautiful mottled effect. Windows are located throughout the house to assure cross-ventilation, with the most glazing on the south side.

BOTTOM All appliances are ENERGY STAR–rated, and the stove is an induction range. The countertops are made of CaesarStone, a quartz material that is nonporous; scratch, heat, impact, and stain resistant; and maintenance free.

Induction Stoves and Cooktops

Unlike gas and electric stoves, induction cookers generate heat directly in the cooking vessel. Cookware must be made of a ferromagnetic metal and have a flat bottom; copper or aluminum pots cannot be used. The magnetic property of the vessels concentrates the induced current in a thin layer near the surface of the pot, which makes the heating effect stronger.

Induction stoves have several advantages. They use less energy, they are safer because the surface isn't hot (and won't burn little fingers), and they heat more quickly, with more consistency. Because they are flat, they are easier to clean. The air around the stove is not hot, reducing cooling requirements in the kitchen. One of the reasons they have become particularly popular is because they don't require gas lines, which could allow for air infiltration into the house. These are not unlike electric stoves, but induction stoves are said to be more efficient.

There are, however, some limitations—only compatible cookware can be used, the top can crack on impact with unspecified types of pots, and aluminum foil will melt if it comes in contact with the cooking surface, which could cause permanent damage to the surface. An internal cooling fan in the stove generates a small amount of noise. The cost of induction stoves is also higher than for electric or gas stoves. Most appliance manufacturers offer induction models. For more information about induction stoves, check the website www.induction-cooktop.com, or for the cooktop in the Modern Cottage, check www.mieleusa.com.

A molding detail (seen near where the wall meets the floor) was added throughout the house to give the walls a finished but still modern look.

Insulated Engineered Wood

Structural insulated engineered wood components are used to prevent thermal bridging (see Unity House, page 162) in framing. The lumber is finger-jointed engineered wood, which is highly stable and won't twist and warp like conventional lumber. Insulation and OSBs are added to the lumber, increasing the R-value (see Stillwater Dwelling, page 67) of two-by-six lumber from 5.5 to 11.5. Insulated headers and plates complete the system, allowing the entire exterior wall system to be thermally broken. By eliminating thermal bridging and improving thermal efficiency of the wall system, the cost of heating and cooling is vastly decreased. This hybrid lumber creates a very stable, highly energy-efficient framing unit. The cost is approximately a dollar per square foot more than traditional lumber. The insulated lumber used for the Modern Cottage and the 4D Home (see page 197) is EnviroWall, a patent pending product from Canada. For further information, check the website www.nordicewp.com.

Radiant Heat: Hydronic vs. Electric

Radiant heat is becoming an increasingly popular heating alternative. It provides clean, even heat, warming objects in the room rather than the air, as forced hot air systems do. When installed correctly, radiant systems provide for greater comfort as heat is spread evenly throughout the heated area. The system can be zoned so only the areas being used are heated, increasing efficiency. Unlike forced hot air systems, with radiant heat no particulates and pollutants are forced into the environment from the blown air. Additionally the system is noise free. Radiant heating systems are imbedded in flooring, ceiling, or wall panels and can even be used to melt snow on driveways and sidewalks. Hydronic or hot water radiant systems can also heat a pool, a spa, or domestic hot water.

There are two types of radiant heat—electric and hydronic. Though they basically work the same way, installations are vastly different and operating costs are different as well. Hydronic systems are more complicated to install because they require a pump and special PEX tubing to circulate water heated by an electric, gas-fired, or oil-fired boiler. They are easily adapted to hydronic solar panels, geothermal systems, and high-efficiency boilers, because they do not require high temperatures to operate. Hydronic systems may be more expensive to install but less expensive to operate. Electric systems are easier and less expensive to install but are more expensive to operate, making them impractical for heating an entire house but effective for small areas, such as bathrooms.

One disadvantage of radiant systems is they take a longer time to heat up an area than other types of systems. Whatever material the system is embedded in acts as a heat sink, absorbing the heat first, before the room gets it. Depending on how big the heat sink is (such as a cold foundation), this could take quite a bit of time. On the plus side, once the heat is turned off, the heat sink will take a similarly long time to dissipate the heat, keeping the area warm for a longer time. To learn more, visit www.radiantpanelassociation.org.

The master bedroom, which is on the first floor for convenience and privacy, has a beautiful view of a meadow.

of glazing. Epoch included a beveled plate on top of the boxes, creating a slope needed for the proper runoff of water.

Timberline Panel Company provided the SIPs to create an R-45 roofing system. In addition to the thermal advantage of SIPs, the panels also served as ready-made overhangs needed as sunshades in the summer, eliminated thermal breaks in the roof joists, and made the installation of the system fast and easy.

A geothermal system was incorporated into the well required at this location because the house is not connected to the local water system. The system heats the water for domestic use and for the

radiant floor heating and cooling system. The excess energy created by the system can also be stored for additional heating and cooling of the water. An electric heating system was included in the house as a backup for extremely cold days. The projected energy cost for the house is $2,836 per year, including heating, cooling, appliances, lights, and hot water. Brenden says that a future owner "could easily use solar PV panels to make this a zero-energy house."

FUTURE CONSTRUCTION

The word "cottage" was used to differentiate this house from the "mansions" that are commonly being built in the area. As in other parts of the country, many of the small farms are being sold off in Columbia County because the younger generation does not want to farm and the land is worth more as a development. Investors are coming in, buying up the land to build McMansions, and changing the bucolic nature of this farm-oriented county.

Brenden and Scot hope to someday build a cluster development of homes, creating a homeowners' association that directly contributed to community supported agriculture (CSA)* on a current farm property. Ideally, the farmer would remain on a portion of the land and the owners of the houses that share the property would help support the farmer by contributing their time and money; they would also share in the crops. The houses on this property would share wells, driveways, windmills, and solar energy, creating a more efficient lifestyle. The Modern Cottage was built as a prototype for the multiple green houses Brenden and Scot would like to build, at an affordable price, to form these communities.

Brenden says he "would like to build houses that would be gentler to the local environment and the community. This would fulfill a lifelong dream of conserving energy and creating more energy-independent communities."

* For further information about CSAs, check the website of the United States Department of Agriculture at www.nal .usda.gov/afsic/pubs/csa/csa.shtml or Local Harvest at www.localharvest.org/csa.

Riley's Rosemary Beach Retreat

Structural Insulated Panels

PHOTOGRAPHER:

Courtland William Richards

ARCHITECT:

Mac Walcott

Watershed

MANUFACTURER:

Premier Building Systems

BUILDER:

Christian Tennant Custom Homes

LOCATION:

Rosemary Beach, Florida

SIZE:

2,100 square feet

HERS RATING: 52

BLOWER DOOR TEST:

0.08 ACH @ 50 Pascals

CERTIFICATION:

LEED-H—Platinum

ENERGY STAR

GREEN ASPECTS:

Walkable community

Low-VOC paints, finishes, and adhesives

Drought-tolerant plantings

Small footprint

Permeable paving

Low-flow bathroom fixtures

Dual-flush toilets

FSC-certified wood

Materials with recycled content

Metal roof

Bamboo flooring

Natural plaster walls

Separate garage

ENERGY ASPECTS:

Insulated concrete form (ICF) foundation
    and some walls (see page 87)

SIPs (see page 87)

ENERGY STAR–rated appliances

ENERGY STAR–rated windows

Tankless water heater

High-efficiency HVAC system

LED and CFL lighting

Concrete flooring

Bahama shutters

Energy-efficient doors

Heat recovery ventilator (HRV)

CARRIAGE
HOUSE LOFT

SECOND FLOOR

CARRIAGE HOUSE

ABOVE The property has two separate structures. The carriage house is on the left, and the main house is on the right.

OPPOSITE At the entrance to the main house, wide overhangs help to block the hot sun during the warm months.

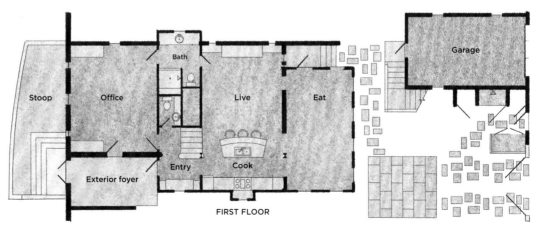

FIRST FLOOR

During a road trip through the Florida panhandle, Donna and Riley Shirey came upon Rosemary Beach. It was love at first sight. Donna says, "It felt like home, lots of wood and warm colors." She and Riley immediately put money down on a lot. This would be their retreat from their rainy, chilly life in Washington State.

DISCOVERING AN ARCHITECT

On a later visit, which took them to Fairhope, Alabama, the Shireys noticed a commercial building that, they say, was just their style. They found out the name of the architect, whose office was conveniently around the corner. Donna and Riley made an immediate connection with architect Mac Walcott and his staff. Without interviewing any other architects, they hired Mac to design their new house—a decision they have never regretted.

GUIDELINES FOR DESIGN

There were many guidelines for construction at Rosemary Beach. The selected lot was to have a small house, under 2,200 square feet, a courtyard, and a one-car carriage house. Energy efficiency was a top priority for the Shireys, builders themselves who have been constructing energy-efficient houses for over twenty years. They wanted this house to be LEED certified. Mac was thrilled at the opportunity to design an energy-efficient house and saw it as a challenge to keep it under the required footage.

The Shireys decided to build this house as they had built so many other houses—with structural insulated panels (SIPs) and insulated concrete forms (ICFs) (see page 87) for the foundation and two of the four walls. The Florida Solar Energy Center documented a blower door test (see New World Hudson Home, page 27) and verified LEED certification.

The house fits in with the style of the other houses in the development but is very different because of the efficiencies built into this construction. The envelope is very tight thanks to the SIPs and ICFs. Large overhangs and traditional Bahama shutters help keep the house cool in the hot, humid weather.

The Shireys initially thought Florida would be the perfect location to create energy with solar panels. But they found out they were not being used in Florida at the time because of the hostile climate. The wind and sand pitted the panels, and the corrosion of metal caused by the salty, damp air made them impractical. Now there are new solar panel technologies available for beach environments.

CONSTRUCTION BEGAN

Donna and Riley hired a local builder and asked him to begin construction on the carriage house. Although the house did have complicated beams, they considered the twenty-four months that it took to build the 425-square-foot structure outrageous. They fired the builder and hired another one, who was able to complete the main house in just less than two years. During that construction, they lived in the carriage house when they visited Rosemary Beach.

A WONDERFUL RETREAT

The Shireys go to their Rosemary Beach Retreat whenever they are able to get away from their busy life in Issaquah, Washington, where they live in the Zero Energy Idea House (see page 144). When they are not using their vacation home, it is in a rental pool, so it can be enjoyed by others.

BELOW The bed in the carriage house is in a cozy area sandwiched between the toilet and shower.

BOTTOM LEFT The carriage house includes this small kitchen and eating area, a loft above, and a small bedroom and bathroom to the rear. The Shireys stayed in the carriage house on their visits to Florida, during the construction of the main house.

BOTTOM CENTER The fans in this guest bedroom and around the main house help to keep people cool without the use of air-conditioning.

BOTTOM RIGHT Having two narrow doors allowed for a wider door opening, giving the space more elegance when open, while still providing privacy when closed.

BELOW The living room and kitchen of the main house are inviting areas to gather, decorated with warm colors and décor. The spaces in the house are generally small, but there are lots of places to be alone or to socialize.

BOTTOM The sun porch off one of the upstairs bedrooms has a sofa with a pull-out bed to accommodate extra guests.

The Shireys call this their "feast room"—a dining area for gathering with family and friends.

BELOW All of the kitchen appliances are ENERGY STAR–rated, and
the cooktop is an induction range, which uses less energy.

Heat Recovery Ventilators (HRV) and Energy Recovery Ventilators (ERV)

When houses are built very airtight, there can be a shortage of fresh air in the house. One popular solution is a heat recovery ventilator, which can minimize energy loss and save on heating and cooling costs. The heated or cooled interior air is exchanged with the exterior fresh air, while transferring some of the heat and coolness generated in the home. Another alternative is the energy recovery ventilator, which functions in much the same way but helps to control humidity. These are often the ventilation choice in hot, humid climates. For additional information, check the website www.energysavers.gov.

Structural Insulated Panels (SIPs)

SIPs are precut sandwich panels—outer panels with insulation sandwiched between them. Most often SIPs are composed of two OSBs (oriented strand boards) with a layer of foam fused between them, but they can include other materials, such as metal, cement board, or wood. SIPs can vary in size, material, overall thickness, and method of connection, and are used as outer walls, floors, and roof components. One of the most important advantages of using SIPs for home construction is the tight, continuous barrier they create against air infiltration. Other advantages are speed and ease of assembly and the quiet interior environment they create. For further information about SIPs or to locate suppliers, check the website of the Structural Insulated Panel Association at www.sips.org.

Insulated Concrete Form (ICF) Foundations and Walls

ICFs are permanent rigid foam forms; they are set into place on-site and concrete is poured and cured between them. They have a high R-value, create consistent insulation because there are no studs to allow thermal bridges, and can reduce energy costs. According to www.icfhomes.com, "Homes built with ICF exterior walls require an estimated 44 percent less energy to heat and 32 percent less energy to cool than comparable frame houses." They are also resistant to rust, rot, fire, and mold and can withstand harsh weather conditions such as hurricanes and tornadoes. The forms are light in weight and most can be set in place without the use of lifting devices. Forms vary in material and construction, but many are made of expanded polystyrene (EPS) or some other form of plastic. For additional information about ICFs check www.icfhomes.com or www.forms.org.

C3 Prefab

Modular

PHOTOGRAPHER:

Mike Schwartz (unless otherwise noted)

ARCHITECT:

Square Root Architecture + Design

MANUFACTURER:

Hi-Tech Housing

BUILDER:

Helios Design + Build

LOCATION:

Chicago, Illinois

SIZE:

2,039 square feet

HERS RATING: 48

BLOWER DOOR TEST:

2.16 ACH @ 50 Pascals

CERTIFICATION:

LEED-H Platinum

ENERGY STAR

Chicago Green Homes & Green Permit
  Programs

Indoor airPLUS Program (see page 92)

GREEN ASPECTS:

Infill lot

Separate garage

Low-flow faucets and showerheads—
  WaterSense labeled

Recycled gypsum board

No-VOC cabinetry, made with recycled
  content

No-VOC paints, stains, and primers

FSC-certified wood

Water catchment

Permeable paving

Public transportation accessible

Concrete foundation with fly ash

Living roof

Fiber cement siding

Reclaimed barn wood siding

Reclaimed hickory flooring

Cork flooring (see page 92)

Fiber cement siding

Recycled corrugated Galvalume siding

ENERGY ASPECTS:

Solar thermal panels

Wired for future photovoltaic panels

Tankless water heater

ENERGY STAR–rated appliances

LED and CFL lighting

High-efficiency windows

High-efficiency ductless mini-split system

Stair tower for natural ventilation

Energy recovery ventilator (ERV)

SECOND FLOOR

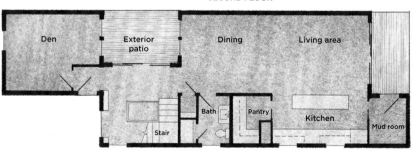

FIRST FLOOR

OPPOSITE ABOVE The modules were lifted about sixty feet in the air to avoid hitting wires and trees. They were set on the already prepared foundation in one day. The street had to be closed off so the boxes could be set. (Photo courtesy of Martin Konopacki)

OPPOSITE BELOW Decks on the upper and lower floors provide expanded outdoor living in this city house.

RIGHT Corrugated Galvalume and fiber cement sidings were selected for their high recycled content and low maintenance. Reclaimed wood from a barn in Ohio is used as an agrarian accent on this clean modern facade.

The C3 Prefab will be the first prefabricated LEED Platinum–certified home in Chicago. This was not an easy or quick quest for Jeffrey Sommers, the principal architect on this project. It was in the works for more than four years. Jeff says his overall goal was "to balance cost and energy efficiency."

INTEREST IN PREFAB

Jeff became interested in building prefab about eight years ago because of the high cost of building in Chicago. He was looking for strategies to control construction budgets without sacrificing the design or performance of the building. In the past, clients had also asked him about incorporating sustainable features into their projects, but didn't have the budget to do so. Jeff wanted to find a way to offer clients a semicustom, high-performance house using a streamlined design process; this would include prefab construction and green features.

Even before Jeff had a client for this project, he designed a prefabricated house incorporating design features previous clients had requested. He initially planned this design to fit into Chicago's affordable housing program and even presented the plans to decision makers at city hall. That project did not materialize, but someone at the meetings introduced him to a woman who had expressed frustration in not being able to build a prefab home in Chicago; that woman turned into his client, Kathy Caisley, an urban planner.

A CLIENT FOR JEFF'S PROJECT

Kathy and her husband, Michael, turned out to be dream clients for Jeff. He says, "They both have really great taste in design, a passion for modern prefab architecture, and a desire for a high level of sustainability in their home." They were also prepared to be pioneers in bringing sustainable prefab design to Chicago, setting a precedent for future prefab houses in urban areas. Kathy and Michael had heard for years that modular would never happen in Chicago, and they were thrilled to find out it was possible. They loved the plan Jeff had already designed and made just minor changes to meet their needs. Since the plan was already designed to be modular, making changes was relatively simple and cost-effective; it just meant moving some interior walls.

BUILDING CHALLENGES

Building a high-end house on an affordable budget was a major challenge. Jeff says, "It took a huge investment of resources within my firm to research materials, work on pricing with contractors and manufacturers, and refine our construction budgets." However, he says that in retrospect the investment in research is paying off because he is now able to provide affordable, sustainable projects incorporating better construction details, materials, and techniques for future houses.

Finding a manufacturer that would construct modules to conform to Chicago's strict building code was another major hurdle. After an exhaustive search, Jeff chose Hi-Tech Housing, a modular manufacturer in Indiana. It took over a year to complete the permitting and general contractor (GC) bidding process; it was difficult for the GCs since they hadn't worked on prefab projects in the past. Jeff functioned as a liaison between the GCs and Hi-Tech to be sure they would meet the requirements to receive structural, mechanical, electrical, and plumbing approval from Chicago's tough trade inspectors.

BELOW LEFT This den area on the first floor has views to the exterior courtyard. The blue door is an example of the homeowners' appreciation for small bursts of primary colors.

BELOW RIGHT These lighting fixtures were chosen because they could use fluorescent or LED bulbs. Kathy says there wasn't a great selection of these fixtures, but she was determined to use LED and fluorescent bulbs in 80 percent of the home's lighting in order to obtain LEED certification.

BOTTOM The Caisleys have a modern sensibility and like the bold use of color often seen in European-style kitchens. They selected green because it would be a dramatic backdrop for food. They chose a refrigerator and dishwasher that could be integrated with the green cabinetry.

BELOW Reclaimed engineered hickory flooring is used throughout the first floor. Cork was used on the second floor because of its affordability and warmth.

BOTTOM This private courtyard area between the living room and the den brings natural ventilation and light into the heart of the home. The area also functions as a private location for the homeowners to enjoy outdoor living.

Cork Flooring

Cork is considered to be an environmentally friendly material because it comes from the outer bark of cork oak trees that can be harvested every nine to fourteen years without harming the trees. Cork is ground up and coated with a nontoxic resin binder. Tiles, sheets, and tongue-and-groove strip flooring are available in a variety of colors, patterns, and thicknesses—the thicker tile is used for flooring because it is more shock and acoustic absorbent. There are lots of advantages to using cork flooring: It's durable; easy to maintain; comfortable underfoot; resistant to moisture, mold, and mildew; easy to install; hypoallergenic; and natural; and it does not absorb odors. The only fly in the ointment is that cork needs to be refinished every eight years.

Indoor airPLUS Program

A house must first be designed to earn the ENERGY STAR label, and then comply with a list of thirty-seven criteria in home design and construction features to protect the home from moisture, mold, pests, combustion gases, and other airborne pollutants in order to qualify for the Indoor airPLUS Program. Certification requires that the house be inspected by an independent third party to make sure it complies with the EPA's guidelines and specifications. For further information about this program check the website www.epa.gov/indoorairplus.

Another challenge was installing the modules in the 25-by-125-foot lot with only three-foot setbacks on either side. There was no room for error when installing the "boxes." A 225-ton crane (with a very calm and experienced crane operator) hoisted the modules into place without a hitch.

BUILDING GREEN

An energy rater joined the team early in the planning process to help "model" design changes to ensure the performance levels the homeowners wanted. Getting LEED certification was not difficult since the house had already been designed with a very energy-efficient envelope and systems. But Kathy says it became a challenge to reach the Platinum level. They decided that to do so they were willing to sacrifice some of the more costly items from their initial wish list, such as using cork flooring instead of hardwood on the second floor, having a built-in staircase instead of a floating one, and having a crawl space instead of a full basement.

Jeff says, "The Chicago Green Homes and Green Permit Programs are really great initiatives in Chicago encouraging homeowners to construct more sustainably, and rewarding qualifying projects with expedited permit processing and permit fee waivers." He chose a ductless mini-split system for heating and cooling (see Hilltop Craftsman, page 135) because it is very energy efficient, inherently zoned, and quiet. Unlike forced-air systems that collect dust and pollens, having a negative impact on the interior environment, mini-split systems are more hygienic and offer more balanced heating and cooling in the home.

LOOKING TOWARD FUTURE CONSTRUCTION

Jeff expects this house to be just the first of many that will be built in Chicago as part of a comprehensive urban renewal project.

The C3 was designed to be highly energy efficient and meet the LEED Platinum and ENERGY STAR standards with low-tech, commonsense solutions in lieu of expensive gadgetry. The focus is a simple, compact, well-insulated design with very efficient systems. Many materials, such as the barn siding and hickory flooring, were reclaimed. Most materials were sourced through local vendors to encourage economic growth within the region.

BUILDING COST

The cost for building this house was $200 a square foot, not including the land and landscaping. Jeff says this is substantially less than other LEED Platinum houses in the area. The exciting part, however, is that the operating costs are less than for other nearby houses. With a HERS rating of 48, it performs 52 percent better than other houses, substantially reducing energy costs. He hopes to be able to build this type of house at an even lower price but says there are trade-offs to building for less. Regardless, Jeff says he is "not willing to compromise on the performance of the home construction."

BUILDING PREFAB

Jeff sees the many advantages that prefabricated housing can provide. He says it can encourage manufacturing in urban areas, help create jobs, save on construction costs, encourage more affordable housing, and provide an indoor environment for people in the construction trades to work year-round, which is currently not the case in climates such as Chicago's. Sourcing materials locally would also encourage economic growth in the region.

Jeff says, "By building homes in a factory, it encourages new economic opportunities in Chicago for the manufacturing and housing sectors. Tradespeople will have the opportunity to be educated in new green construction techniques, while providing housing for themselves and others in the city. Part of being socially responsible is being environmentally conscientious. The C3 Prefab project provides solutions for two major crises facing our world—our finances and our environment. This project is the first modular, sustainable home to be built in Chicago, and our hope is that it will act as a model solution for sustainable, affordable urban housing in other parts of the United States and abroad."

New World Whitman-Annis Home

Modular

PHOTOGRAPHER:

Philip Jensen-Carter (unless otherwise
 noted)

ARCHITECT:

New World Home

MANUFACTURER:

Signature Building Systems

BUILDER:

New World Home

LOCATION:

Oldwick, New Jersey

SIZE:

3,100 square feet

HERS RATING: 46

CERTIFICATIONS:

USGBC LEED-H—Platinum (pending)

NAHBGreen—Emerald (pending)

ENERGY STAR (pending)

Indoor airPLUS Program (pending)

GREEN ASPECTS:

Bamboo flooring

Cork flooring

Low-flow showerheads and faucets—Water-
 Sense labeling (pending)

Dual-flush toilets

Central manifold plumbing system

Ultraviolet (UV) water treatment system

Formaldehyde-free wall insulation

No-VOC paints and finishes

Quartz countertops

Foot control kitchen faucet (see page 99)

Metal roof

FSC-certified framing wood

Reclaimed wood on kitchen island

High-efficiency HVAC system

Recycled brick on chimney veneer

HEPA whole-house filtration system

Fiber cement siding

Formaldehyde-free, FSC-certified kitchen
 cabinets

No Added Urea-Formaldehyde, FSC-certified
 interior doors

Gravel driveway base composed of repurposed
 materials (e.g., countertops)

Fly ash utilized in foundation

MDF interior trim

Composite exterior trim

Composite decking and rails

Permeable walkway pavers

ENERGY ASPECTS:

ENERGY STAR–rated windows and entry door

ENERGY STAR–rated appliances

ENERGY STAR–rated lighting

ENERGY STAR–rated ceiling fans

ENERGY STAR–rated metal roofing

Advanced framing

Insulated prefabricated concrete foundation

Tankless hot water heater

Programmable thermostat

Whole house energy monitor

Direct vent sealed combustion fireplace

Rainwater harvesting system

Spray foam insulation

Passive solar orientation

Integrated roof/wall sheathing panels

Panelized, pre-insulated foundation wall system

Pre-engineered for future solar integration

Heat recovery ventilator (HRV)

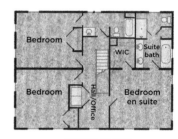

SECOND FLOOR

FIRST FLOOR

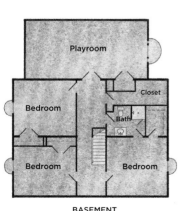

BASEMENT

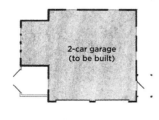

The family wanted their home to fit in with the traditional design of the houses in the surrounding area and also to look like it had been there for one hundred years.

According to Craig Annis, building his and his wife Kate's house was a "family affair" from the beginning to the completion of their home. Together with Kate's parents, John and Christine Todd Whitman, they designed, picked out materials, and even traveled all together to visit the house when it was under construction at the Signature factory. Even the then three children (another was born more recently) came along to check out the structure.

Craig says that with Christine Todd Whitman's concern for the environment, as the former governor of New Jersey and head of the US Environmental Protection Agency (EPA), she was happy to be involved in the construction of this house, which was built to exceed the most stringent environmental standards in the industry.

IN A HISTORIC DISTRICT WITH FAMILY TIES

The house was built on the Whitman farm, which has been in the family for several generations. Oldwick Historical District, where the house is located, was the first historic district in Tewksbury to be listed on the New Jersey and National Registers of Historic Places. The design of the house was planned to fit in with the neighboring traditional farm-style houses but to include all of the modern technology that would make this house more environmentally friendly and comfortable. Craig says one of the advantages of this location is being just across the street from his in-laws' home, with whom he, Kate, and their children spend a great deal of time.

"GREEN" BY DESIGN

The house was designed to be very healthy, constructed with environmentally friendly materials, and also very energy efficient. This was achieved by New World with advanced framing in the factory, passive solar orientation, spray foam insulation, energy-efficient HVAC systems, ENERGY STAR–certified windows, doors, lighting and appliances (see page 99), and a "whole-systems" design approach to building.

The house is targeted to be among the first LEED Platinum and NAHB Emerald factory-built homes in the country. When certifications are achieved, it will join an exclusive group of homes to achieve both Platinum and Emerald certification without relying upon the use of any renewable energy sources such as solar panels, geothermal systems, or wind turbines. The owners are also pursuing EPA Indoor airPLUS (see page 92) and WaterSense (see page 222) certification for their home.

BUILDING MODULAR

Craig says he found New World Home by searching the Internet for sustainable prefabricated construction. He says modular construction was a particularly attractive method because "of the factory quality control, speed of construction and because the wood stays dry, limiting the chance of mold developing in the finished house. A healthy interior environment is a major concern for us because we have four young children." He says that he chose New World Home because they offered the old world design that he and Kate were looking for, they were able to complete the house in six months, and because they provided a multitude of selections to choose from. Craig says most of the sustainable options they chose, such as bamboo floors, quartz countertops, no-VOC paints, and ENERGY STAR appliances, did not come at a substantially higher cost.

BELOW LEFT The Whitman-Annis home is a combination of old-world charm and modern building technology. The driveway is composed of repurposed, chopped-up countertops with a gravel overlay.

BOTTOM This direct vent gas sealed combustion fireplace keeps this cozy room warm in the chilly months. The gaming table in the corner was a wedding gift and one of two built in the world, making it historically significant. The double pane windows are tilt and wash, making them easy to clean.

BELOW RIGHT The house was built in the Signature Building Systems factory under ideal controlled conditions. (Photo courtesy of New World Home)

COMMITMENT TO "GREEN"

"We've been searching the market for many years for an authentic green modular housing company that incorporates traditional architecture," says former governor Whitman. "My family and I were very excited when we connected with New World Home since the company is clearly making great strides in transforming the homebuilding industry."

Literally interpreting the adage "We do not inherit the earth from our ancestors. We borrow it from our children," the Whitmans consider their New World Home an exciting family project, adhering to this saying.

Tyler Schmetterer, cofounder of New World Home, says, "We are thrilled to be working with the Whitman family and furthering our pursuit of achieving historic green milestones in the residential building industry. With our shared commitment to the environment and the support of Governor Whitman and her family, this project should bring greater awareness to the advantages of green modular housing and encourage mainstream use of factory-built construction to provide healthier and more sustainable homes."

BELOW LEFT The Annises wanted to have their bedroom on the first floor for some privacy from their four little boys. The fan in the bedroom helps to circulate both warm and cold air. The antique travel trunk belonged to Craig's grandfather.

BELOW RIGHT Everything in the kitchen was chosen for its sustainability including the quartz countertop, reclaimed wood island, bamboo floors, ENERGY STAR appliances, and kitchen cabinets with no formaldehyde or VOC binders or finishes. The foot faucet (see sidebar) saves on water.

BOTTOM The beautiful wall hanging in the hallway was an antique window, to which a mirror was added. The sign above the entrance to the living room was a gift from Kate to Craig. "Live Free or Die" is the motto of New Hampshire, where Craig grew up. The décor in the casual eating area in the background is a blend of new furniture made from recycled wood and very old fox hunt pictures that belonged to Kate's grandparents.

The elegant coffered ceiling was built in the Signature factory. The dining table was a gift that belonged to Kate's grandparents.

ENERGY STAR

ENERGY STAR is a program administered by the US Environmental Protection Agency that helps to save money and protect the environment through energy-efficient products and practices. This is a voluntary program designed to identify and promote energy-efficient products in order to reduce greenhouse gas emissions. For the home, the program certifies major appliances, lighting fixtures and bulbs, ceiling and bathroom fans, heating and cooling equipment, windows and doors, and home electronics. All told, ENERGY STAR provides labeling on over sixty product categories that meet strict energy efficiency guidelines set by the EPA.

ENERGY STAR–qualified new homes are certified by Home Energy Rating System (HERS) raters who are accredited by a national organization called RESNET. Ratings indicate efficiency on a scale where a "100" is a national energy code compliant home and "0" is a home with no net energy consumption. ENERGY STAR–qualified homes are required to meet a specified HERS Index set for each home, generally targeting total savings of 20 to 30 percent over a minimum code home.

ENERGY STAR also provides assessment tools so homeowners can better understand their individual energy consumption and how to make their homes more efficient. The ENERGY STAR Home Energy Yardstick, found on the ENERGY STAR website (www.energystar.gov) helps homeowners assess the performance of their home against other comparable homes and it links users to guidance on how to reduce energy use in the home. Homeowners enter basic inputs to get their score, including their annual energy consumption in kWh and therms, the size of the house, number of occupants, and the location of the house.

Tax credits are available for existing homes and new construction using renewable energy components through December 31, 2016. Rebates and sales tax exemptions or credits may also be available from some ENERGY STAR partners, which can also be found on the ENERGY STAR website.

Foot Faucets

Although these are used more often for commercial applications, foot control faucets are a great idea for the home. They can prevent the transmission of germs, because hands never have to touch the hand faucet after handling items such as raw meat or after coming in from the garden. They reduce water usage by making it easy to use water in short bursts and to easily turn it off when not being used. Because less water is used, energy is saved in pumping and heating the water. For further information on the foot faucet used in the New World Whitman-Annis Home, check the website www.tapmaster.ca.

The Evolution

Modular/Steel Frame

PHOTOGRAPHER:

D. Randolph Foulds (unless otherwise noted)

ARCHITECT/MANUFACTURER/BUILDER:

Blu Homes

LOCATION:

Lake Tahoe, California

SIZE:

1,500 square feet

CERTIFICATION:

LEED-H—Silver (pending)

GREEN ASPECTS:

Low- or no-VOC paints and finishes

Dual-flush toilets

Low-flow fixtures and showerheads

Bamboo flooring (see page 105)

Fiber cement board siding

Steel frame (from recycled content)

Green recycled concrete countertops

Recycled glass tiles

Small footprint

Cabinets of wood veneer rather than
   solid wood

Ipe decking

Clerestory windows

ENERGY ASPECTS:

Passive solar orientation

LED and CFL lighting

ENERGY STAR–rated appliances

Tankless water heater (see page 105)

High-efficiency HVAC system

Spray foam insulation

High-efficiency windows

Radiant floor heating

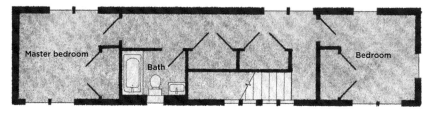

SECOND FLOOR

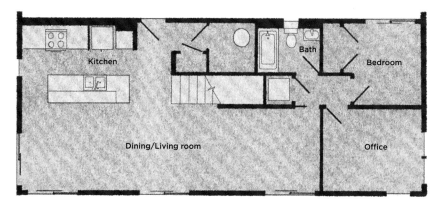

FIRST FLOOR

ABOVE The modular was lifted into place with a crane. In ten days the construction of the house was completed. (Photo courtesy of the owners)

OPPOSITE The house was built to be low maintenance with fiber cement siding. The Josifovska family uses the house for weekend getaways.

Milli and Vanja Josifovska wanted to own a house in southern Lake Tahoe where they could ski with their three children, but they wanted to limit the impact it would have on the environment. Having lived in Sweden much of their lives, they were accustomed to very energy-efficient homes, many of which were built in factories. When they looked around the Lake Tahoe area, they were dissatisfied with the inefficiency and poor materials they were finding in the available houses.

Milli says that because of the short construction season, from June through September, it could take two and a half to three years to build a house on-site in the area. Knowing that many of the houses in Sweden are prefab, they considered this to be an excellent option in the Lake Tahoe area.

CHOOSING THE MODULAR COMPANY

Many of the prefab companies Milli and Vanja looked at had several layers of construction professionals involved; they wanted a company that was "one-stop shopping." They were attracted to Blu Homes because the company would supply architectural, construction, and finishing services for the house.

Milli says that it is a great deal of work to research materials, which requires more time than many homeowners and even some professionals are willing to commit. Blu Home's research on efficient and environmentally friendly resources, says Milli, took much of the personal research out of the equation for her.

DIFFERENT TYPE OF MODULARS

Blu Homes uses a different construction technique from other modular companies. Its houses fold up and are then unfolded on-site. This allows for easier shipment without escort trucks, which are commonly used in transporting modular houses. Also, Blu Homes uses steel frames (unlike some other manufacturers), allowing for larger rooms that have higher ceilings.

INTRINSIC ENERGY

Efficiency was a major criterion for Milli and Vanja. They wanted their house to be environmentally friendly and require a minimum of fossil fuel. Milli says the walls in her house are very thick and solid, similar to houses she is used to in Sweden. When neighbors saw the house unfold, during Blu Homes' unique construction process, they were surprised at how thick the walls were.

The house has four types of insulation—recycled glass batt insulation, spray foam, rigid foam, and structural insulated panels (SIPs) in the roof. Milli says her energy costs are about 60 percent less than in neighboring houses, which are far less efficient.

In addition to the cost of the land, the house cost $320,000 (the foundation cost $20,000). The house took six weeks to build in the factory and just two weeks were needed after it was delivered to "button it up." Milli says there was a lapse in between these periods when the town was not allowing the house to be set, because of a furlough for state workers.

When people come into the house, Milli says, they are surprised that the house is only 1,500 square feet. It feels more spacious, she says, because of the open floor plan, the many large windows, and the eleven-foot-high ceilings. Milli was so pleased with her house, she has become a salesperson for the company.

All the appliances in the house are ENERGY STAR rated. The countertops are made from a recycled concrete material.

The Evolution was the first two-story house that Blu built. The siding on the house is a fiber concrete panel, which requires minimal maintenance. The decking is ipe, a fast-growing hardwood from Brazil, considered a sustainable choice (see Snowhorn House, page 131).

BELOW The open floor plan gives the house a very spacious feeling. The floors in the house are all bamboo, a fast-growing plant, and the lighting is mostly provided by CFLs.

BOTTOM The clerestory window in the bedroom adds to the natural daylighting.

Bamboo Flooring

Bamboo, commonly used today for flooring and cabinetry, is one of the fastest-growing plants in the world and considered a renewable resource. Actually a grass, bamboo stalks are harvested every three to six years and can grow to eighty feet high and six inches or more in diameter. The stalks are split into strips, flattened, and laminated with an adhesive under high pressure to produce planks. Some bamboo is now FSC certified, and most uses nontoxic adhesives. Bamboo is dimensionally stable and harder than oak and maple. For information, see the website www.plyboo.com.

Tankless (or On-Demand) Water Heaters

Tankless water heaters are just that: water-heating systems that require no storage tank, which uses energy continuously to heat the water even when it's not being used. Here's how a tankless water heater works: When a hot water faucet is turned on, cold water is carried through pipes and circulated through a series of coils called a heat exchanger. The water is directly heated by an electric element or a gas burner (gas units typically offer higher flow rates) that heats the water only as long as there is demand. It turns off once the hot water faucet is turned off. Tankless units typically provide hot water at a rate of two to five gallons per minute, depending on the model and the temperature of the groundwater. If demand for hot water will be required simultaneously for several different uses, such as multiple showerheads, dishwashers, and washing machines, two or more units may be needed. Energy savings vary between 8 percent and 50 percent depending on the efficiency rating of the unit and the cost of energy. For additional information about tankless water heaters, visit the Department of Energy's Efficiency and Renewable Energy website at www.eere.energy.gov.

PLACE House

Structural Insulated Panels

PHOTOGRAPHER:

Photos courtesy of PLACE Architects

ARCHITECT:

PLACE Architects

BUILDER:

PLACE Architects and DLH

MANUFACTURER:

Premier Panels

LOCATION:

Kirkland, Washington

SIZE:

2,800 square feet

GREEN ASPECTS:

Cork flooring

Polished concrete

Infill lot (see page 116)

Low-flow faucets and showerheads

Rainwater collection

Rain gardens (see page 111)

Fiber cement siding

Recycled metal roof

Permeable driveway

Recycled-content countertops

Local fiberboard fireplace surround

Formaldehyde-free plywood cabinets

Low-VOC paints

Locally sourced products

ENERGY ASPECTS:

SIPs

Passive solar orientation

Solar hot water panels

Wastewater heat recovery system

Tankless water heater

ENERGY STAR–rated appliances

Hydronic radiant heat

High-performance windows

Staircase stack effect

Ceiling fans

Natural ventilation

Daylighting

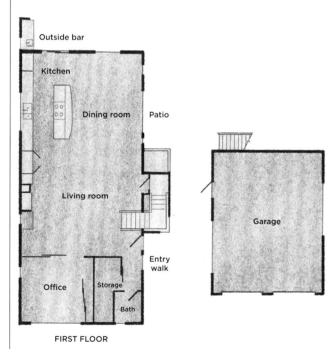

FIRST FLOOR

SECOND FLOOR

OPPOSITE The team sets roof panels into place with a crane. The structural insulated panels come precut with spaces for windows, doors, and chases, and each one is numbered for quick assembly in the field.

BELOW Durable, low- to zero-maintenance cement fiberboard and metal are on much of the exterior, combined with local cedar that provides a natural counterpoint to the more flat, polished manufactured materials.

Monica and Sam Guckenheimer lived in several large houses from London to Boston. Six years after they moved to Seattle, however, they decided they wanted to downsize to a smaller house from a substantially bigger residence in another part of town. They wanted a house with space that they needed rather than wasted space they didn't need. After speaking to several architects who wanted to design a grander-size house, they met architect Heather Johnson, of PLACE Architects, who was devoted to designing highly efficient prefabricated contemporary houses. Heather designed the house for the family of five in a way that utilizes every inch of space.

CREATING A SMALLER FOOTPRINT

To conserve square footage, the design incorporates a flexible allocation of space with overlapping usage. In that way, the house was built smaller, with fewer materials, sitting more gently on the land, and using less energy to heat, cool, and maintain, than a larger house would require.

The roll-up door in the dining area as well as the big sliders at the library/front office close and open to define specific spaces or to blur the boundaries between them. They also allow for good airflow, aiding natural ventilation.

FLEXIBLE USE OF SPACE

Sam's home office provides a space for work, so he can telecommute some days, saving commuting time and gas and giving him more family time. This affords him a more flexible day-to-day lifestyle without cutting into work time.

Shared family spaces upstairs allow bedrooms to be relatively small and still provide work and social space for everyone; these spaces keep everyone interacting without sacrificing opportunities for privacy as well. An open space above the stairs provides a desk and media area, with smaller bedrooms off this common area for private space for each child.

Heather says, "Integration and strong connections between indoors and out provide a feeling of expansiveness inside the house, a connection to nature that is so important to people's health and happiness, and lots of interaction between family members whether they are indoors or outside."

Although many houses today are built with a multitude of bathrooms, the PLACE House has just two and a half, which works fine for this family of five. By sharing bathrooms, fewer fixtures were required, there is less maintenance, and ultimately fewer materials are sent to the landfill.

CONSERVATION OF LAND AND WATER

Care was taken to protect the property when the house was sited. A fir tree was removed to make room for the house, but all the wood from that tree was used for windowsills, stair treads, and the beautiful dining table.

Permeable concrete pavers and Grasscrete were used at the driveway, which significantly reduces rain runoff. The rain gardens (see page 111) catch runoff that does occur and naturally filter the water. Both the house and gardens are oriented on the site to take best practical advantage of the sun, prevailing winds, available shade, and screening from the surrounding trees.

Although Seattle gets good rainfall most of the time, it does have shortages, as do other parts of the country. To conserve water all the bathrooms have low-flow faucets and showerheads and dual-

flush toilets. Water collected from the roof run-off is collected in barrels and used for irrigation of the property.

LIMITING THE USE OF FOSSIL FUEL

SIPs expedited the construction of the outer walls, and they also create a tight envelope with high R-value (see Stillwater Dwelling, page 67). High-efficiency windows add to the energy efficiency of the house while also providing natural ventilation and excellent daylighting.

With the stack effect of the staircase and ceiling fans, air-conditioning is not required. The warm air rises up the stair tower and exits through the window at the top of the stairs, which helps to naturally ventilate the house.

A tankless water heater is used to limit the heat needed for domestic hot water. A wastewater collection system preheats the water coming into bathrooms, with copper coils that wrap around waste pipes to draw out heat and preheat incoming water (see Lancaster Project, page 156). Solar hot water panels heat the water used for the hydronic radiant heating system and the pool.

Monica says, "The house turned out to be everything my husband and I hoped it would be. In addition to wanting to build a very green house, we wanted a house where our children would be comfortable having their friends over. To our great pleasure, our kids' friends love to spend time here and feel right at home—the house is cozy, serene, and a great place to hang out."

All of the woodwork, including the windowsills, stair treads, and
the dining table top, are made from a single fir tree that was on the
property prior to construction. Locally made concrete pavers and
cement fiberboard surround the fireplace, rather than quarried stone.

BELOW The solar panels on the roof heat the water not only for the hydronic radiant floor system but also for the pool. The pool is paved with dark plaster, which absorbs more solar energy than a light color would.

BOTTOM LEFT Grasscrete is a reinforced concrete system with voids created with plastic forms in which grass is grown, and offers an excellent drainage system. The balance of the driveway is made of permeable concrete pavers.

BOTTOM RIGHT The Asian-style bathtub is reminiscent of Monica's childhood in Japan. It is adjacent to a shower with no walls, just a teak floor with a drain. Beautiful views of the Cascade Mountains can be seen from the tub.

Rain Gardens

Rain gardens are landscaped, shallow depressions that allow rain and melted snow to collect and seep naturally into the ground. Native plantings capture the water, and it is naturally filtered through the ground rather than going straight into the storm sewer and into the local water system polluted with pesticides, fertilizers, and other chemicals. As the rainwater percolates into the ground, pollutants are filtered out and broken down. This helps the ecosystem by decreasing sediment in lakes and streams and reducing flooding, while adding beauty to the land-scape. Rain gardens should be located close to the source of runoff, which is generally near downspouts from the roof, adjacent to lawns, or along driveways and walkways.

Green Tags

Green tags are synonymous with carbon off-sets and are available from many organizations. Each new PLACE House comes with a set of corresponding green tags for one year, which are purchased in the owner's name through the Green-e–certified Bonneville Environmental Foundation. These green tags support the creation of renewable energy projects, such as wind and solar farms, to offset the carbon emissions created by fossil fuel energy production. In addition to the carbon emissions produced by PLACE homes, they calculate the carbon emissions of transporting select PLACE house materials from overseas and include those emissions in the green tags as well. Therefore, each PLACE house will be designated "carbon neutral" for one year. To learn more about green tags and Green-e certification, visit the Bonne-ville Environmental Foundation's website at www.b-e-f.org or check the web for other organizations offering green tags.

Greenfab House

Modular

ARCHITECT:

Robert Humble

HyBrid Architecture

MANUFACTURER:

Guerdon Enterprises

BUILDER:

HyBrid Assembly

DEVELOPER:

Greenfab

LOCATION:

Seattle, Washington

SIZE:

1,790 square feet

HERS RATING: 60

CERTIFICATION:

LEED-H—Platinum

Built Green 5-Star (pending)

ENERGY STAR

GREEN ASPECTS:

Urban infill lot (see page 116)

1,500-gallon cistern

Walkable community

Gray water system

Rain garden

Koi pond

Rooftop garden for urban farming

Low-flow water features

No-VOC paints

No formaldehyde-based materials

Drought-tolerant native plantings

Flexible interior partitioning (allows for reconfiguration of interior spaces)

Recycled concrete gabion retaining wall

Recycled-content tiles

Permeable driveway

Vented rain screen (see page 116)

ENERGY ASPECTS:

Passive solar orientation

Advanced framing

Mini-split heat pump for heating and cooling

Programmable thermostat

Energy recovery ventilator (ERV)

Supplemental electric convection heat

Hybrid heat pump water heater

ENERGY STAR–rated appliances

Energy monitoring system

Energy-efficient lighting

Spray foam insulation—soy based

Wired for future photovoltaic panels

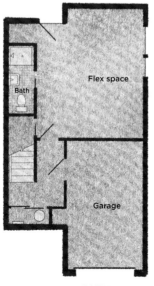

BASEMENT

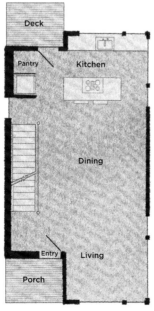

FIRST FLOOR

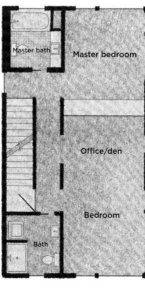

SECOND FLOOR

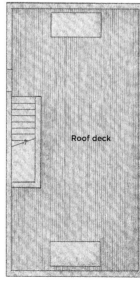

ROOFTOP

OPPOSITE The first module is lifted into place. While the six modules were being built in the factory, the site was excavated and prepared for their delivery.

RIGHT The house was built to have a low impact on the land and use materials that require minimal maintenance, such as the fiber cement siding. Retaining walls were built by filling metal gabion baskets with recycled concrete that was on the property. Robert says it's a way to "soften the look of a typical retaining wall."

Built as a demonstration house in a modular factory in Boise, the modules were constructed in just two weeks, set in six hours, and completed in forty-five days on-site. It was then open to the public for three months before the owners moved in.

Developer Johnny Hartsfield left his nine-to-five job as a landscape architect after being frustrated with how traditional developers and home builders in Seattle were constructing homes that he says were "poorly constructed, badly designed, overpriced, and not at all sensitive to human or environmental health concerns—and the home buyer did not have a choice in this." So after taking a second mortgage on his house to finance the research and development for what was to be the Greenfab project, he spent the next three years working on a healthier, more affordable, environmentally friendly house concept. Early in the process, Johnny met architect and builder Robert Humble, who introduced him to modular and efficient design. Robert showed him how they could integrate these concepts to achieve their financial and environmental goals. Together they worked on the design concept and eventually decided to build their first prototype.

FINDING A LOCATION

A client approached Robert to design a house on an infill lot that was walking distance from town and his office. When the client's plans fell through, Robert already knew the potential of the lot and made an offer to buy it himself. Robert and Johnny decided to proceed to build their prototype on that lot, where Robert and his wife, Nicole, would eventually live.

BUILDING MODULAR

Robert says it made sense to build modular "for cost control and integration of advanced systems. As building envelopes and mechanical systems become more sophisticated it makes more sense to integrate these in a controlled environment." Greenfab invested a great deal of time and money to bring Guerdon Enterprises, the modular factory that was building the model home, up to speed on the green philosophies that form the foundation of the company. The collaboration began back in 2009 when Greenfab invited the factory owner, engineer, and sales representative from Guerdon to Seattle to participate in an all-day brainstorming session with a twenty-person group of design professionals. The team consisted of engineers, architects, green contractors, environmental psychologists, lighting designers, and sustainability consultants.

GETTING THE FACTORY ON BOARD

The Guerdon team was hesitant about building the house once they learned that Greenfab was targeting a LEED Platinum rating and balancing that with affordability. Their concern was that using different materials and systems than usual would interfere with their normal factory operations. They worried that it would hold up the production line, because it would take extra time to procure the green materials and systems, and there would be a learning curve to make something different from what they had been building. In spite of these issues, the factory agreed to build the house and adhere to most of Greenfab's requests.

A LEED rater and verifier visited the factory during the construction process to make sure the factory was meeting all LEED requirements. Most

The kitchen countertop is EcoTop, an FSC-certified product made from a 50/50 fiber blend of 100 percent postconsumer recycled fiber and rapidly renewable bamboo fiber and bound with a clear 100 percent water-based system. It is scratch, heat, and stain resistant.

Vented Rain Screens

Vented rain screens deter rainwater from seeping into the exterior walls, preventing mold and the premature decay of the house. The screens create a gap between the sheathing (protective covering) of a house and the exterior cladding. Vertical furring strips are placed between these two layers, creating an open cavity. There are several advantages to this strategy. First, a path is created so rainwater is not trapped between siding and house wraps, which are supposed to prevent water infiltration but often lose water repellency. Second, the screen equalizes pressure between the interior and exterior of the house when a pressure-equalized rain screen (PER) is used, which means that water is not sucked into the interior of the house from wind-driven rain. Third, water that gets past the cladding is drained out the bottom of the vent or will evaporate. A screen is required at the top and bottom of this vent to prevent insects and other animals from getting into this space and to ensure that air can flow through it. Installing these screens is nominally more costly, but it is an excellent way to prolong the life of the house. For additional information, check the website www.toolbase.org.

Infill Lots

An infill lot is a single vacant property in a predominantly built-up area, which is bounded on two or more sides by existing development and can be "filled in" with a new structure. This can also refer to a lot containing an existing structure that will be removed and replaced with a new structure. Infrastructure and services are generally already in place so bringing in water and electrical lines is not necessary. Infill lots are considered green because they contribute to neighborhood revitalization and increase density without adding additional infrastructure. Certification programs today often offer points for building on infill lots.

BELOW AND BOTTOM Robert preferred to see raw materials, so the railing panel of the staircase is plywood, as is the flooring. While this was Robert's inclination, Johnny says that future clients may choose more finished looks.

Greenfab left the ceiling open to demonstrate where the "marriage walls" come together from the separate modules. Robert says it's also a "way of expressing the nature of the construction," and he feels that "it adds visual appeal to the interior of the home."

requirements Greenfab set for the factory could be met, but some could not. The factory didn't have a large enough demand for FSC-certified wood to justify the annual dues the FSC requires to be part of its network. As demand increases, Guerdon hopes this will change.

Robert says that although his company has been affected by the economy, its "emphasis on advanced building techniques and prefabrication has helped distinguish it from other companies. Today everybody is interested in efficiency whether that be in time, money, or natural resources."

RESPONSIBLE SITE CONSTRUCTION

Several strategies were employed to make sure the site was responsibly used, including rainwater collection, gray water treatment, protecting trees on the property, and managing soil and water runoff. They also used the existing concrete that covered one-third of the vacant lot as the fill for the gabion retaining wall structure.

COST OF ENERGY

The utility bill for the Humbles' neighbors' electricity next door is about $200 a month during the winter months, which is substantially higher than the Humbles' utility bills of $80 a month. Their house is entirely electric, so they have no gas utility bills. Robert says, "The house stays remarkably cool during the summer due to passive ventilation and requires very little heating during the winter due to passive heating and a tight thermal envelope."

SAVING WATER

A 1,500-gallon aboveground water storage cistern captures rainwater for on-site irrigation and toilet

flushing. Three 300-gallon storage basins filter and treat gray water from showers, bathroom sinks, and the washing machine for landscaping. A rain garden (see PLACE House, page 111) filters overflow from the gray water system and koi pond to recharge the groundwater.

OPEN HOUSE

Nicole and Robert agreed to have their house open to the public for three months after it was completed. More than eight hundred people came through the house, and it generated about four hundred sales leads. Greenfab is currently working with clients throughout the United States and western Canada to build future environmentally friendly homes. Johnny says the biggest benefit from opening the house to the public was the chance it gave them "to finally dispel the misconception that modular, prefab homes are cheap and poorly built. As a retailer for modular, prefab homes, this is our biggest hurdle since the majority of people believe that modular homes are synonymous with 'manufactured' homes or your grandma's 'double-wide.' When people came through the door, they had no idea they were in a modular home. To them, it had all the features, qualities, and character of the traditional site-built home they have grown to have confidence in."

The cost for the house was about $150 a square foot—with $90 of that being the cost to the modular factory and $60 for all the finishing work and hookups. Because this was a prototype, Johnny says this house cost more than future houses built to this design will cost. Several of the features were built on-site, such as the cabinets and staircases, which can potentially be built in the factory, bringing down future costs.

Sheth House

Structural Insulated Panels

PHOTOGRAPHER:

M. Ribaudo (unless otherwise noted)

ARCHITECT:

Mark O'Bryan

Art & Architecture

BUILDER:

Blue Brick Renovation + Construction

SUSTAINABLE DESIGN CONSULTANT:

EcoUrban

LOCATION:

St. Louis, Missouri

SIZE:

3,120 square feet plus 576 square feet
(garage with guest room)

HERS RATING: 51

BLOWER DOOR TEST:

0.04 ACH @ 50 Pascals

CERTIFICATION:

ENERGY STAR

LEED-H—Platinum

GREEN ASPECTS:

Infill lot (see page 116)

Detached garage (prewired for a plug-in
electric car)

No-VOC paints, caulks, and sealants

Bamboo flooring

FSC-certified wood (see page 122)

Low-flow showerheads and faucets

Dual-flush toilets

Cabinets with low VOCs, made from local
fallen trees

GREENGUARD-certified quartz countertops
(see page 73)

GREENGUARD-certified bathroom countertops

GREENGUARD-certified kitchen cabinets

Interior doors with 70 percent preconsumer
recycled content

Fiber cement siding

Tile with recycled content

Native landscaping

Permeable pavers

Rain barrel water collection

ENERGY ASPECTS:

SIPs

Prefabricated insulated concrete foundation

Spray foam insulation for sealing

Solar hot water panels

Wired for future photovoltaic panels

ENERGY STAR–rated appliances

ENERGY STAR–rated windows and doors

ENERGY STAR–rated fans

ENERGY STAR–rated lighting

High-efficiency HVAC system

Energy recovery ventilator (ERV)

TPO cool roof (see page 122)

ABOVE The prefabricated SIPs were quickly installed on-site.
(Photo courtesy of Blue Brick Renovation + Construction)

OPPOSITE The lap siding is made of concrete fiber cement,
which is very durable and requires minimal maintenance. All
native plantings were used for the landscaping.

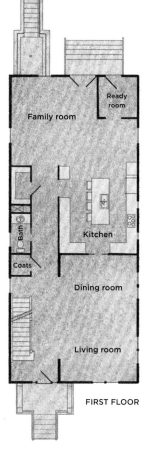

FIRST FLOOR

Family room

Ready room

Bath

Kitchen

Coats

Dining room

Living room

SECOND FLOOR

Master bedroom

Laundry

Closet

Closet

Master bath

Bath

Hall

Bedroom

Bedroom

Bedroom

The Sheth House was designed to be sandwiched between two houses on an infill lot just 33 feet wide. Blue Brick Renovation + Construction craned in prefabricated insulated foundation panels and then structural insulated panels for the walls and roof. With lots of wires, large trees, and houses surrounding the lot, the crane had to lift the sections over 60 feet high in the air to clear all that was around it.

Vihar and Katie Sheth chose this lot in a well-established transitioning St. Louis neighborhood because of its proximity to downtown, its historical relevance, and its social, economic, and cultural diversity. Local attractions include a farmers' market and activities for the whole family held in the nearby park each week.

BUILDING GREEN

When the Sheths decided to build a home to meet their growing space needs, they decided they "were going to do it right." Both Vihar and Katie were always interested in issues surrounding sustainability. The family are all vegetarians, including their son and their dog. Vihar says, "Knowing that the built environment consumes enormous amounts of energy, we set out to build the greenest house possible." It was also important that the house be very functional and that the interior have a healthy air quality.

Because building this house was a huge investment, Vihar and Katie did a lot of research so they would be educated consumers. They began working with sustainable design consultant Jay Swoboda early in 2007 and didn't begin building until April 2010, when they had all their ducks in a row.

They toured many houses and researched narrow-lot house plans. Vihar and Katie had differ-

ent design aesthetics—Vihar preferring more modern design and Katie, more traditional style. They compromised on the exterior look of the house—the more angular style is consistent with modern design, and the lap siding, more traditional. They hired architect Mark O'Bryan to meld their ideas and to work with a structural engineer, to make sure the house would stand up for many years to come.

BUILDING THE HOUSE

Jay introduced the Sheths to several builders in the St. Louis area. They chose Brad Roell of Blue Brick Renovation + Construction, although he was less experienced than some of the others, because he "demonstrated a more tangible commitment to green building."

The Sheths opted for a foundation of prefabricated insulated concrete walls (see Schaller Eco-Home, page 216), which comes with preinstalled insulation rated R-12 (see Stillwater Dwelling, page 67) and steel studs on the inside of the insulation board to make the foundation very stable.

Using prefabricated components for the foundation and walls eliminated a great deal of waste on-site. Brad says that by spending countless hours sorting the waste that was generated throughout the construction process, they were able to divert over 80 percent of it from landfills. The supplier of the structural insulated panels (SIPs) for the walls precuts the panels in the factory and recycles 99 percent of the waste. As a result, practically no waste was generated at the factory or on-site.

To make the "envelope" particularly strong, Blue Brick sprayed foam insulation around all the panels, windows, doors, and other areas that could allow thermal bridging (see Unity House, page 162).

The house is sandwiched between two nearby houses but has a very private yard and patio.

With this building envelope, air infiltration is almost eliminated.

Solar hot water panels were installed on the roof to supply most of the hot water needed for the house. The Sheths plan to add photovoltaic panels in the future to provide all or most of the electricity required for the house.

Brad at Blue Brick provided the Sheths with an extensive manual outlining every detail of their house. It includes manufacturer information on various components, explanations on how everything works, websites to find additional information, maintenance advice, and even suggestions for healthy cleaning products and ways to save energy. This manual could serve as a wonderful blueprint for other builders.

GETTING LEED CERTIFICATION

The Sheths diligently followed the LEED protocol and were determined to reach the Platinum level. They had numerous meetings with their construction team before and during the process to make sure they would be able to meet all the LEED benchmarks. Although Vihar says building the house was like "having another full-time job," he adds that after the house was complete "the end justified the means." The Sheth House is the first custom LEED Platinum house built with SIPs in St. Louis.

Certified Wood

Over fifty certifying organizations world-wide have developed standards for good forest management with third-party auditors, assuring end users that the wood comes from responsibly managed forests. All programs promote chain of custody certification, which follows the wood from beginning to end. There is a chronological documentation of where the wood comes from and where it is being transferred. One of the largest and most commonly used certification programs seen in the United States is the Forest Stewardship Council (FSC). FSC certification assures that areas of special conservation value are protected; that workers' rights, health, and safety are respected; and that no illegal logging is occurring. For additional information about FSC certification, check its website, www.fsc.org.

Cool Roofs

Cool roofs reflect the sun's radiation and emit absorbed heat back into the atmosphere. The roof remains cooler and reduces the amount of heat that is transferred to the house below it, decreasing cooling costs and increasing comfort for the occupants. TPO (thermoplastic polyolefin) is one of the popular cool roofing materials used today. TPO is a product that is a combination of rubber and hot-air-welded seams made from ethylene propylene rubber. TPO is resistant to tears, impact, punctures, fire, and wind uplift, and it's flexible enough to handle thermal expansion and contraction. Attached to the substrate material with adhesive, the roofing forms a strong chemical bond. TPO is considered an environmentally friendly material because it is recyclable, unlike some other types of roofing materials. For further information on cool roofs, check the website www.coolroofs.org.

GREENGUARD Certification

The GREENGUARD Environmental Institute (GEI) was established in 2001 to help consumers improve indoor air quality. It certifies products and materials for low chemical emissions and provides free information for consumers who want to choose healthier products. The kitchen cabinets and bathroom countertops in the Sheth House were GREENGUARD certified. For further information about this program and indoor air quality, check the website www.greenguard.org.

BELOW The solar hot water panels on the roof provide about 85 percent of the hot water required for the house in the summer and 55 percent in the winter.

CENTER Much of the living room furniture was salvaged and restored.

BOTTOM The flooring throughout most of the house is bamboo. The light fixtures and bulbs are all ENERGY STAR rated.

BELOW The countertops are made from quartz, which is stronger than granite and requires no sealants, and they are GREENGUARD certified (see sidebar). The cabinets were manufactured in St. Louis and made of lumber that the company harvested from a maple tree that fell down during a local storm. The cabinet boxes were made from veneer plywood made from FSC-certified wood (see sidebar), stained with water-based stain, and finished with a whey-protein-based clear topcoat. Cabinets were delivered to the site without boxes, to avoid waste.

BOTTOM The countertops are quartz and the cabinets were made from a locally fallen tree. The flooring tiles contain recycled content.

Snowhorn House

Structural Insulated Panels/Steel Frame

DESIGN/BUILD:
Chris Krager
KRDB

LOCATION:
Austin, Texas

SIZE:
3,851 square feet

HERS RATING: 35

BLOWER DOOR TEST:
3.07 ACH @ 50 Pascals

CERTIFICATIONS:
LEED-H—Platinum
Austin 5-Star Green
ENERGY STAR—5 Star

GREEN ASPECTS:
Rainwater storage tank
FSC-certified garapa for siding and decks
  (see page 122)
Low-flow faucets and showerheads
Low-VOC paints, finishes, and stains
Concrete countertops

ENERGY ASPECTS:
SIPs
Photovoltaic panels
Geothermal system (see page 131)
High-efficiency windows
Large overhangs
High-efficiency fireplace
Home automation system
Living wall (see page 151)
Shade awning
Chimney effect stairs with four
  operable skylights
Gas tankless water heaters
ENERGY STAR–rated appliances
ENERGY STAR–rated ceiling fans
Dimmable CFL lighting
Reflective standing seam metal roof
Heat recovery ventilator (HRV)

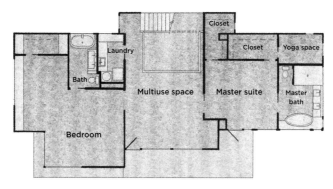

SECOND FLOOR

FIRST FLOOR

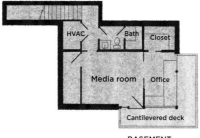

BASEMENT

ABOVE RIGHT The house photographed from the neighboring ravine during construction. The main living space cantilevers over the ravine. The house is nestled into the mature oak canopy on the site. (Photo courtesy of the owner)

BELOW RIGHT The SIPs are delivered to the site. (Photo courtesy of the owner)

OPPOSITE The living wall serves to shade the house from the hot sun, reducing the heat island effect and creating a beautiful natural look. (Photo courtesy of Alison Cartwright)

Owner Josh Snowhorn says his goals in building his home were to create "an efficient home that would assure the health of our family and guests without any compromises, that would have low maintenance costs and represent our modern tastes but with a warm and livable feeling using natural materials, rather than a stark modern bunker."

SELECTING A LOCATION

The Snowhorns wanted to build not only a very efficient green house but one that would limit their overall footprint on the earth. With this goal in mind, they chose a lot that is walking distance from food stores, public transportation, and other conveniences. The location, central to the city of Austin, far exceeded the requirements for LEED points given for proximity to services.

A small house sat on the lot, so with efficiency in mind, the Snowhorns called in Habitat for Humanity to deconstruct the structure and save as many materials as possible. Josh says that many parts of the original house are now used in several other Austin homes.

The lot the Snowhorns chose was in an ideal location but also presented challenges. It backed up on a steep cliff; thus a steel frame was used to support this drop-off. The base of solid limestone made digging supports for the foundation a challenge.

FINDING AN ARCHITECT AND BUILDER

Josh and his wife, Kinga, met with several architects in Austin, but they were impressed with Chris Krager's modern aesthetic and knowledge of green construction. Chris would be a one-stop shop for them, both designing and building their home.

ENERGY EFFICIENCY

The house was built using structural insulated panels (SIPs) for all of the outer walls and the roof. The panels were treated with boric acid to prevent any insect borings, eliminating the need for added pest control later on which would require more toxic methods.

Commercial-type, high-efficiency argon-filled windows were used to keep the envelope airtight. The large sliding doors from the dining room to the outside are lift-and-slide doors, with each panel weighing five hundred pounds; fortunately, because of the clever design, they slide easily for the Snowhorns' two young daughters.

After the outer portion of the house was erected, the entire house was sprayed with a soy-based foam to seal all the cracks and gaps.

A Kalwall panel, more often used for commercial construction, was used at the stairwells. This sandwich panel is reinforced, translucent fiberglass with an aerogel fill. This allows lots of light to pass through but offers an R-20 insulation.

Because the house was constructed to be so tightly sealed, it needed an air exchange system such as a heat recovery ventilator (see Riley's Rosemary Beach Retreat, page 87) to assure a healthy atmosphere inside.

CFL lights are used in most fixtures in the house. In order to find out which dimmable bulbs are the most efficient, Josh bought CFLs from at least ten manufacturers. After testing all of them, he chose the bulb that lasted the longest and gave off the most pleasant light. He selected the Neptun PAR 30, a 19-watt dimmable bulb that he says has the same output as a 60-watt incandescent bulb but lasts far longer. By replacing 60-watt incandescent bulbs (used during construction) with equivalent

Siding for the house and the decking are FSC-certified garapa, a Brazilian wood. The pool is 100 percent chlorine free, using a copper ionization system that clears all impurities in the water while keeping the swimming experience as natural as possible. (Photo courtesy of Alison Cartwright)

Automated skylights at the top of the stairs are integrated with the home automation system. The Snowhorns open them on hot days when the HVAC system is off to vent heat or cooking odors. They are triple-low-E coated and double paned with argon gas filler. The aerogel-filled Kalwall system allows a great deal of light in but is highly energy efficient. (Photo courtesy of Casey Dunn)

dimmable CFLs, Josh says he was able to save over 4,000 watts (4 kilowatts) of load on the house if all of the lights were on.

DAMPENING THE SUMMER SUN

The Snowhorns took every opportunity to dampen the effects of the hot summer sun. Large overhangs were used around the periphery of the house.

Josh says that the living wall concept came from a book by a French landscape architect named Patrick Blanc, who built these walls all over the world. A local landscape architect, Will Pickens, designed the system, which is located on the southwest of the house. This metal-framed wall is separate but connected to the house. Inside the frame is a medium to support the growth of the plants. Drip emitters are placed variously throughout the wall with an irrigation feed on a timer and a special hydroponic injector from a thirty-five-gallon nutrient tank. The idea was to shade the house while creating something beautiful to look at. The living wall has sun-tolerant plants on the outside and shade plants on the inside, so the Snowhorns can walk behind it and see it from the windows of the front bedrooms.

The shade awning, made from nylon tension fabric to resist weather and to blend with the house, was added after the house was finished when the Snowhorns realized that the sun in the central multiuse space upstairs was too strong throughout the day.

CREATING ENERGY

Energy is created by photovoltaic panels on the roof. During peak hours, the panels produce most of the energy required for the house, even feeding some energy back to the local utility company at times. In the evening when no electricity is generated, the electricity comes from the grid. With "net metering" (see Schaller Eco-Home, page 216) the Snowhorns are credited for the energy they produce in excess of what they need.

In order to keep track of the energy being produced by the photovoltaic panels, the Snowhorns installed a home automation system. Even when they travel, they are able to monitor the energy output from their computer or smartphone. Their system also allows them to control their HVAC, security, lights, music, intercom, and heating for the pool and hot tub for efficiency. All of these devices are tied to an Apple TV and various sound components in a centralized system for the whole house, with sound individually controllable from room to room.

A closed thermal system fireplace takes in fresh air from the outside (rather than from the room) for the combustion, and a fan blows air around the outside of the firebox and then blows that heat inside the house. Josh estimates that 75 percent of his winter heating can be supplied with this fireplace.

A geothermal system is tied into the heating and cooling system in the house and pool. Josh says the system is amazingly quiet and efficient, with no outside fans or compressors. It uses 90 percent less electricity than a normal HVAC system. The cost was $90,000 for the house and pool system; luckily for the Snowhorns, the government offers a 30 percent federal tax credit for geothermal systems like this, saving them a good deal of money.

There are two sources of heating water for domestic use. In the warmer months, there is hot wastewater (which is quite pure), a by-product of the geothermal system. In other homes, this water is usually drained outside, but the Snowhorns store this water in a fiberglass-insulated tank and use it as their primary water source. When this water isn't available, they use natural gas–fired tankless water heaters for the house, the pool house sinks and shower, and the painting studio adjacent to the garage.

WATER CONSERVATION

With water being a precious commodity in Austin, the Snowhorns opted to have a five-thousand-gallon tank dug into the ground. The pool installers graciously offered to dig a hole near the pool for the water tank when the pool was being excavated. The rainwater tank is an innovative design using a material that looks like milk crates stacked on top of each other to form a framework. These are placed in a membrane that is wrapped over the crates and

BELOW Kitchen countertops near the cooktop are concrete, and there is a maple butcher block near the sink. (Photo courtesy of Casey Dunn)

BOTTOM The upstairs flex-library space serves as a connector between the bedrooms ans also assists in providing airflow between floors. The foof has four skylights that can be opened (on-site or remotely) to expel warm air when the house gets too hot. (Photo courtesy of Casey Dunn)

then covered with dirt. A pipe collects rainwater from the house roof, and overflow simply pipes into the ravine. In retrospect, Josh says, "I wish we had done a 50,000- to 100,000-gallon underground tank given the water shortages and cost of water in Austin."

The Snowhorns used all low-flow faucets and dual-flush toilets to save on water. To further conserve water, they installed a drip irrigation system, which delivers the water just under the surface of the ground so the soil is saturated with very little evaporation waste.

GETTING CERTIFIED

The Snowhorns opted to have the house LEED certified, "to have the stamp of approval that would quantify [their] hard work." More rigorous for them was getting five-star certification from the local Austin Energy Green Building program. Landscaping became a challenge because the city, like many others, requires local plantings. Grass tends to be an issue, because even normal zoysia tends to take huge amounts of water. Josh convinced the town certifiers to accept *Palisades zoysia* because it had been specifically bred for Texas by Texas A&M University to survive heat and drought.

In the end, Josh says, "We truly love our healthy green home! Our house is filled every day with happy growing children, visiting family, and good friends. We have found that we use every one of our rooms and daily marvel at the bright light–filled home we have created."

Geothermal Systems

Geothermal systems use the earth's constant temperature to maintain that same steady temperature in the home. The technology can supply heating, cooling, and water heating, and it can be used with a conventional duct system or a radiant floor system. Pipes are laid in the ground (either horizontally or vertically) in holes drilled to a depth of as little as six feet to as much as four hundred feet, depending on the site and the homeowner's needs. Open-loop systems use well, pond, or lake water as the energy source; closed-loop systems use an anti-freeze solution sealed inside buried piping. In the colder months, the heat pump absorbs heat from the ground and uses it to warm the air in the house or water in the radiant floor. In the warmer months, the process is reversed, taking heat from the house and transferring it into the ground. Some electric utilities offer incentives for investing in a geothermal system. The geothermal system in the Snowhorn House is used for heating and cooling both the house and the pool, as well as the waste-water by-product for domestic hot water. To learn more, visit www.eere.energy.gov or www.toolbase.org.

Brazilian Hardwoods

Ipe, cumaru, and garapa are the three most readily available high-density tropical hardwood species. All three species are available in FSC and other sustainable-yield forestry chains of custody. Ipe and cumaru are the hardest species (approximately two and a half times harder than oak), and both are Class A fire rated. Garapa is one and a half times harder than oak. These rapid-growing species all reach maturity (120 feet in height) in approximately thirty-five years. Combined with the sustained yield forestry regulations in their growing areas, they are truly a sustainable and renewable resource. No native North American species (or other species worldwide) come close to these species for hardness, density, and durability. The three species are naturally resistant to rot, decay, termites, scratches, and splintering without any chemical treatment. They are smoother than either engineered wood or many other species of wood, which makes them excellent alternatives for decking. Some companies offer twenty-five-year warranties on these woods because they are expected to endure that long and much longer.

Garapa tends to have a yellowish golden color, ipe has a darker brown color, and cumaru varies from reddish browns to yellowy browns. Cumaru is very similar to ipe in terms of physical properties, strength, and hardness, but ipe has a coarser graining (similar to teak). As the woods weather, they become a light silvery gray (like most other wood) unless sealer is used to maintain their natural color.

The wood is used for siding, interior flooring, window frames, and decking. All three woods are less expensive than composite decking. The Snowhorns used FSC-certified garapa for their siding, fencing, and decking (and used the leftover wood to build a tree house).

Hilltop Craftsman

Structural Insulated Panels

PHOTOGRAPHER:

Aaron Barna Photography (unless
    otherwise noted)

DESIGNER:

Peter Bergford

MANUFACTURER:

Premier Building Systems

BUILDER:

Scott Homes

LOCATION:

Olympia, Washington

SIZE:

2,100 square feet

HERS RATING: 37

BLOWER DOOR TEST:

0.65 ACH @ 50 Pascals

CERTIFICATION:

ENERGY STAR

Built Green—5 Star

Indoor airPLUS Program

Builders Challenge

GREEN ASPECTS:

Recycled-content countertops

Linoleum floors

ESP-certified cabinets

Recycled-content carpet tiles

Low-VOC paints and stains

Low-flow faucets and showerheads—
    WaterSense labeled

Low-flow toilets

Storm water cistern

Xeriscaping (see page 207)

Detached garage

ENERGY ASPECTS:

SIPs

ENERGY STAR–rated appliances

Efficient lighting

Triple-pane windows

Ductless heat pump (see page 135)

Tankless water heater

Triple jamb-lock exterior fiberglass
    doors (which insulate and seal better)

Heat recovery ventilator (HRV)

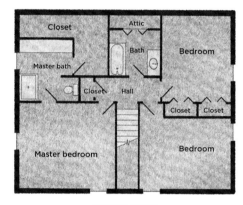

SECOND FLOOR

The garage is detached, which reduces the chance of exhaust fumes entering the house. The owners say that one of the unforeseen benefits of the central area between the garage and the house is that it has proven to be a terrific socializing spot for large and small gatherings.

FIRST FLOOR

The shell of the house was completely finished by mid-September, which was fortunate, since the following season's rain and snow did not stop until May. One of the advantages of building with SIPs is the short time it takes to erect them.

Scott Bergford, the owner of Scott Homes, had been building very efficient houses with SIPs for seventeen years. In recent years he'd heard a great deal of discussion about Passive House standards at his local community green association meetings, so he decided that he wanted to try to meet those standards in a very cost-effective way.

Along came Eileen and Matt Cooper, who were willing to be his guinea pigs as Scott attempted some new methods of achieving even more efficiency than he had in the past. They interviewed several other builders, but were taken with Scott's clear knowledge of effective building systems and his excellent reputation as an active member of the local Master Builders Association and Northwest EcoBuilding Guild.

NONNEGOTIABLE BUILDING CRITERIA

Eileen says, "We wanted to build the most energy-efficient home our small budget would allow." The house had to look and feel welcoming and be oriented so they could enjoy the view of the Olympic mountain range. They wanted a functional layout that would suit their needs currently, as well as throughout the next twenty years. This strategy included having a master bedroom on the first floor, which would work better for them in their senior years.

When Eileen found out the cost of some of the items on her wish list, such as an arboretum and full wraparound porch, she realized she would have to pare the list down to meet her budget. She says Peter Bergford, Scott's son, the designer of the house, ultimately didn't design "the house we day-dreamed about; we got the house we should have."

CREATING A POSITIVE ECOSYSTEM

Scott changed some of the methods that he had used in the past and altered some that other builders used in meeting the Passive House standard. Instead of building with double walls, as some other builders were doing, he opted for thicker structural insulated panels (SIPs). For the flooring and walls, he used ten-inch SIPs (for an R-40 rating), and for the roof he used twelve-inch SIPs (R-50), which were thicker than any panels he had used in the past (R-value indicates an insulation's resistance to heat flow). In addition to achieving a higher R-value, Scott was able to stop thermal bridging (see Unity House, page 162).

Instead of using his usual radiant floor heating system, he opted for a ductless heat pump (see sidebar), which uses much less electricity but produces more heat and cool air per dollar spent. A heat recovery ventilator (see Riley's Rosemary Beach Retreat, page 87) helps distribute the air evenly throughout the house and filters clean air without sacrificing the heat or coolness already generated. Scott says, "When pricing out the Cooper house . . . to my great surprise, this super house cost me less than my normal award-winning product we have been building for years."

Scott says they chose the most efficient triple-pane windows they could find on the American market. Although the fiberglass windows they chose cost more than triple what other windows cost, he says the U-factor (see sidebar) was 0.11 to 0.15 rather than the less expensive models, which are U-0.30 to U-0.35.

Scott discovered that CFL lights gave off more heat than LEDs. He decided to use the CFLs to increase the heat produced by the house. He says

OPPOSITE TOP The orange coating is a breathable membrane system (VaproShield), which Premier Building Systems applied at the factory. This is a water shield that will repel rain from leaking in through the siding. And if the wall assembly is moist, then moisture vapor can migrate out through the membrane, keeping the assembly dry. (Photo courtesy of the owner)

OPPOSITE CENTER AND BOTTOM The Hilltop Craftsman is a story and a half high. After the floor was installed, the walls went up and the second floor and roof were installed. Installation of all the SIPs took just ten working days. (Photo courtesy of the owner)

RESNET (Residential Energy Services Network)

RESNET is an organization that certifies energy auditors and raters, as well as qualified contractors and builders. Its website helps homeowners and builders locate professionals in their area to do energy audits and construct or remodel houses to have excellent energy efficiencies. Raters perform an energy analysis of the house design to achieve a HERS rating, then work with the builder to identify inefficiencies in the design and suggest improvements to ensure the house will meet ENERGY STAR performance guidelines. A blower door test (see New World Hudson Home, page 27) and a duct test, to test the leakiness of the ducts, are performed, then a HERS rating is generated. RESNET has the software program that verifiers use to predict and verify energy efficiencies in the home. For further information about RESNET, check the website www.resnet.us.

U-factor

This rating represents the heat transfer through a window (or door or skylight) and indicates how well the window insulates. This rating may apply to the glass alone or the entire window, which includes the frame and spacer material. The number is measured with a very complicated formula: $BTU/hr \cdot ft^2 \cdot °F$. The formula is the amount of btu (energy) that transfers through a material over time at a given temperature and a given area. The lower the U-factor, the less the window conducts heat, and the better its insulating value; hence, low U-factors signify more energy-efficient windows. U-factors range from about 1.3 for a typical aluminum single-glazed window, to about 0.25 for modern double-pane windows, to about 0.09 for a triple-pane, high-performance glass with low-emissivity coatings. For further information, check the website of the National Fenestration Rating Council at www.nfrc.org.

Ductless Heat Pumps or Mini-split Systems

A popular heating method in Europe and Japan, ductless heat pumps, also known as mini-split systems, are just beginning to be popular in this country as a highly efficient heating and cooling system. They do not require ducts, cost less to install than traditional HVAC systems, and use a fraction of the energy, reducing utility bills by about 25 to 50 percent. Some utility companies offer a rebate for using this system and qualified units are eligible for a $300 federal tax credit. The system is composed of three main parts—an indoor air-handling unit, an outdoor compressor/condenser unit, and a remote control that operates the system. Heat is transferred using refrigerant expansion and compression, in much the same way that a refrigerator works. Because they don't have ducts, they avoid some of the energy losses associated with central forced air heating and cooling systems, particularly those whose ducts are in unconditioned spaces. Mitsubishi Electric (www.mehvac.com) supplied the ductless heat pump for the Hilltop Craftsman house. Similar systems are available from other companies as well. For further information, check the website www.goingductless.com.

LEFT To stay on budget, the Coopers did much of the work on the house—sanding, staining, and installing all the trim, stair banisters, and doors. They also installed the ipe flooring (see Snowhorn House, page 131) in the main room and the carpet tiles in the bedrooms.

RIGHT The carpet in the fireplace room (which Eileen calls "the Snuggery") is handmade Persian and was brought back from one of Matt's deployments in Iraq. Although the Coopers couldn't imagine living in a house without a fireplace, they found out that they didn't really need a fire to keep warm. Their ductless heat pump is extremely efficient at warming the house, as is the ten inches of SIPs below their flooring. Eileen says she expects the fireplace won't be needed more than twice a year since the house is so warm already.

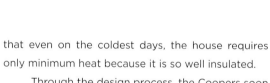

that even on the coldest days, the house requires only minimum heat because it is so well insulated.

Through the design process, the Coopers soon learned that they couldn't change any one part of the house without affecting the rest of the design. For instance, designing a very tight envelope for energy efficiency, in turn demanded alterations to allow for an adequate ventilation system. In highly efficient houses with limited air exchange, it is important to bring healthy, exterior air into the house. They began to understand the concept of "whole house design."

CHOOSING NOT TO CERTIFY THE HOUSE

The cost to employ a local Passive House verifier/certifier was more than the Coopers wanted to spend, and since it wasn't important to them or to

BELOW All appliances are ENERGY STAR rated, and the buffet is made of recycled content.

BOTTOM Since the house is technically a story and a half, there are sloped ceilings in the upstairs rooms. Eileen says she loves sloped ceilings for their coziness and charm, but the plan was developed as a cost-saving technique, more than a design choice. Matt made the bedside tables.

Scott, they all decided not to go through the official process. Scott says the house would have needed some "tweaking" to meet the standards, with more windows on the south side and slightly thicker SIPs. But he says this house gave him the confidence that he could build and certify a Passive House in the future and do it a lot cheaper than builders who used double-walled methods.

RECOVERY OF COST

Eileen estimates it cost between 1 and 5 percent more to build a 2,100-square-foot custom house green than it would to build a house without these features. Because construction of this house was an experiment, Scott had the Washington State University Extension Energy Program run the plans for the house through its RESNET program (see page 135). The report came back that they would make back the extra money they were spending within five years, if energy costs remained the same. If energy costs continue to rise, the payback time period will decrease.

Scott says a typical 2,100-square-foot house in the area costs about $150 to $200 per month to heat during the winter. He predicts the Coopers' house will cost about $70 *a year* to heat.

A "RIGHT" BUILDING EXPERIENCE

Eileen says she "loves how solid the house feels." She uses a Coast Salish word, *hé ladé*, which means "the sense of having everything right," to describe her construction experience. "We were right with our designer/builder, with our choice of building materials, with our design—right as in it was a good, satisfying, proper decision for us and everything worked out for the best."

G·O Logic Home

Structural Insulated Panels/Timber Frame

PHOTOGRAPHER:

Trent Bell (unless otherwise noted)

ARCHITECT:

Matthew O'Malia

BUILDER:

Alan Gibson

LANDSCAPE ARCHITECT:

Ann Kearsley

LOCATION:

Belfast, Maine

SIZE:

1,500 square feet

HERS RATING: 20

BLOWER DOOR TEST:

0.05 ACH @ 50 Pascals

CERTIFICATION:

Passive House (first in Maine, twelfth in
  the country) (see page 142)

LEED-H—Platinum

ENERGY STAR

GREEN ASPECTS:

Low-VOC materials and finishes

Locally harvested timber frame and deck

Standing seam metal roof

Low-flow faucets

Dual-flush toilets

Storm water management

Small footprint

Native plantings

Fiber cement siding

ENERGY ASPECTS:

SIPs

Insulated concrete form (ICF) foundation
  (slab-on-grade)

Triple-glazed windows

Cellulose insulation (blown in)

Roll-down shading for solar control

Passive solar orientation

Photovoltaic panels

Solar thermal hot water system

Concrete flooring

ENERGY STAR–rated appliances

ENERGY STAR–rated lighting

Energy monitoring system

Spin dryer for laundry (see page 142)

Heat recovery ventilator (HRV)

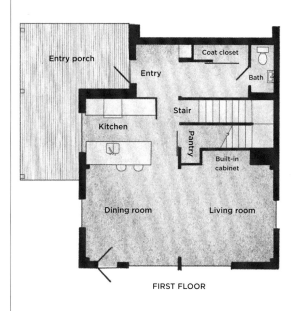

FIRST FLOOR

SECOND FLOOR

OPPOSITE ABOVE The insulated concrete form (ICF) foundation offers excellent energy efficiency, sound attenuation, and durability, and it is fire- and windproof. (Photo courtesy of G·O Logic Homes)

OPPOSITE BELOW The timber frame was erected and then the SIPs were attached to the frame. (Photo courtesy of G·O Logic Homes)

BELOW The standing seam roof on the house is made from recycled metal and holds the photovoltaic and thermal panels. High-performance windows were imported from Germany and are more abundant on the south side of the house to take advantage of thermal rays. Pretinted fiber cement siding was selected for its durability and the minimal maintenance it requires.

After working and studying architecture in Frankfurt, Germany, Matthew O'Malia felt he had learned better ways to build and had acquired the skill to build more efficient houses back home in Maine. He teamed up with general contractor and energy efficiency analyst Alan Gibson to form the company G·O Logic. Each of them had been building energy-efficient projects, but they decided that for their first project together they would step up their effort and build a superinsulated house. Their first venture was the G·O Logic Home, which they hoped would demonstrate that a certified Passive House could be built not only to look attractive and be extremely comfortable, but also to cost no more than $150 a square foot. They chose a rural contemporary design for this first prototype because it would fit in with the local area and be a style familiar to the average homeowner's aesthetic.

THE SCARE FACTOR

Many people are frightened off from building a Passive House because it involves using unfamiliar technology in order to meet the stringent certification requirements. Matt says it was an advantage for G·O Logic to be a design and build company in seeking certification. Together he and Alan planned the project and didn't have to deal with concerns about the implementation of their ideas. Often contractors are deterred from using new techniques that they haven't used in the past, with additional concerns about the cost. At G·O Logic they discussed various ideas, came up with design solutions, and implemented them at a reasonable cost, using both their experience and the knowledge Matt had picked up in Germany.

According to Matt, Passive House standards can often be expensive to meet, unless houses are built in an efficient way. He had the advantage of working in Germany and developing a firsthand familiarity with their building methods and materials. Matt considers many German products to be superior, such as the windows, which he imported for the G·O Logic Home.

THE COSTS

The house was completed for approximately $150 a square foot. Matt says this house was about 5 to 7 percent more expensive than the other local houses, but the difference will be paid off in five or six years. The cost for heating and cooling the house is $300 a year compared with $1,300 to $1,500 a year for the typical house in the area. Although the initial output is slightly higher for a Passive House, the savings over a thirty-year mortgage can be substantial—approximately $170,000 with modest energy inflation.

ENERGY DEMAND KEPT TO A MINIMUM

The warmth required on the coldest night in January, or at peak demand, would be equivalent to the output of a 2,000-watt hair dryer or the heat required to boil a pot of pasta. Designed to use 90 percent less energy than a typical house, the G·O Logic Home was built with an extremely efficient envelope. The windows are triple glazed with an aluminum-clad wood frame. The timber frame has extra-wide spacing for added cellulose insulation; the structural insulated panels have a high R-rating, meaning they are very energy efficient; and the insulated concrete foundation allows no air infiltration. ENERGY STAR–rated appliances and lighting minimize energy use.

The highly efficient windows provide natural daylighting and are operable to allow natural ventilation in the warmer months.

OPPOSITE SIDEBAR Spin dryers are very energy efficient.

BELOW The timber frame is important to the stability of the room, but the wood also adds warmth to the already highly insulated house.

BOTTOM The countertops are butcher block and local Maine granite. All appliances are ENERGY STAR rated; the refrigerator is European size, twenty-four by twenty-four inches, for energy efficiency and to conserve space. A recirculation vent hood was used to save energy.

Passive House

The Passive House Building Energy Standard, or Passivhaus standard, first established in Germany, is now being used in many countries around the world, including the United States. It focuses on reducing energy consumption for space heating and cooling by about 90 percent. The Passive House Planning Package (PHPP) is software that can be used to predict energy usage and losses for individual structures. The requirements are stringent and include maximum heating and cooling demand, total primary energy consumption, and a maximum leakage of air volume per hour at 50 Pascals of pressure, which is measured with a blower door test. Passive houses are designed with superinsulation, high-performance windows, an airtight building shell or "envelope," and the use of an energy recovery ventilator (ERV) to exchange the interior air with fresh outside air. Although some houses do include active solar systems, generating energy is not the primary focus; Passive Houses are designed to save approximately 75 percent of the entire energy used in a building compared to existing building stock. There are currently about thirty thousand structures built to this standard, and it is possible that this may become the energy standard for some countries by 2020. For further information about the Passive House Institute US, check the website www.passivehouse.us.

Spin Dryers

The typical clothes dryer in the United States and Canada uses up to 5,000 watts, or about 6 to 10 percent of the household energy, and it runs for forty to sixty minutes. The spin dryer uses 300 watts and runs for two or three minutes. The G·O Logic Home has a spin dryer in an oversized upstairs closet, which also includes the washing machine, a ventilation system, and a clothesline. Spin dryers are quiet, fast, inexpensive, and portable, and they don't fade or shrink clothes. The downside to these machines is that because they don't use heat, clothes come out damp, and because machines are generally small, only a few items can be dried at one time. Using a spin dryer first can limit the time clothes need in the traditional dryer or on a clothesline to get fully dry. The spin dryer used in the G·O Logic Home was purchased from www.laundry-alternative.com. An alternative site is www.clothesdrygreen.com.

Other elements of the house that minimize energy requirements are a spin dryer (see sidebar) rather than a typical dryer, and concrete floors, which function as thermal mass (absorbing heat and cool air and gently releasing it when it is needed).

A monitoring system in the house gives continuous information on the energy being used, compared to the energy being produced by the photovoltaic and hot water panels. The cost of running each energy item in the house, such as outlets, lights, and the energy recovery ventilator (ERV) (see Riley's Rosemary Beach Retreat, page 87), is consistently available, as is the energy used each hour of the day. This information can be checked on the panel in the house as well as on a computer, when the owners are away.

Large overhangs, often used to protect against hot summer rays, were avoided in this house by placing the house on the lot so that the angle of the sun is very steep in the summer, with solar heat mostly hitting the roof. With limited windows on the east and west of the house, solar gain is avoided in the summer and heat loss is limited in the winter. It gets excellent solar gain in the winter when it is needed.

Concrete flooring functions as thermal mass, absorbing heat during the day and releasing it in the evening, when the sun isn't shining. Roll-down shades disappear between the window and the beam in front of it when not in use. While not limiting the heat of the sun from seeping into the house, they control the glare, allowing 7 percent visibility (which is still good visibility), while maintaining some privacy at night.

ADVANTAGES BEYOND ENERGY EFFICIENCY

Matt says the advantages of a Passive House go beyond the financial and environmental ones. He says the house is extremely comfortable. The air is evenly distributed around the house, there are no temperature swings, the walls and windows are warm to the touch, it's very quiet in the house, and it is never drafty. Even on zero-degree winter days, Matt says it's difficult to know what the temperature is outside because it's so warm and comfortable in the house.

G·O Logic has been busy building houses since its founding in 2008. At a time when many builders in the country are starved for work, the people at G·O Logic believe their business is thriving because they have taken the initiative to find a better way to build. Matt says passive design is most likely the future of home construction, and builders who want to be successful will have to become more educated about energy-efficient construction.

Matt says, "Passive House, now in its infancy in North America, is destined to become the future of construction for cold climates. This level of performance has already been adopted by the European Union as their building energy standard for 2020, and it is only a matter of time before we will see that here at home as well. Interestingly, the main reason for the shift to Passive House will not be because the environment inspires political change; sadly no, the cost of energy will leave no other choices."

The G·O Logic Home received the U.S. Green Building Council 2011 LEED for Homes Project of the Year Award, presented at the 2011 Greenbuild International Conference and Expo in Toronto.

Zero Energy Idea House

Structural Insulated Panels/Prefabricated
 Steel Frame

PHOTOGRAPHER:

Dane Gregory Meyer (unless otherwise noted)

ARCHITECT:

David Clinkston, Clinkston Architects

BUILDER:

Shirey Contracting

LOCATION:

Issaquah, Washington

SIZE:

1,630 square feet

HERS RATING: 29

BLOWER DOOR TEST:

1.79 ACH @ 50 Pascals

CERTIFICATION:

ENERGY STAR

Built Green—5 Star

GREEN ASPECTS:

Low-VOC materials and finishes

Dual-flush toilets

Low-flow faucets and showerheads

Rainwater collection

FSC-certified wood

Recycled-content tile

Salvaged wood flooring

Metal roof

Fiber cement siding

Local materials

Living roof

Planted living wall as a retention wall
 (see page 151)

Drought-tolerant plants

Small footprint

ENERGY ASPECTS:

SIPs

ENERGY STAR–rated appliances

ENERGY STAR–rated lighting

Energy monitoring system

High-performance windows

Insulated concrete form (ICF) foundation

Photovoltaic panels

Solar hot water panels

Wind turbine (see page 151)

Tankless water heater

Hydronic radiant heating

Heat recovery ventilator (HRV)

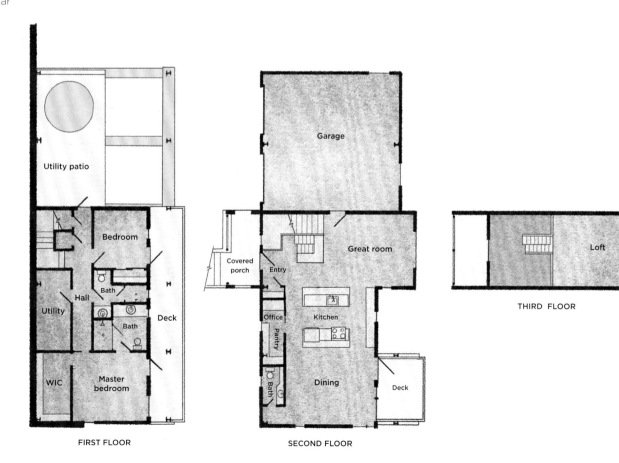

FIRST FLOOR

SECOND FLOOR

THIRD FLOOR

BELOW Many of the green aspects of the house are visible to passersby, such as the living roof, the wind turbine, the solar thermal panels, and the photovoltaic panels.

BOTTOM LEFT On this very steep site, the house is anchored to the hillside by auger cast piles, concrete-grade beams, SIPs, and insulated concrete forms (ICFs). The white is the outer layer of foam, part of the ICFs. This meets the SIPs to create a tight envelope around the house. (Photo courtesy of the owners)

BOTTOM RIGHT The three-thousand-gallon cistern, in the area beneath the garage, slows down the rate at which storm water enters the public system. The runoff water from the roofs and driveway is used not in the home but for irrigating the landscape.

The Zero Energy Idea House not only incorporates much of the newest green, energy, and water technologies available today, but much of it is totally visible from the exterior. The architect, David Clinkston, says that "unlike some houses promoted for sustainable features that require diagrams, text, or a set of headphones and a tour to begin to understand the sustainable features—with this house they are self-evident." To anyone driving by the house, the solar panels, photovoltaic panels, wind turbine, and living roof are easily visible.

Owners Donna and Riley Shirey wanted to build a house that would be a "deep green" state-of-the-art residence that would inspire others to reduce consumption of natural resources and build smaller, more energy-efficient homes. This house would go beyond any other energy-efficient house their company, Shirey Contracting, had built in its nearly thirty years in business. From the start of this project, the firm hoped it would serve as a demonstration house to educate the public as well as the construction industry. This house would showcase the newest technologies, attempt to achieve zero energy use, and do all of this in 1,630 square feet of living space.

THE CHALLENGES

The lot they chose for this project presented serious challenges. The steep slope and environmentally sensitive location was deemed a "critical area" by the town. Clinkston says, "The extraordinarily steep slope was a challenge above and beyond the norm." The Shireys would be among the first homeowners to attempt to meet the city's newly adopted Critical Area Ordinance. Along with the typical building permit required of all houses, a "critical area permit" was needed to build on what they deemed an environmentally sensitive area. With the intense project goals of energy independence, meeting strict environmental regulatory requirements, and the physical challenge of building on a steep slope, it was clear an extended professional design team would be required. The Shireys and Clinkston led a design team of experienced professionals including geotechnical, civil, and structural engineers, a land use planner, a wildlife biologist, two landscape architecture firms, an arborist, and an interior designer.

The Washington State University Extension Energy Program was consulted to make energy recommendations regarding the integration of various elements of the house, such as R-values of the thermal envelope (see Stillwater Dwelling, page 67), size of windows, and mechanical systems. With energy modeling, they helped the Shireys decide to use six-inch SIPs for the walls rather than eight-inch panels. Monitors installed in the house allow them to tweak the house's energy systems in order to improve consumption rates and at the same time collect information to be used by future homeowners.

The house is also currently involved with the US Department of Energy's Building America program, which conducts research to develop "energy solutions that improve efficiency of new and existing homes in each US climate zone, while increasing comfort, safety, and durability."

The local electricity and gas provider, Puget Sound Energy, has also been involved with monitoring the house. When the Shireys produce more energy than they use, the utility company reimburses them for the difference.

All appliances in the house are ENERGY STAR rated. Countertops were constructed with an old-fashioned drain board built in and a metal piece to be used as a trivet next to the stove. Special words, such as "create" and "imagine," were also carved into it.

STARTING CONSTRUCTION

Nine months and $75,000 in consulting fees later, the Shireys were ready to build their home. Luckily Clinkston's sensitivity to the nuances of this site and experience at integrating architectural design with the land and its natural features helped the Shireys get through the process.

Construction of the foundation required fourteen tons of rebar and two hundred cubic yards of concrete, way beyond the requirements of most any other house with this petite footprint.

To avoid having large amounts of water flowing down the steep slope, the team designed an elaborate system of erosion control. To minimize impact to the land, they planted a living roof and wall (see page 151) to reduce storm water runoff and also filter water going back into the municipal system. The living wall also functions as a retaining wall on the side of the driveway. An innovative technique uses mesh tubes filled with composted material to retain sediment for erosion control, and flowers planted in the compost give the area a garden effect. Drought-tolerant plants used for landscaping minimize watering and garden maintenance.

BUILDING AND LEARNING

The Shireys wanted this house to be an educational "laboratory," incorporating the greenest and most sustainable elements now available. The house envelope needed to be energy efficient and systems needed to create as much energy as the house consumed. Plus, it had to include some of the most healthy products, sustainable materials, and water-saving systems available. Clinkston says the Shireys were "the most willing and ambitious clients, when it came to incorporating almost every sustainable technology one can imagine."

The primary framing of the house is prefabricated heavy-gauge steel, made from recycled material that can one day also be recycled. Riley wanted to "see the bones" of the house, so the frame is apparent in many areas inside and outside of the house. The secondary support comes from the structural insulated panels (SIPs).

BELOW The steel frame allows for large open spans without lots of interior structural walls. Riley likes having the steel exposed so the "bones" of the house can be seen.

OPPOSITE Dramatic views of Lake Sammamish and the Cascade Mountains to the east can be seen, due to the extremely steep slope that the house is sited on. This image also shows the full array of photovoltaic panels oriented to the south. (Photo courtesy of Northwest Property Imaging)

CREATING A TIGHT ENVELOPE

The team of architects and specialists began the design of the house with the most energy-efficient envelope they could create. The insulated concrete form (ICF) foundation was fast to install and has an R-value of 22. The walls are six-inch-thick SIPs, creating an R-value of 24; the floor and roof panels are 10½ inches thick and offer an R-40 rating. The high-performance fiberglass windows are efficient and low maintenance and have vapor flashing, an impervious material installed to prevent moisture intrusion.

CREATING AND SAVING ENERGY

Several methods of energy production were incorporated into the design. A helix-shaped wind turbine on the roof catches the breezes off the adjacent Lake Sammamish. Solar hot water tubes on the roof heat the water for domestic hot water, while a high-efficiency air-to-water outdoor heat pump warms the water for the hydronic radiant floor system. Photovoltaic panels produce electricity used to power various items in the house including appliances and lighting.

ENERGY STAR–rated lighting and appliances reduce energy requirements. A wire mesh grid or scrim around the front entry will be planted with vines to block some of the afternoon sun as well as block out bright headlights from passing cars, also creating a separation between the road and the house.

SAVING WATER

The three-thousand-gallon cistern, under the garage on a utility patio, harvests rainwater and slows down storm water from entering the public system. This water can also be used for watering the landscape. Dual-flush toilets and low-flow faucets and shower-heads keep water usage to a minimum.

SUSTAINABLE ELEMENTS

Everything that went into this house was well thought out. Many of the products were produced from recycled and scrap materials. The countertops were produced from damaged shower doors and the bathroom tiles from bamboo scraps. The flooring is a hickory veneer over an engineered substrate, which vastly reduced the use of lumber.

The fiber cement siding, with a fifty-year warranty, and the standing seam metal roofing, with a forty-year warranty, are very durable and long-lasting.

Donna Shirey says, "Our Zero Energy Idea House is a wonderful home—quiet, cozy, and can just about take care of itself. I find it reassuring that the house is creating energy every day. We are giving back to our community and doing a small part in making the world better."

Bathroom tiles were made from bamboo scraps. The toilet is dual flush, and the faucet is low flow.

BELOW The bedroom opens to the upper terrace and beautiful views of the lake.

BOTTOM The loft is accessed via handcrafted steps that are modeled after a ship stair or alternating-step stair. Donna describes the loft as the "away room," a place to get away and enjoy looking outside from the cozy window seat.

Wind Turbines

Wind turbines have been in use since ancient times. Recently wind power is increasingly being used to take the place of fossil fuel to create electricity. Wind power is natural and clean, and it is becoming more financially preferable with the decreasing cost and increased options in turbines. Wind power accounted for 40 percent of all new energy by electric utilities in 2008 and 2009. The Zero Energy Idea House has a helix-shaped turbine, which catches the wind regardless of which direction it is blowing from and generates energy with winds as light as 7.5 mph. For further information about wind turbines, check the website of the American Wind Energy Association at www.awea.org.

Living Walls

Living walls are also known as green walls, eco-walls, and vertical gardens. They are constructed of parallel panels with soil or another growing medium between them, where a variety of vegetation, such as climbing vines, may be planted. Living walls can decrease energy bills by providing insulation and shade on the side of the house, while also reducing outside noise. Evaporation of water on the leaves can also decrease adjacent air temperature. Living walls can improve air quality by providing biofiltration, and can help manage rainwater from the roof, preventing excessive puddling. If edible plants grow on the wall, they can provide food. In addition to all of these advantages, they also add a beautiful, natural look to the structure. Living walls are a perfect solution for houses on small lots where gardens would otherwise not be possible. The Zero Energy Idea House has a living wall that functions as a structural retaining wall on one side of the driveway and a metal scrim, where vines will eventually grow, at the entrance to the house, which screens the house from the street. The house also has a living roof, which functions in essentially the same way as a living wall.

Lancaster Project

Modular

ARCHITECT:

Daniel Smith & Associates Architects

BUILDER:

ZETA Communities

DEVELOPER:

Bill Malpas

LOCATION:

Oakland, California

SIZE:

1,540 square feet

HERS RATING: 0 (see page 156)

CERTIFICATION:

LEED-H—Platinum

GreenPoint Rated

Indoor airPlus Program

ENERGY STAR

DOE's Builders Challenge (see page 156)

GREEN ASPECTS:

Whole-house integrated fresh air system

Infill lot (see page 116)

Low-VOC finishes

No-VOC paints

Concrete floors

Garage exhaust fan

FSC-certified wood

Engineered wood

Fiber cement siding

Low-flow plumbing fixtures

Drought-resistant landscaping

Dual-flush toilets

Near public transportation

Small footprint

Waste diversion and recycling

Recycled glass and cement composite
   countertops

GREENGUARD-certified insulation board

ENERGY ASPECTS:

Passive solar design

Automated energy controller—zTherm

High-efficiency triple-pane windows

Air-to-air heat exchanger

High-efficiency hybrid heat pump

Heat recovery ventilator (HRV)

Wastewater heat recovery system (see page 156)

LED and CFL lighting

ENERGY STAR–rated appliances

Photovoltaic panels

Recycled cellulose insulation

Spray foam insulation

Rigid insulation on exterior of building

Cool roof

Daylighting

Thermal storage basement (with high fly ash content)

ABOVE The first modular is lifted with a crane and set on the prepared foundation. (Photo courtesy of ZETA Communities)

OPPOSITE The house sits on an infill lot in a mixed-use community. (Photo courtesy of Nandita Geerdink)

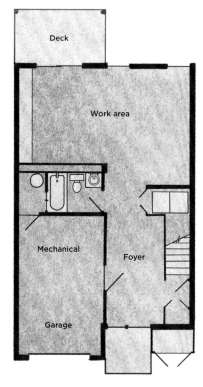

FIRST FLOOR

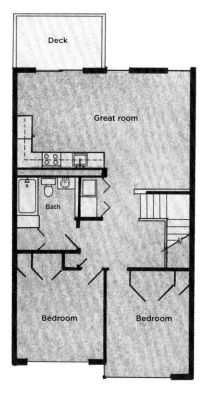

SECOND FLOOR

When they began their business in 2008, the ZETA Communities partners aimed to prove that they could build a net-zero house cost-effectively. The name of their company includes the word "communities" because they believe that a house can be truly sustainable only if the location is considered, including availability of transportation, services, "walkability," and green spaces.

ZETA's Shilpa Sankaran says, "It is our thesis that infill and revitalization of urban communities is the most sustainable way to build." Keeping in mind that important aspect of their plan, the partners chose an infill lot in Oakland for their prototype two-story town house, in a transitional, eclectic, artsy neighborhood that includes factories, artists' studios, residences, and cafés and is close to municipal transportation.

The ZETA team says they can build a house for 5 to 15 percent less than other homes in the area and still produce a much more energy-efficient structure. Although their houses cost less, they say the houses have the same market value as the more expensive ones in the area.

With a HERS rating of 0 (see page 156), by definition the cost for running this home is 100 percent less that of the other, less efficient homes in the area. Because the house produces 20 percent more energy than it uses, the owners actually make money on their energy since California is now one of the states that reimburses homeowners for excess energy.

PLANNING A ZERO-ENERGY STRUCTURE

The three founders of ZETA, Shilpa and sister and brother Naomi and Marc Porat, set out to build the most energy-efficient house possible. All of the other green features they would include would be "icing on the cake." Before they began construction of the Lancaster Project, their first house, they spent six months planning every detail of the design with a team including themselves, the client, an architect, structural and mechanical engineers, a project manager, and building scientists from the Building Science Corporation, a private corporation assigned and funded by the US Department of Energy. According to Shilpa, net-zero standards will be coming to California in 2020 and federally in 2030; they chose to start building net zero now, before it is mandated.

The company's vertical integration, along with the help of local partners, allows them to plan all aspects of the project, from construction of the modules to fabrication of the foundation; setting the house; completing on-site connections of electricity and plumbing; finishing work (including painting and detail work); and monitoring the house's performance. While doing so they can control waste throughout the process, as well as the schedule, the budget, and various construction aspects.

A WHOLE HOUSE APPROACH

A whole house approach was taken, planning every detail of the construction before it was begun. Because this house would be built quickly with modular construction in a factory, there would be little time to change items as they went along.

MODULAR ADDS EFFICIENCY

Shilpa says that building modular added to the energy efficiency of the Lancaster Project. Because they are built on jigs (devices used to hold work during manufacturing), the walls are very straight and the corners tight; these are typically areas prone to air leakage. The open-cell spray foam is regulated

BELOW   The large room downstairs is the work area of the house. (Photo courtesy of Louis Langlois)

BOTTOM LEFT   All windows in the house are triple pane and high performance, adding to the efficiency of the envelope of the house. (Photo courtesy of Louis Langlois)

BOTTOM RIGHT   The skylight at the top of the open stairs brings light in and expels warm air that travels up through the open stairwell. (Photo courtesy of Louis Langlois)

HERS Rating (Home Energy Rating System)

This is a national standard developed by RESNET, a not-for-profit association (see Hilltop Craftsman, page 135). It expresses the energy efficiency of a house compared to a reference house with the same dimensions, in the same climate, built according to the model energy code with a HERS rating of 100. The HERS number indicates how much more efficient that house is than the reference house, so the lower the number, the more efficient the house is. The Lancaster Project is 100 percent more efficient than the reference house. A certified rating provider, working under the supervision of RESNET, determines the individual house rating, which is often used in determining eligibility for some programs, such as ENERGY STAR. Many older homes have a HERS rating over 100, but many new homes are being built more efficiently and are well under 100. The Lancaster Project hits the ultimate goal of 0, signifying that the house produces as much energy as it uses. For additional information about this rating, check the website www.resnet.us.

Builders Challenge of the US Department of Energy

The Builders Challenge is a voluntary program of the US Department of Energy that helps new home buyers identify high-performance homes constructed by the nation's leading builders. Builders who opt to meet this challenge show a commitment to construct homes that are at least 30 percent more efficient than homes constructed to the latest national energy code. Quality features include a comprehensive air sealing and insulation package, advanced windows, a high-performance comfort system, efficient components, and enhanced water protection. Third-party verification by a qualified professional is required to ensure consistent conformance to these program requirements. By simply looking for the Builders Challenge label, home buyers can ensure they are getting leading-edge performance that can easily pay for itself in annual energy savings. For further information or to find builders involved in this program, check the website at www1.eere.energy.gov/buildings/challenge.

Energy-Saving Water Heating

About a third of a home's energy is used to heat water that goes down the drain and is wasted. Two energy-saving methods are used in the Lancaster Project house to save on water heating. First, a wastewater recovery system uses the hot wastewater from sinks, showers, the washing machine, and the dishwasher to heat fresh water. A wastewater coil wraps around the pipe that takes the cold water to the hot water heater and warms that water fifteen to twenty degrees before it reaches the heater. Because the water is partially warmed, the heater requires less energy than it ordinarily would. Second, the hybrid air-source heat pump water heater uses warm air as well as electricity to heat the water. The Department of Energy is tracking the effectiveness of the overall system in the Lancaster Project, including the wastewater recovery system and the hybrid heat pump water heater, to evaluate the effectiveness of some of its innovative methods. For more information about wastewater heat recovery systems check the website www.energysavers.gov. For more about the hybrid heat pump used in this house, check the website www.geappliances.com.

BELOW The open porch on the upper deck of the house offers natural ventilation and private exterior space. (Photo courtesy of Louis Langlois)

BOTTOM All of the appliances are ENERGY STAR–rated, and the countertops are composite made from recycled material. (Photo courtesy of Louis Langlois)

with proper installation around pipes and outlets, also eliminating areas of air infiltration. Ductwork is predesigned in the plan and located in protected areas of the house instead of haphazardly installed on-site in unconditioned areas of the house. Unique to modular construction, foam is installed at the tops of walls, then the roof is immediately installed, creating a tight seal in a place that is usually a vulnerable section of the construction.

The Lancaster Project took three months to complete because it was a prototype in the research and development stage. Today the ZETA Communities team says they can build the same house in a week. They are now operating in a new ninety-one-thousand-square-foot facility, allowing them to do more work in the factory; consequently, whereas the waste for the prototype house was 70 percent less than an on-site construction, it is now 90 percent less.

MINIMIZING THE NEED FOR ENERGY

A variety of creative methods were used to produce this net-zero-energy house. ZETA started with a highly efficient building envelope that would eliminate air infiltration. Two insulation materials were used: spray foam in the interior and rigid foam insulation on exterior walls, which also attenuates sound. The results of this insulation are the following R-value ratings: roof R-39, walls R-25, rigid foam R-5, and floors R-22. The windows are triple glazed, krypton filled, ENERY STAR rated, and R-7.

Energy loads for water heating are vastly reduced with a hybrid air-source heat pump water heater (located in the garage) and wastewater recovery system (see sidebar), which captures sink and shower waste flow for warming incoming water.

ZETA took full advantage of thermal mass by creating a mini thermal storage basement that is two feet high, which stores heat and cool air to be released when it is needed through registers on the first floor. During cool evenings, the cold is stored in the mass and then circulated up into the house during the day when it is hot. In the cooler weather, the warmth is stored in the mass during the day and released in the evening, when it is colder in the house. The advantages of thermal mass were also achieved by means of the concrete flooring on the first floor and the bulky frame.

The airtight building envelope limits air changes, but the ventilation system and exhaust fans keep the air quality healthy. Also, a skylight at the top of the stairs opens to release warm air that rises up through the house.

ENERGY STAR appliances and lighting minimize energy loads. Effort was taken to maximize natural daylighting with efficient glazing on the east and west sides of the house and to achieve proper ventilation with an energy recovery ventilator (ERV).

TRACKING ENERGY

ZETA wanted to track and control the energy being produced and used in the house. At the time they began their business, the partners weren't able to find software that would meet all of these needs. So they developed their own program, called zTherm, which acts as the "brain" of the house. This system controls mechanicals and uses sensors to optimize indoor temperature and humidity. The occupants can monitor and track their energy usage with online controls and a Web interface.

The Department of Energy's Building America project is currently monitoring the house, keeping track of heating and cooling loads, humidity, temperature inside and outside the house, and water use. With input from the homeowners, the staff can provide feedback on energy use. The program's overall goal is to assist builders in reaching more energy efficiency and to track the houses in the program to learn from the methods builders are using. The house has been certified by several organizations and in 2009 won the Green Builder Home of the Year Award.

Michelle Jewett and Peng Soon Cheang, the current owners, happily live and work in this first ZETA home. They say, "The thoughtful design and sophisticated technology used in building our house not only support its sustainability and energy efficiency but also enhance our living experience, creating a tranquil and comfortable environment."

Unity House

Modular/Panelized

PHOTOGRAPHER:

Naomi C.O. Beale

ARCHITECT:

Randall Walter/Hilary Harris

Bensonwood Homes

BUILDER:

Bensonwood Homes

LOCATION:

Unity, Maine

SIZE:

1,930 square feet

HERS RATING: 24

BLOWER DOOR TEST:

1.25 ACH @ 50 Pascals

CERTIFICATION:

LEED Certification—Platinum

ENERGY STAR

GREEN ASPECTS:

Materials with recycled content

Low-VOC paints, stains, and finishes

Small footprint

Low-flow faucets

Dual-flush toilet

Eco-friendly countertops (PaperStone)

FSC-harvested wood furnishings

ENERGY ASPECTS:

Triple-glazed windows

Concrete floors

Passive solar orientation

Photovoltaic panels

Solar hot water panels

Cellulose insulation (see page 162)

Clerestory windows

LEDs and fluorescent lighting

ENERGY STAR–rated appliances

Heat recovery ventilator (HRV)

Energy monitoring system

Energy-efficient air-source pump (for heating and cooling)

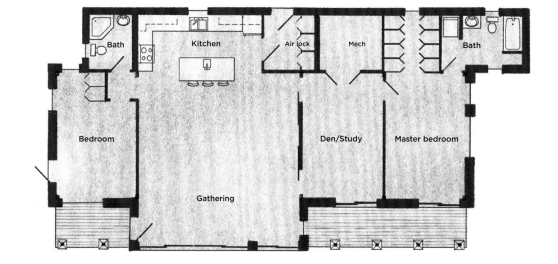

OPPOSITE LEFT   The panels and modular boxes for the home are built in the Bensonwood factory in New Hampshire.

OPPOSITE CENTER   The panels are loaded on the flatbed truck and delivered to the construction site.

OPPOSITE RIGHT   The overhang is a living screen that was planted after the winter to provide shading in the warmer months.

BELOW   The shape of the house is reminiscent of the rustic barns in the Unity area. Although the house went through an icy cold winter after it was constructed, similar to the conditions shown here, it still achieved net zero, actually producing more energy than it used.

T edd Benson has long been known as a pioneer in modern timber frame building. However, in recent years, he decided to try to find an even better, more efficient way of building. In collaboration with Kent Larson at MIT's Open Source Building Alliance, Tedd turned his focus to Open-Built construction, an open wall system (see page 162). Benson's first residential single-family prototype is the Unity House, built for the president of Unity College.

The house was built in the Bensonwood facility in Walpole, New Hampshire, and trucked to the site at Unity College, an environmentally focused school in Maine.

BUILDING GOALS

The goal in building this house was to demonstrate how affordable and environmentally efficient a house could be built using currently available methods and materials. Development of the construction plan took about seven months, prefabrication in the factory about five weeks, closing the house watertight about four days, and on-site overall construction just forty working days. In the process, waste was kept to just three wheelbarrows' worth, rather than the eight thousand pounds typically produced by a house this size.

Because the house is in a college setting, the goals were threefold: to provide a comfortable residence for the college president and his or her family (at that time, Mitch Thomashow and his wife, Cindy); to serve as an educational facility, raising public awareness of new methods of building; and to make the house adaptable for school functions.

The house was designed to allow an interior wall, between the guest room and the living room, to open up and disappear, adding eighteen feet of space to the open common area. A traditional door that goes to the guest room disappears with the wall. This area is then an open space that can accommodate large gatherings.

The Thomashows' additional goals for the house were that it have a small footprint "to demonstrate that you can build a house like this no matter what your income level," and because they are themselves ardent environmentalists, they wanted the house to emit net zero carbons and be built to LEED Platinum specifications.

DESIGNING NET ZERO

The house was designed to be net zero, which means that it produces as much energy as it consumes. Minimal energy is required for heating and cooling because of the tight envelope that was created with the twelve inches of insulation and triple-glazed windows. With R-40 walls, R-67 roof, and R-20 concrete floor, energy loads are kept to a minimum (R-value indicates an insulation's resistance to heat flow).

The photovoltaic panels produce most of the energy that is required; the local utility company provides supplementary electricity when it is needed. When the photovoltaic panels produce excess energy, it is sold back to the utility company. The grid, therefore, acts as a giant battery that can be drawn from in periods of protracted cloud cover.

After being monitored for its first year, the Unity House lived up to its net-zero-energy expectation. Although an ice storm that winter crippled much of New England, and the sun rarely shone, the house still achieved the energy goals set for it.

MULTIPLE CONSTRUCTION METHODS

Construction of this house was executed with several different methods. Some parts of the house that were very dense, such as the kitchen, closets, plumbing, and bathrooms, were built as two modules. Other parts of the house that did not include mechanicals and included wide-open space were built as panels, to avoid shipping lots of air. Some other components, such as beams, girders, and ceiling joists, were cut and prefinished in the factory and were installed on-site like kit-type components. As is true of most Bensonwood houses, there are visible post and beam components, which add to the strength of the design, showcasing the beauty of these natural elements.

MODERN TECHNOLOGY, RUSTIC APPEAL

Because the house is in a very rural community, an attempt was made to bring some rustic elements into the design. Lead architect Randall Walter says that, reminiscent of the old barns in the area, a barn silhouette was given to the house by creating a roofline of integrated photovoltaic panels.

Random lengths of barn siding were dropped from the ceiling in the living and dining areas. The ceiling above the boards was painted white and the small, energy-efficient fluorescent lights bounce off the ceiling and then down through the wood grid, creating a very soft and indirect light. Randall says "this concept was born out of the image of looking at the dappled light that shows through the canopy of trees in the forest or seeing the light come through the little gaps of an old barn." The result is a warm, attractive look but with obvious environmental implications.

Open-Built System

Developed by Bensonwood Homes, the Open-Built system takes the many components that go into a house and puts them together in subassemblies in a factory setting. These are designed using 3-D modeling software that takes into account not only design requirements but also site conditions; seasonable variables, such as solar direction; and climate conditions, such as wind and snow loads. The electrician, plumber, HVAC contractor, and other team members are involved in planning the construction design of the house. A virtual 3-D model is generated prior to construction. The components are then cut very precisely with a CNC (computer numerical control) machine. They are assembled with insulation and a sophisticated wall system, minimizing thermal bridging, preventing water infiltration, and disentangling components, so parts can be accessed later. With systems being layered, anticipating the need for future modifications, homeowners can adapt components to changing lifestyles and install replacement parts easily, while minimizing waste. These subassemblies, including interior and exterior finishes and wire chases, are then shrink-wrapped, palletized, and loaded on trucks for assembly at the building site, where they are quickly joined together. Modules are also loaded on trucks to be installed with panels and other components on-site. This method is efficient and fast, and it creates minimal waste.

Thermal Bridging

This refers to any thermally conductive or noninsulating material (such as metal fasteners or wall studs) that allows the insulation to be bypassed and heat to transfer between the interior and the exterior. Materials that have better insulating qualities and can create a "thermal break" must be used to eliminate this bridge.

Cellulose Insulation

Cellulose insulation is made from about 85 percent recycled newsprint, one of the largest waste contributors to landfills. After it is pulped and treated with boric acid to repel pests, cellulose can be sprayed damp into open walls and attics or blown in dry ("dense packed"). As the density is increased so is the energy efficiency and cost of the insulation. Cellulose reduces heat loss and air leaks, and it boasts a lower "embodied energy" (meaning it takes less energy to produce this insulation than many other types). The installed cost of cellulose is often higher than fiberglass batt insulation but significantly less expensive than any type of foam insulation. For additional information, go to www.cellulose.org.

OPPOSITE The wall behind the dining table is made of OSB and
can be folded back into itself to create a wide-open space for larger
gatherings.

BELOW Lights shine through the wood grid, creating very soft and
indirect illumination.

CONSTRUCTION MATERIALS CELEBRATED

Rather than selecting materials that needed to be finished on-site, such as drywall and ceramic tile, materials were used that didn't need layers of finishes, and
their construction method was left obvious.

Many commercial-grade materials were used in
a way that is rarely seen in residential construction.
OSB, an engineered wood product, is used for one
of the living room walls and presented with a clear
finish so that even this material made of wood fiber
is expressed. It has the appearance of cork, but adds
a more rustic, warm look to the room. Randall says
these rustic materials were "celebrated" rather than
hidden behind other materials or finishes.

In many areas of the house the vertical lines
or seams can be seen, rather than being concealed
under paint or other opaque finishes. The prefinished
MDF (medium-density fiberboard), an engineered
wood formed by compressing wood fibers, is used
for several walls in the house. These panels are easily snapped together on-site. This material is typically
hidden or covered, but here it is used as the finished
material. This was a strategy to reduce construction
time but also to showcase the textures and integrity
of the various walls. In addition, this allows access to
the cavities underneath to make adjustments and fix
mechanicals. When drywall is used, seams are finished, making access difficult and requiring destruc-
tion of the material to make adjustments underneath.

A spiral duct, originating on the warmest side
of the house, facing the south, gathers heat from the
thermal mass and then winds around the living room
area, circulating warm air through the house. The
duct is visible and becomes a design element as well
as a functional element of the house design.

Mitch Thomashow feels confident that his
students will have the values to continue living a
sustainable life when they leave the college. One of
the beams in the living room has a quotation from
John Ruskin: "When we build, let us think that we
build forever." This philosophy is apropos of both
Bensonwood as a construction company and Unity
College as an institution of higher education.

High Desert itHouse

Steel Frame/Steel Panel

PHOTOGRAPHER:

Art Gray Photography

ARCHITECT/BUILDER:

Linda Taalman/Alan Koch

Taalman Koch Architecture

STRUCTURAL ALUMINUM FRAMING

 MANUFACTURER:

Bosch Rexroth

STEEL ROOF DECK MANUFACTURER:

Epic Metals

LOCATION:

Pioneertown, California

SIZE:

1,100 square feet

GREEN ASPECTS:

Materials with recycled content

Recyclable materials (see page 168)

Small footprint

Low-flush toilet

Low-flow faucets

ENERGY ASPECTS:

Passive solar orientation

Photovoltaic panels

Solar hot water panels

Radiant floor heating

High-efficiency lighting

Concrete floors

High-efficiency glass

No HVAC system

Cross-ventilation

ENERGY STAR–rated appliances

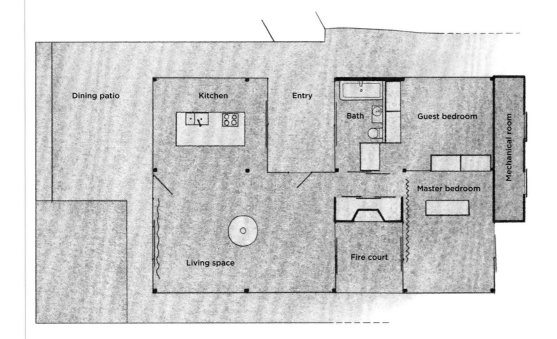

ABOVE Components of the house are custom made and delivered directly from the manufacturer. Parts can be easily bolted together without the need for heavy construction equipment. The parts can someday be taken apart and moved elsewhere.

OPPOSITE The house sits gently on the land among the large boulders, desert scrub, cacti, and piñon pines. In the twilight it is very serene in the desert.

Ever imagine living in a house totally off the grid for water and power? Architects and partners Linda Taalman and Alan Koch did just that. They built a house that generates its own energy with solar photovoltaic and solar hot water panels. A 2,500-gallon tank provides them with water.

For their off-grid prototype, Linda and Alan wanted to build a pre-engineered, "minimal" home that was custom tailored, making a "light touch" on the landscape and acting as a "24/7 resource for self-discovery and inspiration." The itHouse's name comes from the whimsical concept that this type of house will be the next hot thing.

FINDING A LOCATION

They originally planned to build a house for themselves in Los Angeles, where their architectural practice is located. But they were deterred by the high cost of property in town. Having made several outings to the Joshua Tree National Park, they were drawn to the area for its natural beauty and serenity. They decided to purchase five acres of land and built their vacation house on this beautiful rolling terrain, sprinkled with large boulders, desert scrub, cacti, and piñon pines.

They wanted this house to have a low impact on the environment with minimal disturbance to the natural beauty of the desert, be independent of the grid, and create minimal waste.

PREFABRICATED PARTS

The house is prefabricated with an aluminum frame and modular parts, including the basic shell and interior sections. Two people can install the house without the need for cranes or heavy equipment that would have an impact on the land.

The structural system includes a featherweight aluminum framing system and perforated steel decking for the roof, which were both prefabricated and shipped directly to the site, avoiding excessive shipping on multiple occasions. The parts arrive at the site in flat packs and can be rapidly assembled with ordinary household tools. The enclosure system includes high-efficiency glass and insulated walls. The system is bolted together and can be dismantled and moved to another location.

Two courtyards separate the living area and bedroom wing; one has a fireplace and the other is an entry courtyard, a great place to take off shoes.

A cabinet system provides storage and privacy partitions between rooms.

KEEPING THE HOUSE COMFORTABLE

In the colder months, the radiant heated floors warm the house, supplemented by the ceiling-mounted fireplace. The insulated walls and high-efficiency glass minimize the heating requirements. Concrete floors function as thermal mass, helping to heat and cool the house.

In the hot summer months, the overhanging roof blocks the high sun. In the winter, when the rays of the sun are lower, it can penetrate through the glass windows and doors, warming the interior.

Linda and Alan designed the house to be a high-functioning structure, with passive heating and cooling and a strong connection to the environment. Doors are opened on the east or west side of the house in the hot summer to allow for cool breezes, depending on the time of day.

Linda and Alan intentionally designed the off-grid itHouse systems to work efficiently for the majority of the year, leaving out the extreme 1 per-

LEFT The faucet and showerhead are low flow, as is the toilet, in order to conserve water. There is Polygal Polycarbonate cladding behind the shower and tub, exposed concrete flooring, and fluorescent lighting with light gel.

RIGHT The house is completely off the grid, generating its own energy and drawing from a 2,500-gallon water tank.

cent of days when the house would be chilly or too hot. Because they were in a very remote location, it would have been too costly to connect to the grid. If future models are built off the grid, they say they could include more solar panels, a wind system, and integrate a responsible shade screen on the west side of the house. They have designed ten additional houses like their own that are on the grid, which they say is a preferable situation, because the houses can then feed back the extra energy they create and get additional energy when it is required.

HANDS-ON BUILDING

Linda and Alan spent their weekends at the lot building their home. Friends arrived to help. Artist friends Sarah Morris and Liam Glick designed a grid for the walls, made of a commercial vinyl material, that helps to create a barrier between the interior of the house and the outside for privacy. Another designer friend, Elodie Blanchard, created the floor-to-ceiling curtains for the bedroom, bathroom, and living room, which reflect some of the hot sun while maintaining a connection to the beautiful desert scenery. Twelve weekends of work and the house was complete. The final total cost of the house (excluding the cost of the land) was $265,000.

BELOW Curtains are sheer to allow views of the landscape and also to reflect the sun's heat in the summer.

BOTTOM The table is called the "Camping Table" and is solid oak. The lighting is fluorescent with a theatrical gel added to give the kitchen a warm glow.

Ceiling-Mounted Fireplaces

Ceiling-mounted fireplaces are used in houses not only for their sculptural beauty, but also for supplementing the heating system. The Fireorb in the itHouse swivels around so the mouth can face different directions and supplement the solar heating on cold winter days. It is suspended from the ceiling, so it takes up no floor space and can be used in the center of the room. This fireplace can be used even in rooms with high ceilings. The Fireorb used in the itHouse can have a flue up to forty feet long and is available with two fuel options: wood and denatured alcohol (which is ventless). For further information about Fireorbs, check the website www.fireorb.net.

Recycled and Recyclable Content

In this time of tossing the old house into a Dumpster to make room for the new house, Alan and Linda had a different idea. They wanted to create a house whose materials not only contained recycled content, but that also could someday be reused. In an attempt to make their house totally sustainable, they chose parts for the itHouse that are modular and demountable, which means they can be taken apart and used in another house or to modify the current one. Should the house ever be ready to be demolished sometime in the future, very little of it would end up in a landfill. Most of the parts can be easily and efficiently recycled, particularly the steel, but also the glass.

The front porch is a great place to enjoy the outdoors while being shaded by the solar panels.

LEFT The outdoor fireplace keeps the family warm in the evening, when it gets cool in the desert.

RIGHT The grid, made of a commercial vinyl material, on the glass provides for some privacy and creates a barrier between the interior and exterior of the house.

Rock Reach House

Steel Frame

PHOTOGRAPHER:

Lance Gerber

Nuvue Interactive (unless otherwise noted)

ARCHITECT:

o2 Architecture

DEVELOPER/FRAME SYSTEM PROVIDER:

Blue Sky Building Systems

GENERAL CONTRACTOR:

Solterra Development

INTERIOR DESIGNER:

Christopher Kennedy

LOCATION:

Yucca Valley, California

SIZE:

1,000 square feet

GREEN ASPECTS:

Small footprint

FSC-certified cabinetry

Bamboo cabinetry

Gray water system

Steel frame from recycled material (see page 176)

Steel deck

Steel roof

Countertop and backsplash with recycled content

Dual-flush toilet

No-VOC paint

ENERGY ASPECTS:

Photovoltaic panels

Solar hot water panels

High-performance windows and doors

ENERGY STAR–rated appliances

Steel thermal efficient panel (S.T.E.P.) exterior walls (see page 176)

Ceiling fans

Concrete floors

LED lights

Passive solar orientation

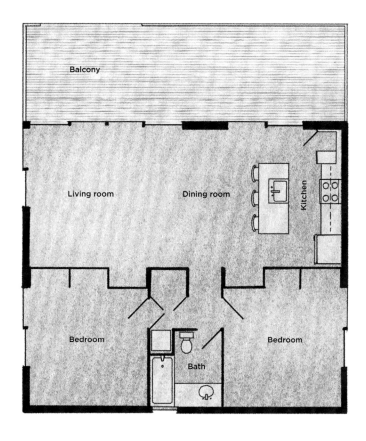

TOP The steel frame was erected in a day and a half and the panels were connected in another day and a half. In five days, the house was weather tight. (Photo courtesy of Blue Sky Building Systems)

BOTTOM After much of the framing was bolted together, the core module, with most of the electrical, plumbing, and mechanical elements, was set in place. Framing was then completed and the outer wall panels were quickly placed. (Photo courtesy of Blue Sky Building Systems)

OPPOSITE The house sits comfortably nestled among the native trees and plants without disturbing the environment.

At four thousand feet above sea level, amid massive weathered boulders and ancient piñon and juniper trees in the Mojave Desert, David McAdam decided to build a prototype all-steel vacation house on a two-and-a-half-acre lot with jaw-dropping views. In order to preserve this pristine site, he needed to build this house so that it would "float" above the rugged terrain.

CONSTRUCTION CHALLENGES

Although this property in Yucca Valley had all the beauty and serenity David would want for a vacation house, it also presented some major challenges. The house is just several miles from the San Andreas Fault, the largest earthquake zone in California. Geotechnical testing is necessary to determine construction requirements in all seismically active locations. He needed to select a construction method that would be resilient to movement.

The hilly terrain is full of boulders, and David didn't want to intrude on this natural beauty. After much research, he opted for a framing method that would require no site grading or disturbance to the land. This would not only save money but would also be gentle to the natural environment. In fact none of the ancient trees or the weathered boulders were disturbed in order to build this house.

Because the desert is so dry, the integrity of any wood used in the construction could quickly be destroyed. David needed to find a material that would survive this harsh arid environment.

A HOUSE OF STEEL

With just a few minor exceptions, the house is constructed of steel. The steel frame is not only seismically safer than wood but also more resistant to the dry desert air. It's a light-gauge galvanized steel (see page 176) that is highly resistant to movement, can "hover" over the terrain, and can literally last forever. It is shaped, cut, drilled, and detailed in a factory, and then labeled and shipped flat to the site, where the parts are rapidly bolted together like an Erector set. The six columns—eight-by-eight-inch structural steel tubes—are anchored to small concrete footings.

The frame was fast to install and is maintenance free, dimensionally stable, and built to endure its environment. Because the steel can clear spans of thirty feet or longer, the house could be designed with wide-open spaces and modified in the future when the homeowner's needs change. The steel that went into the framing material was manufactured with up to 70 percent recycled steel. David likes to say that the home "is made from about six Oldsmobiles."

FILLING IN THE FRAME

David says, "Once we had elected to adapt this system for our frame the other choices were easy. We knew we wanted everything to be highly resistant to the harsh desert environment, to be all but maintenance free, and to be fast and easy to install."

When the frame is in place, it does all of the work in "holding up" the house. Because the frame carries all of the structural loads of the house, the in-fill walls, or "curtain walls," do not have to be structural. Their function is to provide insulation and protection against heat, cold, and wind. For this purpose, David chose the steel thermal efficient panels (see page 176), an insulated panel system. Like the frame, the walls are very light as well as quick and easy to install. The entire house was completed just eight weeks after the footings were installed.

The cowboy soaking tub was constructed using two livestock water troughs with insulation between them and a thin concrete layer.

Steel Frames

There are two main types of steel frames—a light-gauge steel frame, such as the one used on Rock Reach House, and a heavy-gauge structural steel frame. Steel is sometimes used for home construction instead of wood because it is stronger; it can span larger spaces without requiring load-bearing walls in between; and it doesn't shrink, warp, or twist. A large percentage of steel is recycled, and the frame can be recycled again when the structure is at the end of its life, making it a greener material. Additional advantages to using steel are its resistance to fire (it takes longer to burn than wood), mold, rot, and termites. Because steel doesn't have to be treated for insects, it also creates a healthier indoor space.

Steel Thermal Efficient Panels

Generally used for commercial applications, this patented system has been adapted for residential use. The prefabricated insulated exterior wall panels enhance the speed and ease of construction and the durability of the finished structures. The prefabricated panels of the steel thermal efficient panel (S.T.E.P.) system consist of expanded poly-styrene "married" to light-gauge steel studs that stick out about three and a half inches from the insulation. This creates a cavity for utility runs and additional insulation. In Rock Reach House, additional batt insulation was added in that space, which brings the overall R-value (resistance to the passage of heat) for these exterior walls to almost R-30, an excellent rating for walls. The panels arrive from the manufacturer precut and are rapidly and securely attached to a steel frame. They provide good insulation and make it easy for exterior and interior finishes to be attached to them. For further information about this system, check the website www.blueskybuildingsystems.com.

BELOW These beautiful ancient boulders surround the house on all sides.

BOTTOM David says, "No tree died in the service of my home." The coffee table in the living room was made from a downed tropical tree and the dining table top was constructed using recycled wood from old railroad ties; the legs are made of steel.

Prefabricating most of the elements for the house meant very little waste was created on-site. Any waste that was created was sorted and recycled.

MORE METAL

A moisture barrier was added to the exterior of the house and then two types of siding were used. Most of the exterior is covered with corrugated steel with apple vinegar sprayed on it to create a rusted patina. The steel immediately took on the look of a hundred-year-old mining cabin, a nod to the heritage of the Mojave Desert. Other parts of the house are covered with a maintenance-free fiber cement siding.

Steel was a natural option for most of the house, after the framing, walls, and siding were selected. The roof would be standing seam metal and the large cantilevered front deck, perforated steel. Initially David was concerned about the heat of the material when the sun was beating down on it. But because air is able to circulate through the holes in the decking, it doesn't get too hot to walk on.

One of the more unusual items is the cowboy soaking tub. It, too, is metal. David calls it a cowboy soaking tub because of its origin as a livestock feed and water trough and because he thinks there is a notion out there that cowboys might have taken their "Saturday baths" in such things. It consists of a five-foot-diameter galvanized stock tank nested inside a six-foot tank from the same manufacturer. David used spray foam to fill in the gap between the two to create an insulation barrier and capped the foam with a thin concrete layer for aesthetics. There are no jets in the tub, just an input port and a center drain at the bottom for filling, draining, and recirculating water. In the winter, the tub is filled with hot water generated by an electric on-demand tankless water heater that is hidden under the composite wood deck that surrounds it.

OTHER MATERIALS

The only wood in the entire house is found on the interior cabinets, which have bamboo fronts and FSC-certified wood boxes; the interior doors; and the doorjambs.

The floors are all polished concrete. Consequently, other than standard drywall, some batt insulation material, and fiber cement board siding, all materials in the house are metal.

ALL THIS AND ZERO ENERGY, TOO

Not only is the house that David built beautiful and durable, but it is very energy efficient as well. He did all he could to orient the house to take the best advantage of passive solar energy, create a tight envelope, and limit use of fossil fuel and water.

The 2.4-kilowatt solar photovoltaic system generates roughly the same amount of electricity as the house draws from the utility grid. Electric utilities in California are required to buy back any power generated by individual homes, so the local utility pays for the extra power the house generates.

The solar thermal panels generate most of the hot water that is needed in the house. Electricity is used as a backup. The solar panels also provide for space heating the house through an advanced hydronic radiant heating system. With its location four thousand feet above sea level, air-conditioning is rarely required, even in the summer.

OTHER CONSERVATION MEASURES

With water a precious commodity in the desert, measures were taken to conserve its usage. A gray water system disposes of wastewater from the shower, bathroom sink, and washing machine and percolates into the ground, which gives the septic system a smaller footprint. Low-flow faucets and showerhead and the dual-flush toilet limit water use.

Ceiling fans limit the need for air-conditioning, and ENERGY STAR appliances limit electricity use.

David says the challenges of building in this beautiful but problematic location led him to a system that offers great advantages well beyond his own parcel of land. David now has four partners, and the Rock Reach House serves as a prototype for the company, Blue Sky Building Systems, they founded based on the steel frame system.

Recently o2 Architecture won the local AIA top award for its work on the Rock Reach House.

ART House

Modular

PHOTOGRAPHER:

Philip Jensen-Carter
  (unless otherwise noted)

ARCHITECT:

J. B. Clancy
Albert, Righter & Tittmann Architects

ENERGY CONSULTANT:

Peter Schneider
Vermont Energy Investment Corporation

MANUFACTURER:

Preferred Building Systems

BUILDER:

Green Mountain Habitat for Humanity

LOCATION:

Charlotte, Vermont

SIZE:

1,350 square feet

HERS RATING: 35

BLOWER DOOR TEST:

0.40 ACH @ 50 Pascals

CERTIFICATION:

Passive House
ENERGY STAR

GREEN ASPECTS:

Low-flow faucets and showerheads
Salvaged materials
Permeable paving
Close to town
High-density location

ENERGY ASPECTS:

Passive solar orientation
Solar hot water system
Daylighting
Triple-pane windows (see page 182)
Heat recovery ventilator (HRV)
Cellulose insulation
Spray foam insulation—closed cell
Air-source heat pump
ENERGY STAR–rated appliances
Soil heat exchange system
Energy monitoring system
LED and CFL lighting
Insulating shades

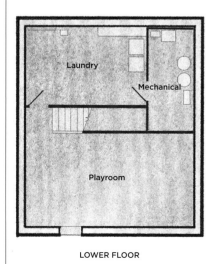

LOWER FLOOR

FIRST FLOOR

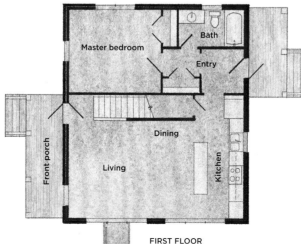

SECOND FLOOR

Energy consultant Peter Schneider and architect J. B. Clancy found themselves in the same Passive House certification class in 2009. Peter told J. B. that he had arranged with Green Mountain Habitat for Humanity in Vermont to build a Passive House. J. B. had a good idea of what the house should look like and made some sketches right there at the class. Soon after, at a Vermont energy efficiency conference, Better Buildings by Design, Peter presented their idea. Chet Pasho, a manager at Preferred Building Systems, attended the talk and suggested his company build the house's modular components. The result was the first certified Passive House for Habitat for Humanity in the country and the first modular Passive House in the country.

BUILDING TO PASSIVE HOUSE STANDARDS

The ART House was designed somewhat differently from many of the other modular houses Preferred Building Systems produces. Six inches of rigid foam insulation was installed outside of the walls in addition to the 5½ inches of densely packed cellulose on the inside of the walls. With the half-inch of sheathing, the walls are twelve inches thick, about six inches deeper than on the average modular or site-built home. Spray foam insulation was added between the foundation and the modular boxes to limit air infiltration. The result of this extensive insulation is R-58 in the walls, R-90 in the ceiling, and R-60 in the foundation (for an explanation of R-value, see Stillwater Dwelling, page 67). Three-quarter-inch strapping was added on the exterior of the insulation to create a vented rain screen (see Greenfab House, page 116) between the insulation and the fiber cement siding.

J. B. and Peter used the Passive House Planning Package, a computer-modeling program, to determine the number and locations of windows on all sides of the house. Windows are triple pane with a U-factor of 0.16 (see Hilltop Craftsman, page 135). Most of the windows were located on the south side, with fewer on the east and west and just two on the north side. This configuration offers the best advantage from passive solar radiation on the south side of the house and minimal loss on the north side, which gets the least amount of sun.

HVAC KEPT TO A MINIMUM

Because the house is so well insulated, minimum heating and cooling are required. A heat pump on the first floor serves to keep the house warm in the winter and cool in the summer. The solar thermal panels on the roof provide hot water for domestic use. A soil heat exchange system using a closed loop system of one-inch PEX tubing around the foundation runs through a small heat exchanger to temper the incoming fresh air before it reaches the heat recovery ventilation system (HRV). (See Riley's Rosemary Beach Retreat, page 87).

Since the house is so airtight, a heat recovery ventilator is used to bring fresh air into the house without losing most of the warmed or cooled air.

CONSTRUCTION SCHEDULE

The house took ten days to build at the Preferred Building Systems factory in Claremont, New Hampshire. On the day it was set in September 2010, the first module was lifted into place at 6:30 in the morning. By 1:30 in the afternoon, all of the parts were erected and the house was buttoned up, so no moisture could get in. It took about eight months for the house to be completed by the Habitat volunteers. The family selected by Habitat was delighted with the end result.

BELOW This light-filled dining area is a comfortable place for family meals. The windowsills are all wider than average because of the extra inches of insulation.

BOTTOM LEFT All of the windows bring lots of sun into this small kitchen area. The viewing screen of the energy monitoring system is shown on the windowsill. All of the appliances are ENERGY STAR rated.

BOTTOM RIGHT Bonded polyester shades were used on the windows to avoid heat gain in the summer and heat loss in the winter. Side tracks—channels where the shade attaches to the sill, preventing light and air from penetrating the room from the edges of the shade—create three layers of dead air, which can add an R-value of as much as 4, doubling or tripling the insulating power of the window and bringing it a little more in line with the highly insulated walls.

Preferred Building Systems' owner, Bryan Huot, says his company "was honored to be part of this Habitat project and to work with such a professional team of people."

Habitat for Humanity

Habitat for Humanity is a nonprofit worldwide organization building simple, affordable housing in partnership with people in need. Together the organization's affiliates "seek to eliminate poverty housing and homelessness from the world and to make decent shelter a matter of conscience and action." Families apply for housing and when selected are required to participate in the construction and pay a down payment for the house along with an affordable monthly mortgage. Habitat accepts donations of money as well as building materials, which are tax-exempt; ReStore outlets sell the building materials to the public at a discount. For further information, check www.habitat.org.

Triple-Pane (or Triple-Glazed) Windows

In order to achieve the high level of efficiency being sought for many houses today, more energy-efficient windows are required—triple-pane windows are helping to meet that demand. These are windows with three layers of glass hermetically sealed with an inert gas—either argon or krypton—trapped between the layers. The third layer, on which low-E coating can be applied, further hinders heat transfer, providing additional efficiency. Reduced heating and cooling costs, increased comfort, and reduced noise pollution are advantages to triple-pane windows. The main deterrent is the higher initial cost, which can vary depending on the windows being used, but this increased cost is recouped over time through energy savings.

Four ratings to consider when evaluating windows are:
- **U-factor** (see Hilltop Craftsman, page 135).
- **R-value** (see Stillwater Dwelling, page 67), which is the inverse of the U-factor.
- **SHGC (solar heat gain coefficient)**; this measures how much solar radiation is admitted through a window. The SHGC is expressed as a number between 0 and 1, the fraction of the heat from the sun that enters through the window glass. The lower the number, the less solar radiation it transmits; the higher the number, the more solar radiation it transmits.
- **VT (visual transmittance)**; this is an optical property that indicates the amount of visible light transmitted through the glass. VT is a number between 0 and 1; the higher the VT, the more light is transmitted.

European triple-pane windows tend to be made out of wood, with wider frames and sashes, and require longer lead times. North American models tend to have narrower frames and sashes and are made of fiberglass, like the Thermotech windows used on the ART House. For further information check www.thermotechwindows.com. An excellent resource guide, including the blog "Musings of an Energy Nerd," is at www.greenbuildingadvisor.com.

The rear (south) side of the house has the most windows. The solar panels on the roof are also well situated to catch as much solar energy as possible.

Passive Craftsman

Structural Insulated Panels

PHOTOGRAPHER:

Jim Tetro (unless otherwise noted)

ARCHITECT:

David Peabody

BUILDER/DEVELOPER:

O'Neill Development

PROJECT MANAGER:

Brendan O'Neill Jr.

SIPS SUPPLIER & INSTALLER:

PanelWrights

SIPS MANUFACTURER:

Insulspan

LOCATION:

Bethesda, Maryland

SIZE:

4,300 square feet

HERS RATING: 37

BLOWER DOOR TEST:

0.48 ACH @ 50 Pascals

CERTIFICATION:

Passive House
ENERGY STAR

GREEN ASPECTS:

No VOCs or formaldehydes in paints,
  adhesives, and finishes

Reclaimed materials

Recycled materials

Separate garage

Low-flow faucets and showerheads

Dual-flush toilets

Fiber cement siding (see page 191)

ENERGY ASPECTS:

Triple-pane windows

SIPs

Geothermal preconditioning coil

ENERGY STAR–rated appliances

Gas-fired water heater with a solar heat
  exchanger

Motorized awning shades

High-efficiency mini-split heat pump

Energy recovery ventilator (ERV)

Energy monitoring system

LED and CFL lighting

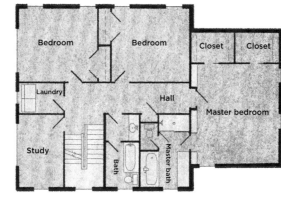

SECOND FLOOR

THIRD FLOOR

FIRST FLOOR

OPPOSITE   The SIPs are lifted up with a crane and set for the roof. (Photo courtesy of O'Neill Development)

BELOW   Passive House standards did not affect the look of the house, designed to fit in with the other homes on the block.

Architect David Peabody first got interested in Passive House (PH) construction when he was searching for good residential energy modeling software. He found the Passive House Planning Package (PHPP), which was developed to assist architects design to the Passivhaus standard, first developed in Germany. David attended a Passive House conference in Germany, and when he returned he went on to take the second class ever offered in the United States in Passive House design. He became certified in the program in 2009.

TEAMING UP TO BUILD PASSIVE

Meanwhile developers Brendan O'Neill Sr. and his son Brendan Jr. were interested in building a green house. David suggested they consider building a PH in the Washington metropolitan area, which would be the first in this location. He encouraged the O'Neills to visit a PH in Urbana, Illinois. They arrived in the Midwest in the perfect conditions—freezing—to experience how well this simple technology could handle extreme temperatures; they were immediately sold. They returned to Washington, enthusiastic to join David in building a PH.

The O'Neills had no previous experience with PH technology, but Brendan Jr., a techie, readily embraced the engineering and technical side of it. He partnered with David in its execution. The O'Neills' focus throughout their company's thirty-six-year history had always been on design. So they insisted that the cutting-edge PH technology be merged with a traditional American style. Brendan Sr. says, "We were pleased when David designed an American 'four square' PH—old meets new."

The challenge for the O'Neills as builders was to "ramp up" their traditional methods to those required to build a PH and to apply them to the humid mid-Atlantic climate. They also had to select subcontractors who would be adaptable to the Passive House concepts. After meeting with the major "subs" and orienting them to the PH concept, Brendan Sr. says, "they were enthusiastic to be part of this pioneering effort and responded well."

Al Cobb, the owner of PanelWrights, a provider and installer of structural insulated panels (SIPs), was brought on board. Al offered to take full responsibility for assembling the shell and meeting the blower door requirement for Passive House certification, which is 0.6 ACH @ 50 Pascals. That was an offer David couldn't refuse.

David says one of the really unique aspects of this project is that it has shown that an architect, such as himself, with just a few weeks of training, and a good contractor can build a PH house using standard materials at a cost increase of just 7 percent over a standard SIP house.

DESIGNING AND BUILDING PASSIVE

David's goals with this house were to show that a PH can look like a traditional American house and be built to sell competitively with standard homes. He says he feels secure that he reached both of these goals with the Passive Craftsman house. "The more important point," David says, "is that this house is cheaper to own than a standard house of the same size in energy and mortgage payments from day one, when purchased under a standard thirty-year mortgage." Heating and cooling energy costs will be less than 10 percent of a standard house (built to current building codes), and the total energy costs will be about 25 percent of the total cost for a standard house.

The countertops in the kitchen are quartz, and the top of the island is bamboo. The cabinets were custom made with plywood created with nontoxic technology using a soy-based adhesive and water-based finishes with no VOCs or urea-formaldehyde.

BELOW LEFT The windows are triple pane and highly energy efficient. The ceilings are nine feet high on the first floor, which adds to the openness of the house.

BELOW RIGHT The flooring throughout is reclaimed oak.

BOTTOM All of the lighting is a combination of LEDs and CFLs.

The focus of building a PH is not to create energy but to create a superinsulated "envelope" that will conserve the energy in the house. Architects have always been interested in insulation, but did not have the standards or energy modeling software that is now available. David says the efficiency required can be achieved in many ways, and these vary with the site and location.

He says, "The biggest challenge from a design standpoint was reinventing the way the home is put together to eliminate thermal bridges [see Unity House, page 162]. From a construction standpoint, the greatest difficulty was in reaching the PH air infiltration standard of 0.6 ACH @ 50 Pascals on a blower door test. It takes care in every step of the process to reach that standard. You'd better have a good thermal imaging camera [see sidebar] on the site and some extra rolls of tape when you do your blower door test."

David and Brendan Jr. with their energy technology specialists were able to meet the PH standards, using 90 percent less energy than a house built to the 2006 IECC code.

The SIP walls contributed to the efficiency of the system, with R-45 (see Stillwater Dwelling, page 67) in the roof and R-36 in the exterior walls. The walls have eight-inch SIPs and an additional 1¼-inch additional expanded polystyrene (EPS) insulation board. The foundation walls are R-44, using four-inch EPS on the exterior of the concrete and additional two-inch EPS on the interior wall; they faced this with 3½ inches of additional fiberglass on the interior. Triple-pane high-efficiency windows give them an R-7 for the overall window assembly.

One of the creative ways David and Brendan Jr. found to save money was on the geothermal "air-pre-conditioning" system. They used 350 feet of PEX tubing the contractor had lying around and made a geothermal ground loop to a heat exchanger. They installed this into the intake air duct to get free energy from the earth to precondition the incoming air year-round. The total cost for this system was under $1,000, and the little pump that continuously circulates the water in the tubes uses only about 11 watts of energy, less than a 15-watt lightbulb.

The house is currently being monitored with sensors on all of the mechanicals so the owners will be able to keep track of where energy is coming from and how it is being used. This information can be tracked on a computer or even an iPad. Absolute Power & Control developed the software for this house and will make it available for other PHs built in the future.

FUTURE OF PASSIVE HOUSE CONSTRUCTION

When asked about the future of Passive House construction, David says, "When the 'foreign-ness' of Passive House wears off, the word gets out about the return on investment, and the excellent way these houses perform, I believe the construction industry will begin moving in this direction." He says the two critical factors that will affect how fast that happens will depend on "how the real estate appraisal community introduces into their calculations the significantly lower energy costs associated with these houses, so that production builders will have a financial incentive to add the extra construction costs it takes to make a PH, and how fast energy costs rise."

The Passive Craftsman is the first PH to be built in the Washington, DC, area. For more information about this house, check passivehouse.greenhaus.org.

The porch is consistent with the traditional look of the local houses. The roof on the porch is standing seam, made of recycled metal.

BELOW Custom cabinetry with storage and display components form the dividers between rooms.

BELOW Large overhangs and retractable awnings on windows on the west side of the house limit solar gain in the warmer months. Since optimal solar orientation wasn't possible on this site, alternate accommodations were made to create the most ideal heating and cooling situation possible.

BOTTOM This thermal image taken of the Passive Craftsman shows leaks at a window, which were subsequently taped. (Photograph courtesy of David Peabody)

The Advantages of Fiber Cement Siding

More and more builders today are switching from wood siding to fiber cement in the form of lap siding, panels, shingles, and trim. There are many reasons for its popularity. Unlike wood, fiber cement doesn't rot, warp, or crack, and it is resistant to woodpeckers, termites, and other pests that damage wood siding. It is also noncombustible and resistant to hail and high winds. One of the best advantages is the easy maintenance and the long life that these sidings add to the house, especially if the product is prefinished. Fiber cement is also a very green product, made of mostly natural ingredients (cement, sand, water, wood pulp), and is incredibly durable. For further information about the siding used on the Passive Craftsman, check the website of James Hardie: www.jameshardie.com.

Thermal Imaging (or Thermography)

Thermal imaging is an informative visual tool that helps homeowners and builders see where heat is being lost on the exterior of the house. An image of the house, called a thermogram, taken with a thermal imaging camera, can help identify variations in temperature. This can include air leakage through chimneys, attics, wall vents, and poorly sealed windows and doors. Since heat loss can account for up to 50 percent of the energy consumption in the home, identifying those areas and making improvements in the structure can reduce required energy and save on utility bills. Thermal imaging proved valuable with the Passive Craftsman in finding areas of the house that required additional sealing. When a house is very tight and there is little air exchange, an energy recovery ventilator or heat recovery ventilator is strongly suggested (see Riley's Rosemary Beach Retreat, page 87).

4D Home

Modular

PHOTOGRAPHER:

Jim Tetro (unless otherwise noted)

MANUFACTURER:

Epoch Homes

ARCHITECT/BUILDER:

Team Massachusetts

Massachusetts College of Art and
   Design and University of Massachusetts Lowell

LOCATION:

Solar Decathlon, Washington, DC

SIZE:

946 square feet

GREEN ASPECTS:

Cork furniture

Recycled composite tiles

No-VOC paint and adhesives

Low-flow faucets and shower

Small footprint

Locally sourced materials

Fiber cement siding

ENERGY ASPECTS:

Photovoltaic panels

Passive solar orientation

Solar hot water panels

Triple-pane windows

Heat recovery ventilator (HRV)

Spray foam insulation

LED and CFL lighting

ENERGY STAR–rated appliances

16 SEER heat pump

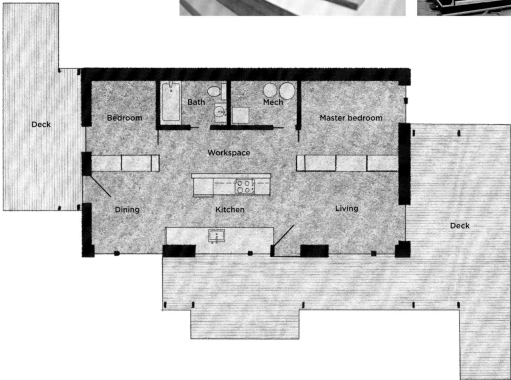

OPPOSITE LEFT The scale model was built by Team Massachusetts to display at the International Builders show in 2011. (Photo courtesy of Julie Chen)

OPPOSITE RIGHT The house was preassembled at the Epoch Homes lot in New Hampshire before it was disassembled and brought to the District of Columbia in September 2011 for the Solar Decathlon. (Photo courtesy of Leila Gonzalez)

BELOW The siding of the house is fiber cement, which requires minimal maintenance. The metal roof is also very durable and adds to the simplicity of the design. (Photo courtesy of Julie Chen/Team Massachusetts)

The simple gable form of the 4D Home was inspired by New England architecture. Though the look of the house is traditional, the workings are a bow to the future, designed to be completely solar powered and even give energy back to the grid. Team Massachusetts envisioned their house for an eco-conscious family of three and designed two bedrooms to accommodate them. They wanted to integrate efficient technology and passive strategies without compromising simplicity.

PASSIVE DESIGN

Although the house cannot be certified without a permanent location, it was designed to meet Passive House standards, with focus on the building envelope. Care was taken to design a house that is airtight, avoids thermal bridging, has efficient placement of windows, and is superinsulated. Two types of insulation fill a twelve-inch cavity in the wall—with eight inches of blown-in fiberglass and four inches of closed-cell polyurethane spray foam resulting in R-56 walls, an R-57 floor, and an R-60 roof (see Stillwater Dwelling, page 67). The triple-pane tilt/turn windows have an R-value of 10 in the glazing and 2.2 in the wood frame.

BUILDING MODULAR

Although the house was manufactured by Epoch Homes in its factory in New Hampshire, the students produced a good portion of the structure. Night and day they spent the month of August at the factory to get the house built. Because the students knew this house had to be reassembled at the Solar Decathlon and then its final destination, modular was the most efficient and energy-saving method of building the house.

INNOVATIVE SOLAR PANELS

Most photovoltaic and solar hot water panels are mounted independently on the roof or on the grounds. The innovative technology used on this house has the solar thermal panels mounted directly on the back surface of a photovoltaic module. As the photovoltaic panel's temperature increases from exposure to sunlight, heat is transferred from the panel to the liquid flowing inside the solar thermal panel. The heated liquid is pumped to a hot water tank, where its heat is transferred to the domestic hot water system. The temperature of the photovoltaic panel is lowered during the process, and therefore its efficiency and electrical energy output are increased slightly, compared to an unpaired panel.

A TRELLIS WITH DUAL ROLES

The asymmetrical timber trellises on the sides of the house echo the structure's gable form. The array is offset from the roof, forming a covered entryway and providing seasonal shading for the southern facade, which helps decrease heat gain and reduce the air-conditioning requirement. This configuration also helps to cool the panels through increased airflow beneath the array.

The trellises extend the dimensions of this small house, helping define the exterior space. The team says, "Many New Englanders are hesitant to change, especially when it comes to solar power, but by integrating the panels into the architecture and by creating a multifunctional trellis, we think that we have created a successful transition."

A TRUSS, BOTH FUNCTIONAL AND BEAUTIFUL

The striking truss in the center of the house is a major architectural element designed and built by

Solar Decathlon

Since the Solar Decathlon began in 2002, thousands of students from colleges in the United States and around the world have designed and created houses that both collect and convert sunlight into usable energy and provide all the conveniences of a traditional family home. The event is sponsored by the US Department of Energy's Office of Energy Efficiency and Renewable Energy, partnered with the National Renewable Energy Laboratory (NREL). The event occurs on alternate years in the United States, and others will also take place in Madrid in 2012 and China in 2013.

It is difficult not to be inspired by the innovative, beautiful, energy-efficient houses at the event and by the bright students who give tours of their houses. They have vast knowledge of the mechanics of their houses and explain all of the systems and considerations behind the design decisions to visitors. This is a great educational opportunity for the public to experience the variety of prefabricated building methods, systems, materials, and techniques that can be used to build more sustainable, healthy, and efficient homes. There are ten contests within the competition, based on several categories: architecture, market appeal, engineering, communications, comfort, hot water, appliances, home entertainment, and energy balance. This year affordability was added. In light of the dismal current economy, it is appropriate that affordability is now a focus for the teams of students.

According to Richard King, director of the Solar Decathlon program, "Our outreach is in the millions. The three thousand students participating in this event will go out into the world, get jobs, and I believe will change the world." King goes on to say, "Solar and energy-efficient houses will become the norm in our near future, not the distant future." For further information, check the website www.solardecathlon.gov.

BELOW The southwestern section of the house gets maximum daylighting without the panel overhangs in that area. The red standing seam roof can be seen where the panels end.

BOTTOM The rear room was set up as a master bedroom, but with the partition opened it can expand the living room/entertainment space. Students at the Massachusetts College of Art and Design created all of the artwork throughout the house.

the students. It separates the private areas (bedrooms and bathroom) from the public areas (living room, dining room, and kitchen). The truss provides bracing for the roof modules and functions as a track for the movable walls. Both the trellis and the truss were built out of Nordic Enviro≡Lam, an engineered wood made up of treetops and side cuts that are typically scrapped in the milling process. This product can span over forty feet, which is the length of the house, making it ideal for the truss.

FLEXIBLE INTERIOR AREA

The birch wood moving partitions add great flexibility in reconfiguring the interior space of the house. Walls on either side of the house can be moved to open up one or both bedrooms, creating a large gathering area for entertaining. The walls contain large storage space and on the rear of one of the walls is a desk/work area, making the walls fully functional as well as flexible.

BUILDING A HOUSE FOR THE FUTURE

The team created the 4D Home as a prototype that could easily be duplicated. The goal was an affordable net-zero home that adapts to a family's changing needs. They wanted this house to serve as a precedent for homebuilders and designers to encourage them to create future affordable housing in New England.

The 4D Home was built in four modules in the Epoch factory in less than a month. The team says it can be assembled in less than a day with a very streamlined design. With cost being an important element in the competition, as well as in society as a whole today, the total cost for the house was estimated to be $267,000.

The house fared well in several categories and ended up ninth in the overall competition. After the Solar Decathlon event, the house went to a family in central Maine.

4D Home

Kenmore Road House

Insulated Concrete Panels

PHOTOGRAPHER:

Kent Corley (unless otherwise noted)

ARCHITECT:

Jay Fulkerson

MANUFACTURER:

Ideal Precast

BUILDER:

Anchorage Building Corporation

LOCATION:

Chapel Hill, North Carolina

SIZE:

2,550 square feet

BLOWER DOOR TEST:

0.54 ACH @ 50 Pascals

CERTIFICATION:

Passive House

National Green Building

   Certification Program—Emerald

GREEN ASPECTS:

Infill lot

Public transportation accessible

Low-VOC trim and hardwood floors

No-VOC paint

Dual-flush toilets

Low-flow faucets and showerheads

On-site harvested wood for trim (tulip

   poplar)

Native plantings

ENERGY ASPECTS:

Passive solar orientation

Precast concrete panels (see page 203)

LED and CFL lighting

High-efficiency triple-glazed windows

   and doors

Ceiling fans

Tankless water heater

Energy recovery ventilator (ERV)

Two ductless 25 SEER heat pumps

All ENERGY STAR–rated appliances

Electric induction cooktop

Condenser dryer (self-contained to

   eliminate venting)

Open-cell foam and cellulose insulation

Deep overhangs

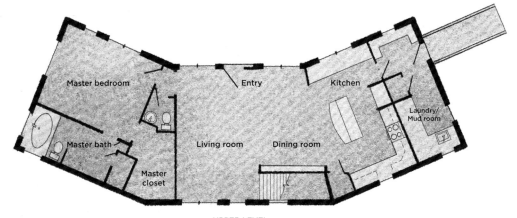

UPPER LEVEL

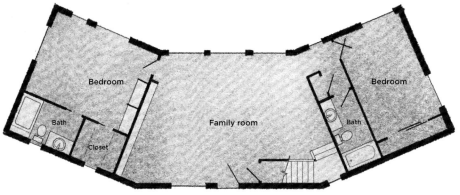

LOWER LEVEL

OPPOSITE The insulated concrete panels are lifted with a crane and set in place. (Photo courtesy of Jay Fulkerson)

BELOW "Sundial" siting of the house was done with the front door square to the sun at solar noon every day of the year, to achieve the best solar orientation possible. The excavation maximizes daylight at the lower level of the house and the two bridges allow entry into the main living section on the upper level.

Jenny Owens and Casey Shaw, owners of a passive materials supply company, are totally committed to moving their community and the country toward much more efficient dwellings. Owning a piece of property next to their current house, they decided they wanted to build a house that was in line with their environmental objectives. They contacted Anchorage Building Corporation, which has an excellent reputation for eco-friendly construction, to build this new home.

BRINGING AN ARCHITECT ON BOARD

Chris Senior, one of the owners of Anchorage, contacted Jay Fulkerson, having seen his name associated with the North Carolina Sustainable Energy Association. Chris and his partners, Vernon Little and Kevin Murphy, were looking for an architect to work with who had the same passion for energy efficiency, passive solar design, and sustainability that they had.

Ever since Jay read Edward Mazria's *Passive Solar Energy Book* in 1979, when he was starting architecture school, these concepts have dominated all of his designs—both in school and with his clients, who have generally had the same interests.

The Anchorage owners got together with Jay, and they all decided that they could work well together. Both Jay and Anchorage had independently worked with precast concrete in the past and recognized the potential of building with concrete panels because of the speed of construction and the economic advantage.

BUILDING PASSIVE

Chris began working on getting his Passive House certification and introduced Jay, Jenny, and Casey to the concept. Jay says he "immediately recognized this as the same superinsulation concept from the post–oil embargo, mid- to late seventies, but with attention to introducing fresh air to the house that those superinsulated houses never addressed. This made them miserable places to live because of the stale air, full of off-gassed particulates and carbon dioxide."

Jay currently designs only very efficient houses because, he says, "attention to where the sun is, daylighting, orientation, energy efficiency, thoughtful use of materials—these are the foundations for what I would call 'good design,' regardless of the architectural style. The Passive House concept meshes well with this definition of 'good design.'

"The energy recovery ventilator systems included in Passive Houses," he adds, "are the key to making the concept work as both extremely energy efficient but also healthy places to live because the total volume of air in the house is replaced every two hours. Being inside Jenny and Casey's house feels as if you're standing outside, the air feels so fresh and clean."

It was clear to the whole team that precast panels were well suited to a Passive House construction because of their insulation and elimination of thermal bridging (see Unity House, page 162). Ideal Precast fabricated the panels for both the foundation and the aboveground exterior walls. Its factory is just a few miles from the house site, so the short transport distance added to the sustainability of the structure. The company reengineered its standard panel to boost the R-value by several points (see Stillwater Dwelling, page 67) and to eliminate thermal bridging.

Jenny and Casey's house was the first house to use the new panel design. Unlike some concrete

ABOVE The siting of the house maximizes passive solar energy.

BELOW This is the front of the house. The area was excavated to allow full southern exposure and lots of light to come into the lower level. Without this excavation, the lower level would have had no windows on this side and no direct daylight. The next step in the construction was putting the roof on, and then the windows were installed to "dry in" the house. (Photo courtesy of Jay Fulkerson)

panel systems, this one does not have an interior second layer of concrete, which made these panels substantially less expensive than ones with concrete/insulation/concrete. Instead a second, non-load-bearing two-by-four wall was built parallel to the interior surface of the concrete panels, and cellulose insulation was blown into the gap. This construction created space for the additional insulation, made it easier to run electrical wiring behind the wall, and provided a surface on which the homeowners could easily hang pictures.

ACHIEVING ENERGY EFFICIENCY

In order to efficiently heat and cool the house, "sundial" siting of the house was done. This positioning ensures that the front door is square to the sun at solar noon every day of the year, to achieve the best solar orientation possible.

The superinsulation of the panels resulted in R-45 walls, an R-60 roof, and an R-20 floor slab. The triple-pane windows are R-7.3, exceeding ENERGY STAR standards by more than 100 percent. Also, the tankless gas water heater is mounted on the exterior of the house to eliminate air infiltration and to keep gas out of the house.

Jenny and Casey's heating bills from this past winter, a cold one, were $30 to $35 a month. Jay says, "It's very easy to achieve at least an 80 percent savings on heating and cooling in a certified Passive House, but with just a little more attention one can get to 90 percent."

Electricity use is also kept to a minimum. The Kenmore Road House is lit entirely with LEDs and CFLs, and it makes good use of natural light.

The Kenmore Road House includes many more windows than some Passive Houses being built today. Jay says that designs that eliminate too many windows "lose sight of the whole idea that houses are for people to live in. When you lose the connection with the exterior I think the interior spaces become unappealing, dreary, and badly daylit, turning lots of people off to the whole idea of Passive House or energy-efficient design."

USING LOCAL CONTENT

In addition to the panels coming from a local manufacturer, the wood for the trim, shelves, and windowsills came from poplar trees that were cut down on the site to create space for the house construction. The mill that cut and kiln-dried the wood was less than an hour away, an example of the sustainable use of materials and minimal embodied energy in that trim. Jay says, "The bulk of the energy for this trim is in the form of solar energy to grow the tree—we need to have a much greater dependence on solar energy (and other renewable energy sources), rather than on oil that comes from parts of the world where the profits from oil sales are ultimately used to control and oppress the people who live there."

OPPOSITE The dining table is an antique, which came from an old monastery. All appliances are ENERGY STAR rated, including the electric induction cooktop.

BELOW Clerestory windows (see Stillwater Dwelling, page 67) in the living room bring in added light.

BOTTOM The depth of the walls can be seen in the window above the bathtub. Windowsills and interior trim are all made of poplar from a downed tree at the site.

Precast Concrete Panels

Long used for commercial construction, precast concrete panels offer a variety of advantages for home construction as well. Concrete's thermal mass (see Sungazing House, page 207) and airtight nature reduce heating and cooling requirements, resulting in significant energy savings. Manufacturers produce these panels in most regions of the country, which limits shipping costs, makes panels readily available, and helps keep them competitively priced. Because they are built in a controlled environment, they are of uniformly high quality and weather does not create delays in manufacturing or delivery. Most panel systems arrive on-site with embedded connections, allowing a smaller installation crew and requiring a lower learning curve to install. Outer walls can be erected in several hours, depending on the size of the house. The concrete mix is customized, as is the amount of embedded foam insulation, in order to best suit local conditions. Design options are unlimited—they can be built in a wide variety of sizes, styles, and finishes. Concrete panels get stronger over time as the concrete cures and can be built on immediately, unlike poured-on-site foundations, which must be cured for at least a week before construction can continue. Precast concrete panels typically use less concrete than equivalent poured-on-site concrete walls because the precast panels are thoughtfully engineered to take advantage of the reinforced concrete's structural qualities.

Concrete panels are considered a green product because there is no waste (concrete is highly recyclable); they can handle structural loads, reducing the need for other structural components; and they are very energy efficient. Precast panels last far longer than typical wood-framed walls with exterior siding, and they require minimal maintenance. They are resistant to impact, insects, severe weather, and fire. In the Kenmore Road House, the first-floor walls were erected in four hours, and the second-floor walls went up in eight hours, a week after the lower-level concrete slab was laid and upper-level wood-framed floor was constructed.

Solar Hemicycle Design

Frank Lloyd Wright first coined the term "solar hemicycle" when he designed the second Jacobs House in Middleton, Wisconsin, which was completed in 1949. A pioneer in passive solar design, Wright designed a half-circle-shaped house, with its southern facade bent around a circular garden and open to absorb the winter sun through glass doors and large windows. Wide overhangs block the sun in the summer. The rear side of the house was partially buried in the ground to avoid energy loss. Wright went on to use this concept in several of his later designs. Jay Fulkerson adapted this concept in designing the Kenmore Road House.

Condenser Dryers

One of the best ways to dry laundry is to air-dry it on an outdoor line; it uses no electricity and leaves clothes smelling very fresh. However, when it's cold outside, line drying may not be a possibility. Another option is condenser dryers. Not as popular in this country as in Europe, these dryers are distinguishable not by appearance but by the lack of venting.

Condenser dryers are becoming a more popular alternative for Passive Houses in particular because without venting to the outside there is less chance of air infiltration; without ducts, there is less leakage of already heated or cooled air. These units are also quieter and use less electricity to operate than traditional vented dryers. However, they may be more costly than vented models and have a longer lead time to purchase and get parts for. Condenser dryers also require regular cleaning of the condensing unit. For additional information, check the website www.creativelaundry.com. For more about the Bosch dryer in the Kenmore Road House, check the website www.bosch-home.com/us.

Sungazing House

Structural Insulated Panels

PHOTOGRAPHER:

Scot Zimmerman (unless otherwise
noted)

ARCHITECT:

Jean-Yves Lacroix

Lacroix Design

BUILDER:

Garrett Strong

Tall Pines Construction

ENVIRONMENTAL ENGINEER:

Troy Harvey

Heliocentric

LOCATION:

Park City, Utah

SIZE:

3,720 square feet

HERS RATING: 12

BLOWER DOOR TEST:

0.77 ACH @ 50 Pascals

CERTIFICATION:

LEED-H—Platinum

National Green Building
Certification Program—
Emerald

ENERGY STAR

GREEN ASPECTS:

Xeriscaping (see page 207)

Cool reflective roof

Steel siding

Rainwater collection tanks for storing
heat

Dual-flush toilets

Low-flow faucets and showerheads

Drip irrigation

Low-VOC paints, adhesives, stains, and
finishes

Formaldehyde-free cabinetry

Materials with recycled content

ENERGY ASPECTS:

Passive solar orientation

SIPs

Solar hot water panels

Photovoltaic panels

Radiant floor heating

Motorized window blinds

Temperature sensors

High-efficiency windows

Wastewater heat recovery system

Wide overhangs

Prefabricated insulated foundation

ENERGY STAR–rated appliances

High-efficiency heat pump

Insulated hot water pipes

Thermal mass

LED lighting

Heat recovery ventilator (HRV)

MERV 13 filters

Energy monitoring system

Clerestory windows

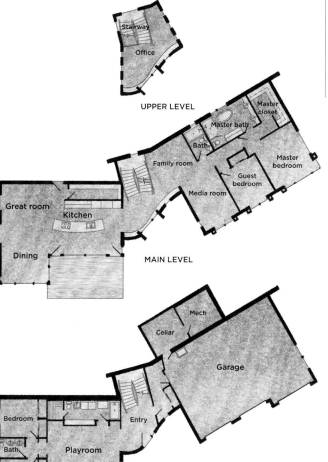

UPPER LEVEL

MAIN LEVEL

LOWER LEVEL

Even on the coldest Utah days when temperatures go down to minus eleven degrees, the Sungazing House never drops below fifty-eight degrees inside. Svetlana and Kevin O'Meara wanted to build a house that created a small carbon footprint but didn't look "trendy."

They hired Jean-Yves Lacroix, with an excellent knowledge of Passive House construction, to design the house. Svetlana says Jean-Yves' "like-mindedness" regarding airtight construction was "grounds for our partnership with him."

With homebuilder Garrett Strong of Tall Pines Construction on board, they planned a house that would take advantage of every opportunity to save energy, conserve water, and preserve the desert location.

Not only did the owners want to generate all of the energy needed for the house with solar hot water panels and photovoltaic panels, but they also wanted to capture as much passive energy as possible.

PASSIVE SOLAR

Orientation of the house was calculated so that the front door faces due south. Much of the front portion of the house is made up of glazing—highly efficient windows and glass doors. The rear and sides of the house have less glazing to prevent heat from escaping.

Deep overhangs prevent direct sunlight from entering the house in the warmer months when the sun is high above the horizon. In the winter months the sun is lower, so that even with the overhangs, the house benefits from the solar rays.

Structural insulated panels (SIPs) were used for the construction because of their high efficiency. Instead of using more typical six-inch-thick SIPs, the O'Mearas opted for twelve-inch panels (which cost just 10 percent more), creating R-48 walls, and they used sixteen-inch-thick panels in the ceiling. Roof panels have an extra four inches of expanded polystyrene foam insulation with an R-value of 68 (see Stillwater Dwelling, page 67).

On the north side of the house is a concrete facade, which is sometimes called a "sink wall." It goes from the basement and ends about two-thirds of the way up the second floor. This wall serves as thermal mass, which means that heat and coolness are absorbed and released when it is needed (see sidebar). The use of thermal mass is taken to a whole new level in the Sungazing House. The sink wall at the rear of the house is sixteen inches thick with twelve inches of expanded polystyrene foam applied to the exterior. It also contains 150 gallons of "phase change wax," which has ninety times the capacity of concrete to absorb and release heat. The wall absorbs heat that escapes from the house, and the twelve inches of space between the wall and the house serves as additional insulation. This helps to keep the house at an even temperature.

ACTIVE SOLAR MAXIMIZED

Solar hot water panels on the roof are used to heat the radiant floors and domestic water. The panels also heat the rainwater in two five-thousand-gallon tanks belowground, used for heat storage.

Photovoltaic panels produce energy for the home's electricity use. The house is connected to the electrical grid, and at times the panels produce more energy than the house needs. When this happens, energy is passed along to the utility company, reducing the owner's energy bill. This is referred to as "net metering."

BELOW   All appliances in the kitchen are ENERGY STAR rated, and
the light fixtures are LED.

BOTTOM   Gorgeous views of the Swaner Preserve, with its wild moose
and coyotes, can be seen from every room in the house. Ceiling fans
in several areas help to limit the need for additional cooling.

Xeriscaping

Xeriscaping is a term used to describe land-scaping that reduces or eliminates the need for watering. This is achieved with native plantings that are easily adapted to the local environment and can thrive without a great deal of maintenance. They often flourish without pesticides and fertilizers that could get into the water supply. Xeriscaping is particularly necessary in dry areas, where drought-tolerant plantings are native, don't require watering, and will survive through periods of water restrictions. In addition to enhancing the appearance of a house, native plants reduce runoff, save water, and reduce the pollution created from lawn mowers. For further information, check the website www.plantnative.com.

Thermal Mass

Thermal mass is generally solid matter (although it can also be liquid) that can absorb and store warmth and coolness. Concrete, brick, and stone are examples of high-density materials that have the ability to store and release energy back into a space. In a home, flooring, fireplaces, and walls with a high thermal mass can help to heat and cool the interior space. In winter, the solar energy is stored during the day and released at night when the air temperature drops in the house, as the material attempts to reach an equilibrium with the interior air. This heat released into the house reduces the energy required for heating the interior space. During the summer, heat is absorbed by the solid surfaces, keeping the space more comfortable during the day and reducing the need for air-conditioning.

BELOW The staircase is designed to create a stack effect, bringing warm energy up through the house. In the summer, the heat rises and is expelled through the upper windows, helping to cool the interior.

BOTTOM The dining room has beautiful views of the natural terrain.

To make sure that every bit of solar energy is utilized, the prefinished steel siding on some areas of the house has tubes filled with a mixture of water and glycol (an antifreeze). The tubes capture the solar heat and in turn they heat the gutters and downspouts that go to the rainwater collection tank, so they don't freeze.

An energy monitoring system (EMS) tracks and manages all of the energy in use by orchestrating the various home systems to optimize both performance and comfort. The EMS is able to select the lowest energy method that meets the capacity requirements given the outdoor and indoor trend conditions.

Temperature sensors inside and outside the house help determine where energy is needed and can respond quickly rather than squandering energy. Thermostats are tied to the Internet so the owners can always find out how much energy is being used currently and historically and can adjust the temperature in the house remotely through an iPad.

PRODUCING HOT WATER AND CONSERVING ENERGY

All hot water supply pipes are insulated to prevent heat loss before the water reaches its destination. A heat recovery system is attached to the wastewater drain in the master bathroom. This heated wastewater from showering and bathing is circulated around the incoming water pipes to preheat the water they carry and limit energy use (see Lancaster Project, page 156). A recirculation system is connected to the upstairs bathrooms in the house. Hot water is available when it is needed, so a person doesn't have to let the water run for a while waiting for it to become hot; this can be both an inconvenience and a waste of water. Typically this type of

The SIPs are delivered to the construction site. (Photo courtesy of Kevin and Svetlana O'Meara)

system, with a continuous loop of hot water pipes, wastes a great deal of energy; to prevent this, there are sensors in bathrooms, so that when someone enters the bathroom the hot water is quickly brought to the pipes, rather than running continuously.

Solar hot water panels store heat in the underground water storage tanks, which provide the water for the radiant floor heating.

PROTECTING THE LAND

The O'Mearas chose to build a much smaller house than is typical in this area to limit their impact on the land. They also were careful to preserve the trees on the ten-acre property during construction.

Being in the desert, the O'Mearas wanted to include water conservation features in the design. With xeriscaping (see page 207) and drip irrigation, water use is limited. The water for the drip system comes from the rainwater collection tank. If there's a shortage of rain, water is pumped to the system from the well. Plants are grouped together so water can be directed to particular areas rather than randomly spread around the entire property, which is typical of traditional irrigation systems.

Using prefabricated components and diligently planning all details of construction meant that the house could be built with limited waste. No Dumpsters loaded with scraps were taken to the landfill, although several were used for LEED-certified recycling.

THE FINAL PRODUCT

Although the homeowners have not lived in the house for a full year yet, the cost of maintaining this house is far less than for other houses in the area. Kevin says the average utility bill for a comparably sized house in the area is about $400 a month; he says his house receives no utility bill at all.

The result of this meticulous construction is a house that the owners say "is sealed so well the wind doesn't push air through our walls or create cold drafts." And with all of the healthy (low-VOC) products used, Svetlana says her chronic nasal stuffiness has gone away, and Kevin says his skin feels better with less mechanical heating.

Svetlana says, "After living in the house over the winter, we can say with confidence that a well-insulated building envelope, the correct positioning in relation to the sun, and features such as overhangs blocking the sun in the summer will be enough to significantly cut the energy bills, both heating and cooling. These features won't cost much more, and any educated builder can build such a house." She adds, "The people we met in the process and worked with made the experience quite enjoyable, and we would do it again in a heartbeat!"

GreenBuilder magazine chose the Sungazing House as the Green Home of the Year in 2010. The house also won the NAHB Green Building Award for single-family custom homes.

Schaller Eco-Home

Structural Insulated Panels

PHOTOGRAPHER:

Philip Jensen-Carter (unless
    otherwise noted)

MANUFACTURER:

Timberline Panel Company

BUILDER:

Dave Nugent

Green Works Builders

ENERGY CONSULTANT:

Revival Homes

LOCATION:

New Hartford, Connecticut

SIZE:

2,700 square feet

HERS RATING: 4

BLOWER DOOR TEST:

0.40 ACH @ 50 Pascals

CERTIFICATIONS:

ENERGY STAR—5+ Stars

GREEN ASPECTS:

Salvaged materials

Bamboo flooring

Fiber cement siding

Steel roofing

Rainwater collection

Native plantings

No-VOC paint

Dual-flush toilets

Waterless urinal

ENERGY ASPECTS:

Passive solar orientation

SIPs

Energy recovery ventilator (ERV)

Precast insulated concrete foundation
    (see page 216)

Concrete flooring

Solar hot water panels

Photovoltaic panels

LED and CFL lighting

ENERGY STAR-rated appliances

Earthbox (see page 216)

Motion sensors (to limit light usage)

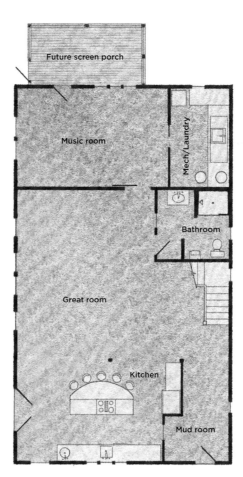

FIRST FLOOR

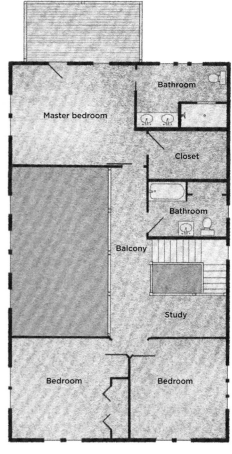

SECOND FLOOR

OPPOSITE TOP A crane lifts the SIPs into place. (Photo courtesy of Karann Schaller)

OPPOSITE BOTTOM The SIPs and radiant heating tubes of the earthbox are in place. (Photo courtesy of Karann Schaller)

BELOW The box-shaped design of the house, combined with the open floor plan, is energy efficient because it is easier to heat and cool than houses that are sprawling or have many separate rooms. This design is also ideal for passive solar design, because one long side of the rectangular house can be oriented facing south, to optimize solar gain.

Karann and Jeremy Schaller were living in Portland, Oregon, when they decided to relocate east to be closer to their family. They had long been intrigued with sustainable design and construction, but their interest grew when they decided to move to Connecticut and build a house. They were committed to building an affordable, sustainable home that approached zero energy use.

Karann and Jeremy designed their eco-home themselves with Karann taking charge of the technical details because of her background in environmental engineering and Jeremy taking charge of the aesthetics, with his specialty in graphic design.

Their plan was to be as self-sufficient as possible, even raising chickens so they could have fresh eggs.

UTILIZING PASSIVE ENERGY TECHNIQUES

Karann and Jeremy's priority was to build their house to be very energy efficient but also as affordable as possible. They meticulously researched and planned every aspect of the house to limit their need for external energy. They sited the house on the property for the best passive solar orientation and designed the shape of the house to limit their energy requirements. Karann says, "The simple 'box' design is very cost-efficient to build and has an open floor plan that is easy to heat and cool. The barn shape also fits into the New England aesthetic."

Karann saw the process of building the house as an integrated design, with all the parts having to function together to be energy efficient. The prefabricated foundation not only limited the impact on the property and reduced the cost of the foundation, but it was also a convenient way of incorporating the earthbox (see page 216) into the design. The structural insulated panels, along with energy-efficient windows, helped create an extremely tight envelope, reducing their need for heating.

Because the house is so tightly sealed, an energy-efficient heat recovery ventilator (HRV) is used to prevent the presence of moist and stale air in the house. In the process, it recovers the heat from the air being vented from the house and warms the fresh incoming air in the cooler months.

The many windows on the south of the house capture the passive solar energy. Windows are more limited on the northern side to limit heat loss. Large overhangs protect the house from the sun, which is high above the horizon in the summer. In the winter when the sun is lower on the horizon, the sun floods the house and provides some solar gain. The thermal mass of the concrete floors and earthbox helps to store solar energy and also reduces heating costs.

The cupola is an important element in the design. Remote-controlled windows in the cupola allow heat to escape, creating a chimney (or stack) effect in the summer, while providing the whole house with a wash of light throughout the year. The house does not have an air-conditioning system. Karann says the house is quite comfortable in the summer without one.

Clotheslines have gone out of fashion in many areas of the country, but among the energy conscious, they are having a resurgence. Karann and Jeremy use a machine dryer in only the coldest part of the year; the rest of the time they hang their laundry on the clothesline in their backyard. According to the Department of Energy, clothes dryers top the list of appliances with high-energy usage.

The interior doors in the house were purchased from a salvage store. Several features were low-cost common construction materials, such as the hog wire fencing used as part of the railing system and the Galvalume corrugated metal on the ceiling of the first floor. Both are in keeping with the aesthetic of the barn design of the house.

BELOW LEFT All of the appliances in the kitchen are ENERGY STAR rated. The countertops on the kitchen island are made of Medex, a wood composite material that is stained and then has a water-based poly on the top to protect it.

BELOW RIGHT The sliding barn door hardware in the master bedroom and music room was a creative solution for areas where pocket doors weren't possible and swinging doors would have been awkward. The solid wood doors were salvaged and also inexpensive.

BOTTOM LEFT Karann has calculated that having the urinal in the house saves three thousand gallons of water a year.

BOTTOM RIGHT The treads on the stairs were salvaged from an old barn, and the flooring on the second floor is bamboo, a highly renewable resource. Hog wire fencing, purchased at the Tractor Supply store, was used for the rail system.

ACTIVELY UTILIZING SOLAR ENERGY

The Schallers received state and federal incentives to install solar hot water panels, which are located in their backyard. They purchased those panels because the payback for them was fairly quick. On the other hand, they decided to lease the thirty-eight photovoltaic panels on the roof, through the Connecticut Clean Energy Fund's Solar Lease Program, because they would not be able to get the funding through their construction loan to include the $52,000 it would cost to buy the system. The leasing program required no upfront costs and had very favorable terms and conditions. They expect the photovoltaic panels will provide 100 percent of the electrical needs of the house.

The solar hot water panels are hooked up to the radiant floor system, which keeps the house comfortable most of the year and also heats the water for domestic use. On days when excess hot water is produced, it is stored inside the earthbox heat sink in the radiant tubing, where the large thermal mass absorbs and reradiates the heat at night. An efficient propane tankless water heater (see The Evolution, page 105) provides backup water heating when it is needed. Propane is delivered to an eighty-gallon tank in their yard between December and March, when they need to supplement the water heating.

LIMITING CONSTRUCTION COST

The Schallers incorporated several common inexpensive building materials to limit the cost of construction. The handrail system for the staircase and outside balcony railing was constructed using hog wire fencing, which was not only inexpensive but also consistent with the barn look of the house.

Karann likes the look of old tin ceilings so she chose Galvalume corrugated metal for the ceiling in the first floor. The material was inexpensive and easy to install, and allows workers to easily access wiring and mechanicals in the space above.

Another cost-cutting measure was to use salvaged materials. The pleasingly funky interior doors would have cost about $300 each if the Schallers had bought them new, but these reclaimed office doors cost just $50 apiece. Other salvaged items include some of the light fixtures, the cabinetry in their bathroom and laundry room, the treads on the steps, and the wainscoting in the mudroom, which came from a deconstructed barn.

Because some of the materials were prefabricated and others salvaged, only one Dumpster was required during construction, instead of the multiple Dumpsters that are used on many construction sites.

SAVING WATER

With two males in the house, the Schallers decided to install a waterless urinal. Karann has calculated that they are saving three thousand gallons of water each year by having the urinal. The only water that is required for the fixture is for cleaning it. All faucets and showerheads in the house are low flow, further saving water.

KEEPING ON A BUDGET

Karann and Jeremy's primary goal was to demonstrate that a zero-energy home should not require expensive and redundant technologies, HVAC systems, or more building materials. They also should not create more construction waste, than a traditionally built house. Karann and Jeremy believe zero-energy homes should be built in such a way that the homeowners can recoup their construction costs through the energy efficiency of the home.

The Schallers are most proud of their ability to achieve near zero energy use while keeping the budget of the house under $125 per square foot. This negates the theory that building green will cost substantially more money.

Connecticut has net metering (see page 216), so the Schallers get a bill from the utility company each month that shows how much power they sold to the utility (daytime generation minus daytime use) and how much power they purchased (nighttime use). Karann says that if they didn't use their hot tub (a medical necessity for Jeremy) they would break even, generating as much energy as they use.

This house won second place in the Connecticut Zero Energy Challenge, with a HERS rating of just 4.

Precast Insulated Concrete Foundations

Since noninsulated basements account for a large percentage of the heat loss in a house, it's important that the foundation minimize energy loss. Wet basements also can lead to mold and other airborne fungus problems, so it's also important to prevent the transfer of moisture through the exterior wall. Precast concrete foundations are walls that are concrete, fused with a layer of insulation in the factory. A metal frame along the interior surface provides an extra cavity for inserting additional insulation and an attachment for drywall. The panels are lifted into place with a crane. The product saves time, because the foundation does not need to be left for days to cure, as with traditional concrete foundations. The low water-to-cement ratio helps prevent moisture from coming through the walls. The R-value, a measure of the foundation's ability to insulate, depends on the system used and the additional insulation added. For further information about the precast insulated system used in this house, check the website www.superiorwalls.com.

What Are Earthboxes?

An earthbox is a bed of compacted sand under the concrete slab or lower level of the house. In the Schaller Eco-Home, it is three feet deep and contained within the insulated concrete foundation. The function of the earthbox is to create a large thermal mass in the house that serves to regulate temperatures; it helps the house to cool down slower in the heating season, or to warm up slower in the cooling season. Once the Schaller earthbox and slab reach a desired temperature—sixty-six to seventy-two degrees, depending on the season—it takes a long time for the temperature in the house to change without adding heating or cooling. In the Schaller Eco-Home, they took the earthbox idea a step further by embedding radiant tubing halfway down (eighteen inches deep in the compacted sand); it then serves as a "solar heat dump." When the solar hot water tank gets fully charged on a sunny day (up to 150 degrees), a sensor triggers the pump on the radiant loop in the earthbox and sends heat down into it, serving two purposes: relieving heat pressure on the tank and indirectly storing that heat in the earthbox where it will reradiate back up into the house slowly overnight. This scenario works well nine months out of the year: in spring, summer, and fall. In winter, it's just too cold, and the Schallers have to burn propane to keep the house warm enough. In summer, air-conditioning is not required. Their first summer, the house stayed surprisingly cool because it is well insulated, and the solar collector system did not put too much heat into the earthbox because the solar thermal panels are angled for winter sun, not summer sun. They are shaded more in the summer, and the earthbox and concrete slab are able to regulate the temperature well.

Net Metering

This is a technique whereby homeowners have a meter that rolls back when they are generating their own home energy, so that they receive a credit on their energy bills. Many states now allow net metering; some of them have restrictions on qualifying facilities (e.g., commercial or residential), type of energy (e.g., solar or wind), and size of the system. Several states offer credit toward future bills for excess generation of energy and others periodically reimburse the customer for excess energy, either monthly or at the end of the annual billing cycle. Some states charge a fee for net metering and some states restrict such fees. There are still many states that do not have net metering programs. For additional information by state, check the website of the State Environmental Resource Center: www.serconline.org/netmetering/stateactivity.html.

SmartHome Cleveland

Structural Insulated Panels/Panelized

PHOTOGRAPHER:

Courtesy of the Cleveland Museum of
Natural History (unless otherwise
noted)

ARCHITECT:

Chuck Miller

Doty & Miller Architects

SMARTHOME PROJECT COORDINATOR:

David Beach

BUILDERS:

Chris Kontur

CPK Construction

Jeff Walters

Panzica Construction

PASSIVE HOUSE CONSULTANT:

Mark Hoberecht

HarvestBuild Associates

LOCATION:

Cleveland, Ohio

SIZE:

2,800 square feet (interior space is 300
square feet less)

CERTIFICATIONS:

Passive House (pending)

Enterprise Green Communities
(for further information about
this program check the website
www.greencommunitiesonline.org)

GREEN ASPECTS:

No combustion sources (furnace, fireplace, etc.)

Low-VOC paints and materials

Detached garage

Fiber cement panel siding

Wheat straw interior doors

Reclaimed materials

Recycled glass countertop

Dual-flush toilets

Low-flow faucets and showerheads—
WaterSense labeled

Rain garden

Cistern for rainwater collection

Permeable pavers

ENERGY ASPECTS:

Passive solar orientation

Solar thermal hot water

SIPs

Triple-pane windows

Solar-reflective roof shingles

Energy recovery ventilator (ERVs)

Ductless air-source heat pump

ENERGY STAR–rated appliances

LED and fluorescent lighting

Insulated concrete form (ICF) foundation (in permanent location)

Induction cooktop

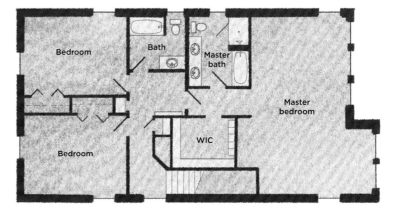

SECOND FLOOR

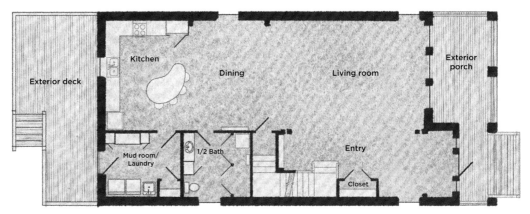

FIRST FLOOR

Siding is fiber cement, which requires minimal maintenance.
Landscaping around the house includes native plantings, a rain garden,
and permeable pavers (see Lakeside Green Cottage, page 46).

The SmartHome Cleveland was built as a prototype, complementing a major climate change exhibit at the Cleveland Museum of Natural History. The goal of building the house was to "provide a real and tangible example of how people can reduce greenhouse gas emissions, not just incremental reductions, but the major reductions that are necessary for our environment," according to David Beach, the director of sustainability at the museum. The house was built using the latest advances in green construction techniques and materials. Miraculously this very efficient house was completed in two months.

HAVING AN INFLUENCE ON THE REGION

The house was built to meet the Passive House (PH) standard of 90 percent less heating and cooling energy; certification is pending now that it has been moved to a nearby permanent location less than a mile away. The listing price for the house is $329,000.

In building this house, the museum hoped to bring innovative building technology to northeast Ohio, influencing future construction in the region and promoting economic development. The museum is already working with a neighborhood development organization in Cleveland to share the lessons of the SmartHome and help to build a smaller and more affordable PH in the future. David says he hopes this house will demonstrate that a Passive-built house can also be beautiful.

DESIGNING A GREEN HOUSE

Chuck Miller, lead architect on the project, says he worked with a large team of collaborators—builders, energy specialists, and a landscape architect—who took a holistic approach to building this house, con-

sidering all aspects of the design before beginning construction. Meeting the PH certification requirements was a primary design goal. Chuck says, "The Passive House construction method creates a new level of comfort and quality, beyond the strict cost savings realized. The home is quiet, without drafts, very durable, and will retain its value over a long life span."

He adds, "This house represents one more way that the green building movement has grown up. Anyone who thought green building was a short-lived fad can just look around today to see how it has penetrated our culture. Ten years ago we could not have assembled such a knowledgeable and experienced team of professionals to get this done. It makes me optimistic about the future of green building and sustainable practices in our everyday lives."

BUILDING AN AIRTIGHT ENVELOPE

A double-layered approach was taken for the building envelope. First a panelized system was used with cellulose insulation. Structural insulated panels (SIPs) were installed on the exterior of the structure to create an overall R-50 (see Stillwater Dwelling, page 67) wall assembly. In comparison, Ohio's building code requires a minimum sidewall insulation of R-13.

Highly efficient triple-pane windows were added, with R-11 insulation value in the glass. The entire building envelope was tightly sealed to prevent draftiness, and insulation was inserted at key points in the walls to prevent thermal bridging (see Unity House, page 162). The house is expected to meet the PH criterion of 0.6 ACH @ 50 Pascals when a blower door test is performed at its permanent location. Because the house is so airtight, a highly

BELOW A SIP being lifted into place.
(Photo courtesy of Chuck Miller)

BOTTOM An open floor plan promotes terrific circulation of
airflow throughout.

efficient energy recovery ventilator was installed to bring fresh air into the house.

The superinsulation, air sealing, and high-performance windows combine to create a house that is expected to maintain its heat even in the coldest Cleveland winters. In lieu of a conventional furnace, the house is equipped with a small ductless air-source heat pump (see Hilltop Craftsman, page 135), which requires minimal energy.

FUTURE OF PASSIVE CONSTRUCTION

The museum's project experts estimate the upfront premium for building this house was 10 to 20 percent more than a conventional one. However, they stress that there is a long-term savings in operating and maintenance costs associated with this type of efficient house. The savings in energy is expected to be dramatic, especially if the cost of fuel continues to rise. They say, "The cost premium should be reduced as more energy-efficient products become available in the United States, and the building industry becomes more familiar with the concepts."

Miller says, "I believe this is the model of future home building in this region. Energy costs will surely be rising dramatically, making older homes less affordable to own and occupy. The initial cost of some of the materials and systems in the SmartHome are currently too high for some new homes today. However, a rise in demand for these innovative building concepts will inevitably drive entrepreneurs to create competitive products and materials, making them much more affordable."

WaterSense Labeling

WaterSense is a voluntary partnership program of the US Environmental Protection Agency (EPA). The WaterSense label is available for water-efficient bathroom faucets, toilets, flushing urinals, showerheads, and new homes that are independently certified to meet the EPA's water efficiency and performance criteria. Irrigation specialists are eligible for WaterSense partnership after completing the professional certification program to ensure their knowledge of water-efficient landscape irrigation system design, installation, and maintenance. When purchasing any of the above items, homeowners should look for the WaterSense label. For additional information see www.epa.gov/WaterSense/about_us/watersense_label.html.

Combustion Woes

Open combustible items, such as most fireplaces and gas stoves, create carbon monoxide and particles (the by-products of combustion). Venting is then required to maintain a healthy air quality in the home. By eliminating all items creating combustion, venting is not required and a potential path for energy loss is eliminated. When houses are airtight, with very limited air exchange between the interior and exterior of the house, ERVs and HRVs (see Riley's Rosemary Beach Retreat, page 87) should be added to ventilate with fresh air without losing the warm or cool air already created in the house. An electric induction cooktop, such as that used in the SmartHome Cleveland, avoids creating combustion gases in the house and also conserves energy (induction stoves are 10 percent more energy efficient than conventional electric stoves).

BELOW LEFT   The house moved from the original location at Wade Oval to its permanent site on Wade Park Avenue, less than a mile away. (Photo courtesy of Chuck Miller).

BELOW RIGHT   The kitchen is equipped with all ENERGY STAR–rated appliances and LED lighting. The induction cooktop does not require venting of combustion gases, helping to keep the house tightly sealed. The island countertop is IceStone, made of 100 percent recycled glass in a cement medium. This is the only durable surface material to date to receive Cradle to Cradle certification (see Green Retreat, page 53).

BOTTOM   The master bedroom contains a comfortable sitting area.

Taliesin Mod.Fab

Structural Insulated Panels

PHOTOGRAPHER: Bill Timmerman
(unless otherwise noted)

FACULTY ARCHITECTURAL GUIDANCE:

Michael P. Johnson

Michael P. Johnson Design Studio

Jennifer Siegal and Laura McAlpine

Office of Mobile Design

DESIGNER/BUILDER: Students from the
Frank Lloyd Wright School of Architecture

PROJECT MANAGER: Christian Butler

MANUFACTURER: Premier Building
Systems

LOCATION: Scottsdale, Arizona

SIZE: 528 square feet

GREEN ASPECTS:

Low-flow water fixtures

Dual-flush toilet

Rainwater collection

Gray water system (see page 229)

Natural ventilation

Materials with recycled content

Small footprint

Drought-resistant plantings

Fiber cement panels

ENERGY ASPECTS:

Passive solar orientation

SIPs

Photovoltaic panels

LED lighting

Tankless propane water heater

Induction cooktop

High-efficiency windows

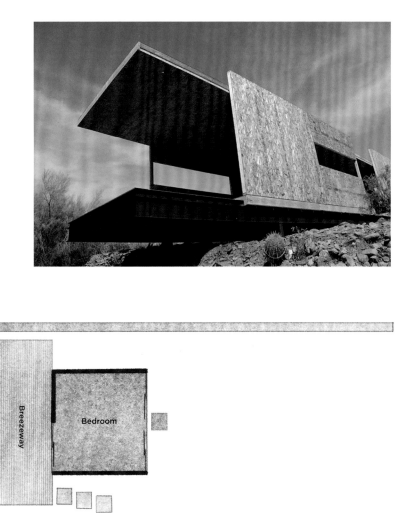

OPPOSITE The SIPs were prefabricated off-site and then erected by students from the Frank Lloyd Wright School. The metal chassis touches the ground in only six locations, limiting the impact on the land. (Photo courtesy of Christian Butler)

BELOW The house was built on a previously damaged area of the desert. The project included revegetating with native plants before constructing the house.

As a design-build exercise, fifteen students at the Frank Lloyd Wright School built this experimental prototype and guest space for visiting faculty and staff in 2008. The site for the project is a previously damaged section of Taliesin West, home of the Frank Lloyd Wright School of Architecture.

Just as Frank Lloyd Wright used this location in Arizona for his winter residence, moving to Taliesin in Wisconsin in the summer, so does the school. This house is closed up in the summer and reopened in the winter when the students and faculty return.

PREFABRICATING THE PROJECT

The property where the house now stands was damaged when the school had an archives building erected nearby. By prefabricating this project, the students avoided further harm to the property. They hand-carried the prefabricated parts down a three-foot-wide, 125-foot-long pathway to the site, rather than risking damage from heavy equipment. The metal chassis that the house rests on touches the ground with only six metal four-by-four-inch posts, further minimizing the impact to the site and not disturbing the natural flow of water on the property. A survey of the natural habitat in a five-hundred-foot radius was done. A plan was then executed to design a structure that was complementary with that land. Native plant revegetation made the property consistent with the area, and additional native plantings helped to revitalize the land further.

The project took six months to complete, with all parts of the house constructed by students, with the exception of the electrical system and membrane roof.

PASSIVE AND ACTIVE SOLAR ENERGY

Careful planning by students and faculty helped ensure a cohesive, sustainable project that incorporates passive and active solar systems and sustainable materials.

Placement of the house optimizes passive solar energy and natural breezes for ventilation and cooling. The floor, walls, and roof, constructed using structural insulated panels (SIPs), create a tight envelope, maintaining heat and cool air in the house. The breezeway between the main living space and bedroom, and the sliding doors on either side, encourages air circulation through the house. The path of the sun helps passively heat the house during the cool desert winters. Heating is supplemented on very cool evenings with a space heater in the bedroom.

The house is connected to the university's grid and often sends energy back to this grid, since it is used only sporadically as a guest space and doesn't often use all of the energy it produces. The excess energy helps to offset the structure's electrical expenses.

WATER IN THE DESERT

Since water is a scarce resource in the desert, the Taliesin Mod.Fab was designed to maximize the effectiveness of the water system and minimize consumption. Rainwater collected from the roof in a cistern, along with the gray water (see page 229) from the house, provides landscape watering. Native and drought-resistant desert plants are used for the landscaping, limiting the water requirements. Low-flow plumbing fixtures and the dual-flush toilet further reduce water usage.

The bedroom is separated from the kitchen, bathroom, and living area by a breezeway.

BELOW LEFT The kitchen includes an induction cooktop, which uses less energy, and a high-efficiency refrigerator, which was donated to the project. The countertop is made of a composite stone.

BELOW RIGHT The deck area is a place to enjoy nature. It is made of a fiberglass grid that permits viewing through it, down to the landscape.

BOTTOM RIGHT The bedroom is separated from the main living area by a breezeway, which helps to create a mix of indoor and outdoor space.

CREATING ENERGY

Photovoltaic panels provide the energy required for the house. A tankless water heater reduces the electricity required, as do the highly efficient appliances and LED lighting. SIPs keep the house well insulated, limiting energy loss.

INTERIOR FINISHES

The interior finishes of the house were carefully chosen not only for their beauty but also to minimize the impact on the environment. The surfaces, such as the countertops, are durable but also include recycled content. Maintenance is minimized with materials such as concrete insulated siding and ceramic floors.

A RESIDENCE AND LEARNING CENTER

Project manager Christian Butler admits some visitors don't like having the bathroom on the other side of the house and don't like going down the long narrow path to the house, but in general the response to the design has been very positive. The concept of this house was adapted for another site in Ashland, Oregon. Although that house is aesthetically similar, it was adapted for long-term living and the Northwest climate: It is larger, it has a fuller kitchen and a washer and dryer, and it does not have the breezeway. The original house can be visited on the student-led Taliesin West Desert Shelter Tour on Saturdays at 1:30 P.M. from November through mid-April.

Gray Water Systems

The national average for public-supplied domestic water use in the United States was 99 gallons per person per day in 2005.* Gray water systems recycle wastewater from showers, sinks, and washing machines for landscaping and flushing toilets. This type of system reduces demand on the water supply and can reduce the pressure on sewage treatment centers, because the soil can help purify the water. Wastewater can also be used to heat incoming water, reducing demand on water heaters. Homeowners interested in installing a gray water system in their home should check with their local building office for regulations regarding water reuse.

---

* "Estimated Use of Water in the United States in 2005" USGS Circular 1344: http://pubs.usgs.gov/circ/1344/, page 19.

This is a view looking toward the bedroom wing of the house.
The freestanding solar collectors provide all of the energy needed
for the house.

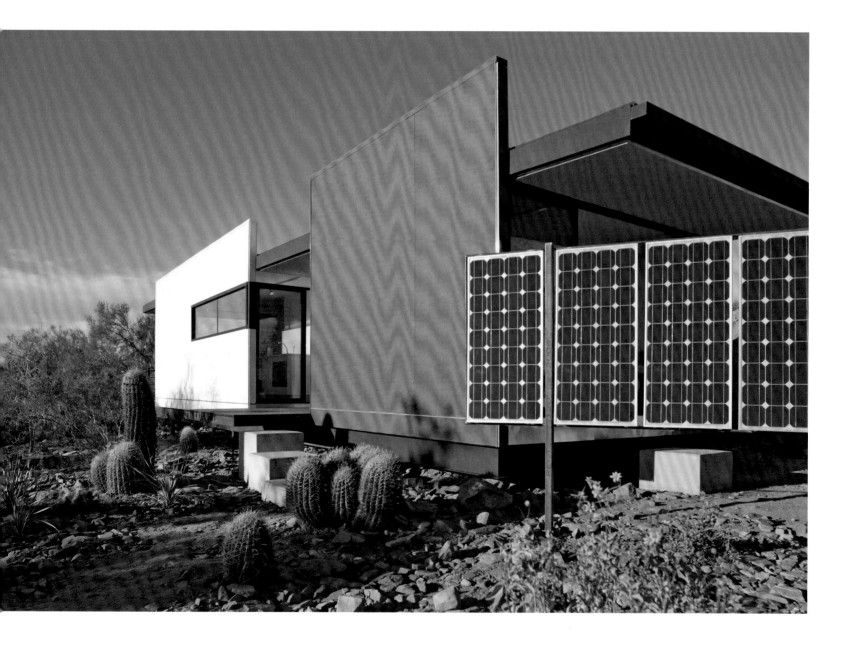

Index of Important Terms

The following green and energy-saving concepts, systems, certifications, and products are discussed in the sidebars of the chapters featuring the houses specified below.

Bamboo Flooring—The Evolution, page 105

Blower Door Test—New World Hudson Home, page 27

Brazilian Hardwoods—Snowhorn House, page 131

Builders Challenge of US Department of Energy—Lancaster Project, page 156

Built Green—Green Retreat, page 53

Ceiling-Mounted Fireplaces—High Desert itHouse, page 168

Cellulose Insulation—Unity House, page 162

Certified Wood—Sheth House, page 122

Clerestory Windows—Stillwater Dwelling, page 67

Combustion Woes—SmartHome Cleveland, page 222

Condenser Dryers—Kenmore Road House, page 203

Cool Roofs—Sheth House, page 122

Cork Flooring—C3 Prefab, page 92

Cradle to Cradle (or C2C)—Green Retreat, page 53

Direct-Vent and Vent-Free Fireplaces—The Sea Breeze Cottage, page 40

Ductless Heat Pumps or Mini-split Systems—Hilltop Craftsman, page 135

Earthboxes—Schaller Eco-Home, page 216

Energy-Saving Water Heating—Lancaster Project, page 156

ENERGY STAR—New World Whitman-Annis Home, page 99

Fiber Cement Siding—Passive Craftsman, page 191

Foot Control Faucets—New World Whitman-Annis Home, page 99

Geothermal Systems—Snowhorn House, page 131

Gray Water Systems—Taliesin Mod.Fab, page 229

Green Tags—PLACE House, page 111

GREENGUARD Certification—Sheth House, page 122

Habitat for Humanity—ART House, page 182

Heat Pumps—The Sea Breeze Cottage, page 39

Heat Recovery Ventilators (HRV) and Energy Recovery Ventilators (ERV)—Riley's Rosemary Beach Retreat, page 87

HERS Rating (Home Energy Rating System)—Lancaster Project, page 156

Indoor airPLUS Program—C3 Prefab, page 92

Indoor Air Pollution—New England Farmhouse, page 31

Induction Stoves and Cooktops—Modern Cottage, page 77

Infill Lots—Greenfab House, page 116

Insulated Concrete Form (ICF) Foundations and Walls—Riley's Rosemary Beach Retreat, page 87

Insulated Engineered Wood—Modern Cottage, page 78

LED Lighting—Lakeside Green Cottage, page 46

Living Walls—Zero Energy Idea House, page 151

Manifold Plumbing Systems—New World Hudson Home, page 27

Mini-duct Air Distribution—Newport Beach House, page 72

Net Metering—Schaller Eco-Home, page 216

Nontoxic Mattresses—New England Farmhouse, page 31

Open-Built System—Unity House, page 162

Panelization—New England Farmhouse, page 31

Passive House—G·O Logic Home, page 142

Permeable Paving—Lakeside Green Cottage, page 46

Post and Beam/Timber Frame Construction—Green Retreat, page 53

Precast Concrete Panels—Kenmore Road House, page 203

Precast Insulated Concrete Foundations—Schaller Eco-Home, page 216

Radiant Heat: Hydronic vs. Electric—Modern Cottage, page 78

Rain Gardens—PLACE House, page 111

Recycled and Recyclable Content—High Desert itHouse, page 168

Recycled Rubber—Superb-A House, page 60

RESNET (Residential Energy Services Network)—Hilltop Craftsman, page 135

R-value—Stillwater Dwelling, page 67

Salvaged Materials—Lakeside Green Cottage, page 46

Smart Home Systems—Stillwater Dwelling, page 67

Solar Decathlon—4D Home, page 196

Solar Hemicycle Design—Kenmore Road House, page 203

Solar Shingles—The Sea Breeze Cottage, page 39

Spin Dryers—G·O Logic Home, page 142

Steel Frames—Rock Reach House, page 176

Steel Thermal Efficient Panels—Rock Reach House, page 176

Structural Insulated Panels (SIPs)—Riley's Rosemary Beach Retreat, page 87

Tankless (or On-Demand) Water Heaters—The Evolution, page 105

Thermal Bridging—Unity House, page 162

Thermal Imaging (or Thermography)—Passive Craftsman, page 191

Thermal Mass—Sungazing House, page 207

Triple-Pane (or Triple-Glazed) Windows—ART House, page 182

U-factor—Hilltop Craftsman, page 135

Vented Rain Screens—Greenfab House, page 116

WaterSense Labeling—SmartHome Cleveland, page 222

Wind Turbines—Zero Energy Idea House, page 151

Xeriscaping—Sungazing House, page 207

Resources

NEW WORLD HUDSON HOME

Architect
New World Architecture
http://newworldhome.com

Manufacturer
Haven Custom Homes
195 Airport Road
Selinsgrove, PA 17870
877-744-2836
www.havenhomes.com

Builder
New World Home
http://newworldhome.com

Interior Designer
Katie Ridder
432 Park Avenue South, 11th floor
New York, NY 10016
212-779-9080
www.katieridder.com

Garden Designer (Manhattan)
Jon Carloftis
www.joncarloftis.com

Suppliers
Mohawk EverStrand (recycled carpeting)
Mohawk GreenWorks (recycled wood flooring)
www.mohawkflooring.com

Kohler (bathroom fixtures)
www.us.kohler.com

Superior Walls (insulated concrete foundation)
www.superiorwalls.com

OWL (energy monitoring)
www.theowl.com

Benjamin Moore Paints
www.benjaminmoore.com

Fabral (steel roof)
www.fabral.com

Takagi (tankless water heater)
www.takagi.com

Andersen Windows
www.andersenwindows.com

Armstrong (cabinets)
www.armstrong.com

James Hardie (fiber cement siding)
www.jameshardie.com

Johns Manville (insulation)
www.jm.com

Tapmaster (foot pedal)
www.tapmaster.ca

Caesarstone (countertops)
www.caesarstoneus.com

Atlantic Premium Shutters
www.atlanticpremiumshutters.com

Teregren (countertops)
www.teragren.com

PureWood (decking)
www.purewoodproducts.com

NEW ENGLAND FARMHOUSE

Manufacturer
Connor Homes
1741 Route 7 South
Middlebury, VT 05753
802-382-9082
www.connorbuilding.com

Project Architect
Steve Haskell
Connor Homes

Green Architect
Stephanie Horowitz
ZeroEnergy Design
156 Milk Street, Suite 3
Boston, MA 02129
www.zeroenergy.com

Builder
Aedi Construction
384 Main Street
Waltham, MA 02452
www.aediconstruction.com

Interior Designer
Lisa Kauffman Tharp
978-505-1310
www.ktharpdesign.com

Suppliers
James Hardie (fiber cement siding)
www.jameshardie.com

Green Mountain Window Company (windows)
www.greenmountainwindow.com

Marvin Windows and Doors (doors)
www.marvin.com

Simpson Door (doors)
www.simpsondoor.com

Mythic Paint
www.mythicpaint.com

ECOS Paints (organic paint and wood finishes)
www.ecospaints.net

Myson (radiators)
www.mysoninc.com

Waterworks (Hancock vessel sink)
www.waterworks.com

Duravit (toilets)
www.duravit.us

Barn Depot (barn doors)
www.barndepot.com

White Lotus Home (mattresses and bedding)
www.whitelotus.net

Iron Horse Standing Seam Roofing
www.ironhorseroofing.com

Longleaf Lumber (antique flooring)
www.longleaflumber.com

J. Aaron (concrete countertops)
www.jaaroncaststone.com

Eco Home Center of New England (green building materials)
www.ecohcne.com

THE SEA BREEZE COTTAGE

Architect
Don Aheron
Nationwide Homes
1100 Rives Road
P.O. Box 5511
Martinsville, VA 24115
800-216-7001
www.nationwide-homes.com

Photography
David Brown
Brown Photography
4004-M Spring Garden Street
Greensboro, NC 27407

Manufacturer/Builder
Nationwide Homes
800-216-7001
www.nationwide-homes.com

Interior Designer
Margie Wright
Nationwide Homes

Suppliers
Generac (backup generator)
www.generac.com

Dow (Powerhouse solar shingles)
www.dowsolar.com

Behr (paint)
www.behr.com

DuPont (Corian countertops)
www2.dupont.com

Rheem (HVAC system and tankless water heater)
www.rheem.com

BASF (closed-cell foam insulation)
www.basf.com

ET2 (lighting)
www.et2online.com

Progress Energy (lighting)
www.progress-energy.com

Moen (faucets)
www.moen.com

Briggs (dual-flush toilets)
www.briggsplumbing.com

Lasco (bathtub)
www.lascobathware.com

Heat & Glo (fireplace)
www.heatnglo.com

LAKESIDE GREEN COTTAGE

Photographer
Peter Baker
www.peterbaker.net

Designer
Dennis Feltner
601 McDonough Street
Sandusky, OH 44870
419-656-3839

Frame and SIP Designer
Brian Faulkner
Riverbend Timber Framing/Insulspan

Contractor
Tom Dearth
Dearth Contracting
617 Park Avenue
Bellevue, OH 44811
419-483-2856

Manufacturer
Insulspan (SIPs)
www.insulspan.com

Riverbend Timber Framing
www.riverbendtf.com

Suppliers
Advantage ICFs (foundation)
www.advantageicf.com

Frank's Green Speak (Frank Baker's blog)
www.franksgreenspeak.com

Chautauqua on Lake Erie
www.lakesideohio.com

Lakeside Environmental Stewardship Society
http://lakesideohio.com/organizations/main/environmental_stewardship_society

Plasti-Fab (flexible insulation)
www.plastifab.com

Andersen Windows
www.andersenwindows.com

PFB (insulation)
www.pfbcorp.com

GREEN RETREAT

Photographer
Patrick Barta Photography
2821 Market Street, Suite A
Seattle, WA 98107
206-343-7644
www.bartaphoto.com

Project Manager
Tom Schuch
Lindal Cedar Homes
253-217-2049

Contractor
MC Construction Consultants
5219 North Shirley Street, Suite 100
Ruston, WA 98407
360-456-6307
www.mcconstruction.com

Building Package
Lindal Cedar Homes
4300 South 104th Place
Seattle, WA 98178
800-426-0536
www.lindal.com

Garden Design
Virginia Hand
315 Howe Street
Seattle, WA 98109
206-443-8856
www.virginiahanddesign.com

Interior Design
Debra Ching
Seattle, WA

Salvage and Deconstruction of the Old Home
Olympia Deconstruction
120 State Avenue, PMB#179
Olympia, WA 98501
360-545-3007
www.olydecon.com

Third-Party Verifier (for certification)
Pam Worner
Green Dog Enterprises
14119 82nd Place NE
Kirkland, WA 98034
206-883-6688
www.greendogenterprises.com

Suppliers
IceStone (bathroom counters)
www.icestone.biz

EcoBatt (insulation)
www.ecobatt.us

Sunlight Woodenworks (cabinetry)
876 East Johns Prairie Road
Shelton, WA 98584
360-426-1393

EcoHaus (cork flooring)
www.ecohaus.com

Fiberon (composite decking)
www.fiberondecking.com

SUBERB-A HOUSE

Photographer
Art Gray Photography
171 Pier Avenue, #272
Santa Monica, CA 90405
310-663-4756
www.artgrayphotography.com

Architect
Minarc
www.minarc.com

Builder
Core Construction
1049 Willard Avenue
Glendale, CA 91201
818-548-5714

Manufacturer
mnm.MOD
www.mnmmod.com

Engineer
C. W. Howe
www.cwhowe.com

Suppliers
Vent Vue Window Products
www.ventvue.com

DuPont (Corian countertops)
www2.dupont.com

Gaggenau (appliances)
www.gaggenau.com

EcoSmart Fire (fireplace)
www.ecosmartfire.com

K-tect (manufacture of panels)
www.k-tect.com

US Architectural Products (exterior siding)
www.architecturalproducts.com

Wetstyle (bathtub)
www.wetstyle.ca

KWC (plumbing fixtures)
www.kwcamerica.com

FSB (hardware)
www.fsbna.com

STILLWATER DWELLING

Architect/Builder
Stillwater Dwellings
3950 6th Avenue NW
Seattle, WA 98107
206-547-0565
www.stillwaterdwellings.com

Manufacturer
Guerdon Enterprises
5556 Federal Way
Boise, ID 83716
208-345-5100
www.guerdon.com

Suppliers
Benjamin Moore Paints (Aura paint)
www.benjaminmoore.com

TOTO (dual-flush toilets)
www.totousa.com

General Electric (hybrid electric heat pump water heater)
www.geappliances.com

Control 4 (monitoring system)
www.control4.com

Sierra Pacific with Cardinal (windows and glass)
www.sierrapacificwindows.com

Trane Heat Pumps (heat pump)
www.traneheatpumps.org

EcoSmart Fire (freestanding fireplace)
www.ecosmartfire.com

SolarWorld (PV panels)
www.solarworld-usa.com

NEWPORT BEACH HOUSE

Photographer
Scott Mayoral
Mayoral Photography
310-270-5563
www.mayoralphoto.com

Manufacturer
Profile Structures
13926 Carmenita Road
Santa Fe Springs, CA 90670
562-921-2551
www.profilestructures.com

Design Architect
KieranTimberlake
420 North 20th Street
Philadelphia, PA 19130
215-922-6600
www.kierantimberlake.com

Builder and Construction Drawing
LivingHomes
2910 Lincoln Boulevard
Santa Monica, CA 90405
310-581-8500
www.livinghomes.net

Interior Designer
Kristin Kilmer Design
7223 Willoughby Avenue, Suite 108
Los Angeles, CA 90046
310-409-9190
www.kristinkilmerdesign.com

Suppliers
Suntech (PV panels)
www.suntech-power.com

Klip BioTechnologies (exterior siding)
www.kliptech.com

Rinnai (tankless water heater)
www.rinnai.us

Andersen Windows
www.andersenwindows.com

Owens Corning (blown-in insulation)
www.owenscorning.com

Sherwin-Williams (paint)
www.sherwin-williams.com

Broan-Nutone (automatic ventilation)
www.broan.com

Grundfos (tankless water heater)
www.grundfos.us

Kohler (toilets and faucets)
www.us.kohler.com

Trex (decking)
www.trex.com

Crossville (glass tiles)
www.crossvilleinc.com

Humabuilt (wheat-core doors)
http://greenindustryresource.com

DuPont (Zodiaq countertops)
www2.dupont.com

Hi-Velocity Systems (air distribution)
www.hi-velocity.com

Lyptus (flooring)
www.lyptus.com

Whirlpool (appliances)
www.whirlpool.com

KitchenAid (appliances)
www.kitchenaid.com

Lightolier (lighting)
www.lightolier.com

MODERN COTTAGE

Photographer
Philip Jensen-Carter
914-815-8239
www.jensencarter.com

Builder
Modern Cottage
2715 State Route 23
Hillsdale, NY 12529
914-450-3279
www.moderncottage.net

Architect
Turkel Design
617-868-1867
www.turkeldesign.com

Manufacturer
Epoch Homes
P.O. Box 235
107 Sheep Davis Road
Pembroke, NH 03275
603-225-3907
www.epochhomes.com

Suppliers
Timberline Panel Company (SIPs)
7 Pearl Street
Cambridge, NY 12816
518-665-8128
www.timberlinepanels.com

Serious Windows
www.seriouswindows.com

Nordic Engineered Wood
(Enviro-Wall System)
www.nordicewp.com

Miele (appliances)
www.mieleusa.com

Caesarstone (kitchen counters)
www.caesarstoneus.com

PaperStone (bathroom counters)
www.paperstoneproducts.com

IKEA (kitchen cabinets)
www.ikea.com

RILEY'S ROSEMARY BEACH RETREAT

Photographer
Courtland William Richards
www.courtlandrichards.com

Architect
Walcott Adams Verneuille Architects
One South School Street
Fairhope, AL 36532
251-928-6041
www.wavarchitects.com

Builder
Christian Tennant Custom Homes
10952 E. County Highway 30-A, Suite A
Panama City Beach, FL 32413
850-231-9502
www.ctcustomhomes.com

Suppliers
Premier Building Systems
www.premiersips.com

Perform Wall (ICFs)
www.performwall.com

Crate & Barrel (furniture)
www.crateandbarrel.com

Marvin (windows and doors)
www.marvin.com

Kohler (bathroom fixtures)
www.us.kohler.com

American Clay (natural plaster)
www.americanclay.com

C3 PREFAB

Photographer
Mike Schwartz
www.mikeschwartzphoto.com

Architect
Square Root Architecture + Design
4656 North Leclaire Avenue
Chicago, IL 60630
www.squarerootarch.com

Manufacturer
Hi-Tech Housing
1103 South Maple Street
Bristol, IN 46507
574-848-5593
www.hi-techhousing.com

General Contractor
Helios Design + Build
224 North Ada Street
Chicago, IL 60607
312-224-9200
www.heliosdesignbuild.com

Energy Consultant
Sylvan Shank
The Sylvan Company
773-301-1459

Financing
GreenChoice Bank
www.greenchoicebank.com

GreenRater/Energy Rater
Energy Diagnostics
395 East 500 North
Valparaiso, IN 46383
219-464-4457
www.energydiagnosticsinc.com

Landscape Architect
KMS Gardens and Design
www.kmsgardensanddesign.com

Solar Panel Design and Installation
Solar Service
7312 North Milwaukee Avenue
Niles, IL 60714
847-647-9312
www.solarserviceinc.com

Mechanical Consultant and Installation
Ardmore Fresh Air
5967 North Elston Avenue
Chicago, IL 60646
773-631-9160
http://ardmorefreshair.com

Window Consultant
Murphy's Windows and Sunrooms
10359 South Pulaski Road
Chicago, IL 60655
800-640-6873
www.murphyswindows.com

Interior Design and Furnishings
Angela Finney-Hoffman
Post 27
1819 West Grand Avenue
Chicago, IL 60622
312-829-6122
www.post27store.com

Suppliers
Fujitsu (ductless mini-split HVAC
system)
www.fujitsugeneral.com

THV Compozit Windows & Doors
www.thv.com

EcoUrban Collection (kitchen and bath
cabinetry)
www.ecourbancollection.com

Lightology (lighting consultant and
sales)
www.lightology.com

Colori Eco Paint Boutique (low-VOC
paint)
www.colorichicago.com

Firestone (UnaClad corrugated
Galvalume siding)
www.firestonemetal.com

James Hardie (fiber cement siding)
 www.jameshardie.com

Daltile (floor and wall tile)
www.daltile.com

RenewAire (ERV)
www.renewaire.com

Noritz (tankless water heater)
www.noritz.com

NEW WORLD WHITMAN-ANNIS HOME

Architect
New World Architecture
www.newworldhome.com

Builder
New World Home
www.newworldhome.com

Manufacturer
Signature Building Systems
www.signaturecustomhomes.com

Suppliers
James Hardie (fiber cement siding)
www.jameshardie.com

Trex (decking)
www.trex.com

Azek (railing)
www.azek.com

ThermaTru (front door)
www.thermatru.com

Masonite (interior doors)
www.masonite.com

Executive Cabinetry (kitchen cabinets)
www.executivecabinetry.com

Merillat Classics (bathroom cabinets)
www.merillat.com

Caesarstone (countertops)
www.caesarstoneus.com

American Fluorescent Corp. (lighting)
www.americanfluorescent.com

Kohler (bathroom fixtures)
www.us.kohler.com

Benjamin Moore Paints
www.benjaminmoore.com

Englert (standing seam, Galvalume metal roof)
www.englertinc.com

Andersen Windows
www.andersenwindows.com

Rohl (kitchen sink)
www.rohlhome.com

Tapmaster (foot pedal)
www.tapmaster.ca

Dragonfly (bamboo flooring)
www.dragonflybamboo.com

DMI (cork flooring)
www.dmikc.com

Daltile (tiles)
www.daltile.com

Monessen (fireplace)
www.monessenhearth.com

KitchenAid (appliances)
www.kitchenaid.com

Viqua (filtration system)
www.viqua.com

Zip System (integrated roof/wall sheathing panels)
www.zipsystem.com

Superior Walls (foundation wall system)
www.superiorwalls.com

Glen-Gery Brick (chimney veneer)
www.glengerybrick.com

Lamington General Store (antiques)
www.lamingtongeneralstore.com

THE EVOLUTION

Photographer
D. Randolph Foulds Photography
www.drandolphfouldsphotography.com

Architect/Manufacturer/Builder
Blu Homes
760 Main Street
Waltham, MA 02451

500 Third Street, Suite 230
San Francisco, CA 94107
866-887-7997
www.bluhomes.com

Suppliers
Andersen Windows
www.andersenwindows.com

Viessmann (boiler)
www.viessmann-us.com

EcoUrban Collection (countertops and cabinets)
www.ecourbancollection.com

Smith & Fong (Plyboo bamboo flooring)
www.plyboo.com

PLACE HOUSE

Architect
PLACE Architects
Seattle, WA, and Vancouver, BC
778-279-7274
www.placehouses.com
www.placearchitects.com

Manufacturer
DLH Inc General Contracting
44021 SE Tanner Road, Suite A
North Bend, WA 98045
425-888-1853
www.dlhinc.com

Interior Designer
Sally Oien
The Oien Collaborative
Seattle, WA
206-617-8907

Suppliers
PaperStone (countertops)
www.paperstoneproducts.com

Grasscrete (pervious driveway)
www.grasscrete.com

Edge Concrete (permeable concrete pavers)
www.edgeconcretellc.com

James Hardie (fiber cement siding)
www.jameshardie.com

Northwest Door (garage door)
www.nwdusa.com

Ecohaus (cork flooring)
www.ecohaus.com

Minka Group (Minka-Aire ceiling fan)
www.minka.com

Tech Lighting
www.techlighting.com

GREENFAB HOUSE

Architect/Site General Contractor
Robert Humble
HyBrid Architecture
1205 East Pike Street, Suite 2D
Seattle, WA 98122
206-267-9277
www.hybridarc.com

Developer
Greenfab
6532 Phinney Avenue N
Seattle, WA 98103
877-846-4445
www.greenfab.com

Modular Manufacturer
Guerdon Enterprises
5556 Federal Way
Boise, ID 83716
208-345-5100
www.guerdon.com

Structural Engineer
Davido Consulting Group
15029 Bothell Way NE, Suite 600
Lake Forest Park, WA 98155
206-523-0024
www.dcgengr.com

Mechanical Engineer
Ecotope
4056 9th Avenue NE
Seattle, WA 98105
206-322-3753
www.ecotope.com

Sustainability Consultant
Conservation Services Group
9655 SE 36th Street, Suite 202
Mercer Island, WA 98040
206-682-0624
www.csgrp.com

Integrated Water Management
Living Systems Design
211 NW 201st Street
Shoreline, WA 98177
206-546-3119
www.harvestrain.net

Interior Designer
Staged By Design
2440 6th Avenue South
Seattle, WA 98134
www.stagedbydesign.com

Landscape Designer
In Harmony Sustainable Landscapes
23622 Bothell-Everett Highway
Bothell, WA 98021
425-486-2180
www.inharmony.com

Suppliers
EcoTop (countertops)
www.kliptech.com

IKEA (sinks and appliances)
www.ikea.com

Fujitsu (mini-split heat pump)
www.fujitsugeneral.com

Convectair (backup electric heater)
www.convectair.com

Nuheat (radiant heating)
www.nuheat.com

James Hardie (fiber cement siding)
www.jameshardie.com

NuBe Green (furniture)
www.nubegreen.com

Gaco Western (water-based insulation)
www.gaco.com

Grasscrete (permeable paving)
www.grasscrete.com

Sierra Pacific (windows)
www.sierrapacificwindows.com

General Electric (hybrid electric heat pump water heater)
www.geappliances.com

Panasonic (WhisperComfort ERV)
www.panasonic.com

TED (energy monitoring)
www.theenergydetective.com

SHETH HOUSE

Photographer
M. Ribaudo
St. Louis, MO

Architect
Mark D. O'Bryan
Art & Architecture
314-629-4531

Builder
Blue Brick Renovation + Construction
2757 Wyoming Street
St. Louis, MO 63118
314-772-3644
www.bluebrickconstruction.com

Sustainable Design Consultant
Jay Swoboda
EcoUrban
906 Olive Street, Suite PH9
St. Louis, MO 63101
314-231-0400 ext. 4
www.ecourbanstl.com

Landscape Architect
Randall W. Mardis
Landscape Technologies
67 Jacobs Creek Drive
St. Charles, MO 63304
636-928-1250
www.landscapetechnologies.net

Suppliers
Superior Walls (foundation)
www.superiorwalls.com

Enercept (SIPs)
www.enercept.com

Quaker Windows & Doors (windows)
www.quakerwindows.com

Velux (skylights)
www.veluxusa.com

Therma-Tru (doors)
www.thermatru.com

Panasonic (fans)
www.panasonic.com

American Standard (programmable thermostat and heat pump)
www.americanstandard-us.com

Grass Elements (bamboo flooring)
www.grasselements.com

Green Tech (porcelain tile)
www.ergontile.it

Mwanzi Company (cabinets)
www.mwanzi.com

Sherwin-Williams (paint)
www.sherwin-williams.com

James Hardie (fiber cement siding)
www.jameshardie.com

Cambria (countertops)
www.cambriausa.com

SNOWHORN HOUSE

Photographers
Casey Dunn
www.caseydunn.net

Alison Cartwright
www.alisoncartwright.com

Architect/Builder
Chris Krager
KRDB
1101 East 6th Street, Suite A
Austin, TX 78702
512-374-0946
www.krdb.com

Landscape Architect
Will Pickens
Prado Design
www.pradodesignllc.com

Project Architect
Mike Diani
KRDB

Project Manager
Brad Deal
KRDB

Suppliers
R-Control (SIPs)
www.r-control.com

APC Metal Works (steel frame)
1412 East 5th Street
Austin, TX 78702

WaterFurnace (geothermal system)
www.waterfurnace.com

Kalwall (insulating wall panel)
www.kalwall.com

AMX (automation system)
www.amx.com

Weiland Sliding Doors and Windows
www.weilandslidingdoors.com

Rhino Windows by Gerkin
www.rhinoaustin.com

Bodart and Gonay (fireplace)
www.b-g.be

Sherwin-Williams (paint)
www.sherwin-williams.com

Rinnai (tankless water heater)
www.rinnai.us

Velux (automated skylights)
www.veluxusa.com

Innovative Water Solutions (rainwater system)
www.watercache.com

Vintage Material Supply Company (millwork and doors)
www.vintagematerialsupply.com

Habitat for Humanity Deconstruction Services
www.re-store.com/deconstruction/index.php

Vermont Natural Coatings (floor and other finishes)
www.vermontnaturalcoatings.com

Carrier (Infinity air purifier)
www.residential.carrier.com/products/airquality/aircleaners/purifier.shtml

Miele (kitchen appliances)
www.mieleusa.com

Sub-Zero/Wolf (downdraft cooktop blower)
www.subzero-wolf.com

Enphase (solar voltaic system)
www.enlighten.enphaseenergy.com

Austin Energy Green Building program
https://my.austinenergy.com

HILLTOP CRAFTSMAN

Photographer
Aaron Barna Photography
Olympia, WA
360-970-7001
www.aaronbarnaphotography.com

Designer
Peter Bergford
Scott Homes
www.scotthomes.com

Builder
Scott Homes
3016 10th Avenue NE
Olympia, WA 98506
360-357-9167
www.scotthomes.com

Suppliers
Premier Building Systems
www.premiersips.com

Serious Windows
www.seriouswindows.com

Mitsubishi Electric (Mr. Slim ductless heat pump)
www.mehvac.com

Lifebreath (HRV)
www.lifebreath.com

Navien (tankless water heater)
www.navienamerica.com

PaperStone (countertops)
www.paperstoneproducts.com

G·O LOGIC HOME

Photographer
Trent Bell Photography
207-807-5044
www.trentbell.com

Architect/Builder
Matthew O'Malia
Alan Gibson
G·O Logic Homes
P.O. Box 567
137 High Street, 3rd floor
Belfast, ME 04915
207-338-1566
www.gologichomes.com

Landscape Architect
Ann Kearsley
58 Fore Street
Portland, ME 04101
207-756-8899
www.annkearsley.com

Structural Engineer
Albert Putnam
183 Park Row, Suite 1B
Brunswick, ME 04011
207-729-6230
www.albertputnam.com

Suppliers
ReVision Energy (alternative energy systems)
www.revisionenergy.com

EGE (windows)
www.ege.de/en

Winter Panel (SIPs)
www.winterpanel.com

eMonitor (energy monitoring)
powerwisesystems.com

Laundry Alternative (spin dryer)
www.laundry-alternative.com

IKEA (kitchen cabinets)
www.ikea.com

Freshwater Stone (local granite counter)
www.freshwaterstone.com

ZERO ENERGY IDEA HOUSE

Photographer
Dane Gregory Meyer
706 Sixth Avenue
Tacoma, WA 98405
253-572-9809
www.danegregorymeyer.com

Architect
David Clinkston
Clinkston Architects
135 First Avenue West
Seattle, WA 98119
206-286-2000
www.clinkstonarchitects.com

Builder
Shirey Contracting
230 NE Juniper Street
Issaquah, WA 98027
425-427-1300
www.shireycontracting.com

Landscape Architect
Windrose Landscape Architecture
111 West John Street, Suite 203A
Seattle, WA 98119
206-274-5979
www.windroseseattle.com

Structural Engineer
Swenson Say Fagét
2124 Third Avenue, Suite 100
Seattle, WA 98121
206-443-6212
www.swensonsayfaget.com

Interior Design
Autumn Donavan Design
206-795-1088

Living Roof Design
Triad Associates
12112 115th Avenue NE
Kirkland, WA 98034
800-488-0756
www.triadassoc.com

Suppliers
Insulspan (SIPs)
www.insulspan.com

ARXX ICF (foundation)
www.arxx.com

A&R Solar (solar panels)
www.aandrsolar.com

Milgard Windows & Doors
www.milgard.com

VaproShield (VaproFlashing)
www.vaproshield.com

Miele (appliances)
www.mieleusa.com

Flux Studios (wood mosaic tiles)
www.fluxstudios.com

Helix Wind (wind turbine)
www.helixwind.com

Kingspan (Thermomax solar collectors)
www.kingspansolar.com

Sherwin-Williams (paint)
www.sherwin-williams.com

Warmboard (radiant heat)
www.warmboard.com

Applied Organics (living wall)
www.appliedorganics.net

SunPower (PV panels)
http://us.sunpowercorp.com

Triad Association (vegetated roof)
www.triadassoc.com

James Hardie (fiber cement siding)
www.jameshardie.com

The Unico System (air-to-air heat pump)
www.unicosystem.com

Bellmont Cabinet Co. (cabinets)
www.pacificcrestindustries.com

LANCASTER PROJECT

Photographers
Louis Langlois (interiors)
Nandita Geerdink (exterior)

Architect
Daniel Smith
Daniel Smith & Associates Architects
1107 Virginia Street
Berkeley, CA 94702
510-526-1935
www.dsaarch.com

Builder/Manufacturer
ZETA Communities
1550 Bryant Street, Suite 855
San Francisco, CA 94103
415-946-4084
www.zetacommunities.com

Structural Engineer
Tipping Mar
1906 Shattuck Avenue
Berkeley, CA 94704
510-549-1906
www.tippingmar.com

Energy Design
John Straube
Building Science Corporation
30 Forest Street
Somerville, MA 02143
978-589-5100 ext. 5296
www.buildingscience.com

Green Certifications
Ann Edminster
Design AVEnues
115 Angelita Avenue
Pacifica, CA 94044
650-355-9150
http://designavenues.net

Interior Design
Sandra Slater
Sandra Slater Environments
650-566-0550
www.sandraslater.com

Suppliers
Serious Windows
www.seriouswindows.com

General Electric (hybrid electric heat pump water heater)
www.geappliances.com

Airiva (HRV)
www.suncourt.com

Icynene (insulation)
www.icynene.com

Caesarstone (countertops)
www.caesarstoneus.com

UNITY HOUSE

Photographer
Naomi C. O. Beal Photography
139 South Freeport Road
Freeport, ME 04032
207-710-9478
www.naomicobeal.com

Builder/Manufacturer
Bensonwood Homes
6 Blackjack Crossing
Walpole, NH 03608
877-203-3562
www.bensonwood.com

Architect
Randall Walter
Bensonwood Homes

Suppliers
AvanTech OSB (living room paneling)
www.huberwood.com

Thermotech Windows (windows and doors)
www.thermotechwindows.com

PaperStone (countertops)
www.paperstoneproducts.com

groSolar (PV panels)
www.grosolar.com

Crown Point Cabinetry (kitchen cabinets)
www.crown-point.com

Dow Building Solutions (roof insulation)
www.building.dow.com

HIGH DESERT ITHOUSE

Photographer
Art Gray Photography
171 Pier Avenue, #272
Santa Monica, CA 90405
310-663-4756
www.artgrayphotography.com

Architect/Builder
Linda Taalman/Alan Koch
Taalman Koch Architecture
1570 La Baig Avenue, Unit A
Los Angeles, CA 90028
213-380-1060
www.taalmankoch.com

Manufacturers
Bosch Rexroth (structural framing materials)
www.boschrexroth.com

Epic Metals (steel roof deck)
www.epicmetals.com

3form (resin panels)
www.3-form.com

Structural Engineer
Gordon L. Polon
1718 22nd Street
Santa Monica, CA 90404
310-998-5611

Suppliers

Metal Window Corporation (windows and doors)
www.metalwindowcorp.com

Evergreen Solar (solar panels)
www.evergreensolar.com

Fireorb (chimney)
www.fireorb.net

3form (backsplashes and resin wall panels)
www.3-form.com

Polygal (cladding)
www.polygal-northamerica.com

Bulthaup (kitchen)
www.bulthaup.com

Duravit (bathroom fixtures)
www.duravit.us

Grohe (bathroom fixtures)
www.groheamerica.com

ROCK REACH HOUSE

Photographer
Lance Gerber
Nuvue Interactive
www.nuvueinteractive.com

Architect
o2 Architecture
1089 N. Palm Canyon Drive, Suite B
Palm Springs, CA 92262
760-778-8165
www.o2arch.com

Developer/Frame System Provider
Blue Sky Building Systems
17530 Ventura Boulevard, #201
Encino, CA 91316
www.blueskybuildingsystems.com

General Contractor
Solterra Development
700 East Tahquitz Canyon Way, Suite C
Palm Springs, CA 92262
www.solterrahomes.com/

Interior Designer
Christopher Kennedy Design
870 Research Drive, #10
Palm Springs, CA 92262
760-325-3214
www.christopherkennedy.com

Suppliers
Milgard Windows & Doors
www.milgard.com

The Modern Fan Company (ceiling fan)
www.modernfan.com

Smith & Fong (Plyboo bamboo doors, panels, and drawers)
www.plyboo.com

Yolo Colorhouse (no-VOC paint)
www.yolocolorhouse.com

Veranda Composite Decking
www.verandadeck.com

Vetrazzo (recycled glass countertops and backsplashes)
www.vetrazzo.com

ART HOUSE

Photographer
Philip Jensen-Carter
914-815-8239
www.jensencarter.com

Architect
J. B. Clancy
Albert, Righter & Tittmann Architects
262 Washington Street
Boston, MA 02108
617-451-5740
www.alriti.com

Builder
Green Mountain Habitat for Humanity
Burlington, VT
www.habitat.org

Modular Manufacturer
Preferred Building Systems
143 Twistback Road
Claremont, NH 03743
603-372-1050
http://buildingsystems.com

Energy Consultant
Peter Schneider
Vermont Energy Investment Corporation
802-658-6060 ext. 1141

Suppliers
Thermotech (windows)
www.thermotechfiberglass.com

Sunward (solar hot water panels)
www.gosunward.com

Zehnder (HRV—ComfoAir 350)
www.zehnder-systems.com

Whirlpool (appliances)
www.whirlpool.com

Bosch (washer and dryer)
www.bosch-home.com/us

Dow (XPS and Thermax rigid foam insulation)
www.building.dow.com

Huber (Zip System exterior sheathing)
www.zipsystem.com

Mitsubishi Electric (Mr. Slim air-source ductless heat pump)
www.mehvac.com

James Hardie (fiber cement siding)
www.jameshardie.com

Gordon's Window Decor
www.gordonswindowdecor.com

PASSIVE CRAFTSMAN

Photographer
Jim Tetro
2975 Hunters Branch Road, #322
Fairfax, VA 22031
703-268-5514
www.jimtetro.com

Architect
David Peabody
Peabody Architects
3417 Halcyon Drive
Alexandria, VA 22305
703-684-1986
www.greenhaus.org

SIPs Installation
PanelWrights
808 French Road
Shenandoah Junction, WV 25442
304-876-0265
www.panelwrights.com

Builder
O'Neill Development
11 Russell Avenue
Gaithersburg, MD 20877
301-840-9310 ext. 103
www.oneilldev.com

Mechanical System
Dan Foley
Foley Mechanical
8390 Terminal Road, Unit I
Lorton, VA 22079

Mike LeBeau
Conservation Technologies
4804 Oneota Street
Duluth, MN 55807
218-722-9003
www.conservtech.com

Suppliers
Insulspan (SIPs)
www.insulspan.com

Zehnder (ERV—ComfoAir)
www.zehnder-systems.com

Mitsubishi Electric (Mr. Slim mini-split system)
www.mitsubishicomfort.com

Lochinvar (gas boiler)
www.lochinvar.com

Viessmann (hot water tank)
www.viessmann-us.com

Caesarstone (kitchen countertops)
www.caesarstoneus.com

Walmer Enterprises (kitchen cabinets)
www.walmerenterprises.com

Sunair (retractable awnings)
www.sunairawnings.com

Thermotech Windows
www.thermotechwindows.com

James Hardie (fiber cement siding)
www.jameshardie.com

Absolute Power & Control (monitoring system)
www.absolutepowerandcontrol.com

4D HOME

Photographer
Jim Tetro
2975 Hunters Branch Road, #322
Fairfax, VA 22031
703-268-05514
www.jimtetro.com

Builder
Team Massachusetts:
Massachusetts College of Art and Design
www.massart.edu
University of Massachusetts Lowell
www.uml.edu

Modular Manufacturer
Epoch Homes
P.O. Box 235
107 Sheep Davis Road
Pembroke, NH 03275
603-225-3907
www.epochhomes.com

Suppliers
CertainTeed (fiber cement siding, decking, and insulation, including CertaSpray)
www.certainteed.com

Nordic Engineered Wood (Enviro-Lam and I-joists)
www.nordicewp.com

Makrowin (windows)
www.makrowin.sk/en/

Kohler (fixtures)
www.us.kohler.com

Bosch
www.bosch-home.com/us

NuAir (ERV)
www.nuair.com

Mitsubishi Electric (heat pump)
www.mehvac.com

Drexel Metals (roofing)
www.drexmet.com

SunDrum Solar (hybrid solar thermal panels)
www.sundrumsolar.com

SunPower (PV panels)
http://us.sunpowercorp.com

Solectria Renewables (inverters)
www.solren.com

Cambia (furniture)
www.cambiawood.com

KENMORE ROAD HOUSE

Photographer
Kent Corley
Kent Corley Photography
919-616-7679
www.kentcorley.com

Architect
Jay Fulkerson
Jay Fulkerson, Architect
2122 Ridgewood Road
Chapel Hill, NC 27516
919-933-3996
www.jfarch.com

Builder
Anchorage Building Corporation
919-928-2664
www.anchoragebuildingcorp.com

Concrete Panel Manufacturer
Ideal Precast
7020 Mt. Herman Church Road
Durham, NC 27705
919-801-8287
www.idealprecast.com

Suppliers
Passive House Materials (Passive House materials supplier)
919-357-4121
www.passivehousematerials.com

Serious Windows
www.seriouswindows.com

Sherwin-Williams (paint)
www.sherwin-williams.com

Fujitsu (heat pumps)
www.fujitsugeneral.com

UltimateAir (ERV)
www.ultimateair.com

SUNGAZING HOUSE

Photographers
Scot Zimmerman
800-279-2757
www.scotzimmermanphotography.com

Jacob Kauppila
www.jacobkauppila.com

Architect
Jean-Yves Lacroix
Lacroix Design
9024 North Jeremy Ranch Road
Park City, UT 84098
435-602-9014
www.lacroix-design.com

Builder
Garrett Strong
Tall Pines Construction
P.O. Box 980776
Park City, UT 84098
435-640-5136
www.tallpinesconstruction.com

Environmental Engineer
Heliocentric
12401 East Wilderness Road
Salt Lake City, UT 84121
(801) 453-9434
www.heliocentric.org

Suppliers
Premier Building Systems
www.premiersips.com

Serious Windows
www.seriouswindows.com

Schüco (solar thermal panels)
www.schueco.com

Trina Solar (PV panels)
www.trinasolar.com

Venmar CES (HRV)
www.venmarces.com

Thermador (appliances)
www.thermador.com

Drexel Metals (siding)
www.drexmet.com

Columbia (low-VOC paint)
www.columbiapaint.com

Next Generation Lighting Supply (LED lights)
www.nglscorp.com

SCHALLER ECO-HOME

Photographer
Philip Jensen-Carter
914-815-8239
www.jensencarter.com

Builder
Green Works Builders
38A Church Street
New Milford, CT 06776
860-355-2639
www.greenworksbuilder.com

Building and Energy Consultant
Revival Homes
New Hartford, CT
www.revivalhomes.net

SIPs
Timberline Panel Company
7 Pearl Street
Cambridge, NY 12816
518-665-8128
www.timberlinepanels.com

Suppliers
Andersen Windows
www.andersenwindows.com

Superior Walls (foundation)
www.superiorwalls.com

Takagi (tankless water heater)
www.takagi.com

Venmar Eko (heat recovery ventilator)
www.venmar.ca

James Hardie (fiber cement siding)
www.jameshardie.com

Smarthome (home automation system)
www.smarthome.com

Radiant Floor Company
www.radiantcompany.com

Sherwin-Williams (paint)
www.sherwin-williams.com

ReCONNstruction Center (salvaged materials)
www.reconnstructioncenter.org

Urbanminers (salvaged materials)
www.urbanminers.com

Kohler (urinal)
www.us.kohler.com

Tractor Supply Company (hog wire fencing)
www.tractorsupply.com

SMARTHOME CLEVELAND

Architect
Chuck Miller
Doty & Miller Architects
600 Broadway Avenue
Bedford, OH 44146
440-399-4100
www.dotyandmiller.com

SmartHome Project Coordinator
David Beach
Cleveland Museum of Natural History
1 Wade Oval Dr.
Cleveland, OH 44106
216-231-4600
www.cmnh.org

Builders
Jeff Walters
Panzica Construction
739 Beta Drive
Mayfield Village, OH 44143
440-442-4300
www.panzica.com

Chris Kontur
CPK Construction
8051 Vesta Avenue, Suite 3
Northfield, OH 44067
330-467-5918
www.cpkus.com

Energy Consultant
Mark Hoberecht
HarvestBuild Associates
Columbia Station, OH
440-236-3344
www.harvestbuild.com

Energy Systems
Ed Shank
Comfort Systems USA
www.comfortsystemsusaohio.com

Landscape Architect
Mike McAndrews
Knight & Stolar
216-391-0910
www.kslarch.com

Suppliers
SureTight (SIPs)
www.suretight.com

Stark Truss Company (preengineered wood trusses)
www.starktruss.com

Energate (windows and exterior doors)
www.energate.com

Mitsubishi Electric (heat pump)
www.mehvac.com

CertainTeed (shingles)
www.certainteed.com

James Hardie (fiber cement siding)
www.jameshardie.com

Zehnder (ERV)
www.zehnderamerica.com

Dovetail Solar and Wind (PV panels)
www.dovetailsolar.com

Sherwin-Williams (paint)
www.sherwin-williams.com

PNC (sponsorship)
www.pnc.com

Advanced Fiber Technology (cellulose
insulation)
www.advancedfiber.com

Insulation Systems (Fomo spray foam
insulation)
www.insulationsystems.net

David Yasenchack Timber Framing
and Design (living room arch)
www.dytimberframing.com

General Electric (appliances)
www.geappliances.com

IceStone (countertop)
www.icestone.biz

Moen (faucets and showerhead)
www.moen.com

TOTO (dual-flush toilets)
www.totousa.com

Unilock (permeable pavers)
www.unilock.com

Rain Brothers (cistern)
www.rainbrothers.com

TALIESIN MOD.FAB

Photographer
Bill Timmerman
Timmerman Photography
212 South 18th Street
Phoenix, AZ 85034
602-403-1441
www.billtimmerman.com

Faculty Architectural Guidance
Michael P. Johnson
Michael P. Johnson Design Studio
www.mpjstudio.com

Jennifer Siegal and Laura McAlpine
Office of Mobile Design
www.designmobile.com

Designer/Builder
Students from the Frank Lloyd Wright
School of Architecture
www.taliesin.edu

**Dean of Frank Lloyd Wright School
of Architecture**
Victor Sidy

Suppliers
Premier Building Systems
www.premiersips.com

Rinnai (tankless water heater)
www.rinnai.us

Arcadia (fixed glass frames)
www.arcadiainc.com

Glaz-Tech Industries (fixed glass)
www.glaztech.com

Milgard Windows & Doors (sliding
door systems)
www.milgard.com

Caesarstone (stone countertop)
www.caesarstoneus.com

Landscape Development (landscape
installation)
www.landscapedevelopment.com

TOTO (toilets)
www.totousa.com

Teka USA (kitchen sink)
www.teka.com

Floor Gres (living space tile)
www.floorgres.it

Cree (LED lighting)
www.cree.com

Agate Steel (structural steel)
www.agateinc.com

Design Within Reach (furniture)
www.dwr.com

IKEA (cabinets)
www.ikea.com

Sub-Zero/Wolf (appliances)
www.subzero-wolf.com

Ky-Ko (roofing system)
www.kykoroofing.com

Pittcon Industries (aluminum trim)
www.pittconindustries.com

Editor: Laura Dozier
Designer: Darilyn Lowe Carnes
Production Manager: Kathy Lovisolo

Library of Congress Cataloging-in-Publication Data

Koones, Sheri, 1949-
 Prefabulous + almost off the grid : your prefabulous path to building
an energy-independent home / Sheri Koones ; foreword by Robert Redford.
   p. cm.
  Includes index.
  ISBN 978-1-4197-0325-6
1. Ecological houses—United States. 2. Dwellings—Energy
conservation. 3. Sustainable architecture. I. Title. II. Title:
Prefabulous and almost off the grid.
  TH4860.K66 2012
  690'.8047—dc23

                              2012008324

Text copyright © 2012 Sheri Koones
Front cover photograph © Trent Bell Photography
Back cover photographs © Art Gray (top); © Eric Roth (middle);
© Matthew Stannard, Stillwater Dwellings (bottom)

Printed and bound in Hong Kong
10 9 8 7 6 5 4 3

Abrams books are available at special discounts when purchased in
quantity for premiums and promotions as well as fundraising or educational
use. Special editions can also be created to specification. For details,
contact specialsales@abramsbooks.com or the address below.

ABRAMS
THE ART OF BOOKS SINCE 1949
115 West 18th Street
New York, NY 10011
www.abramsbooks.com